Josquin des Prez and His Musical Legacy
An Introductory Guide

Willem Elders

Josquin des Prez
and His Musical Legacy
An Introductory Guide

LEUVEN UNIVERSITY PRESS

Translation of Preface, Chapters 1-6 and Epilogue: *Paul Shannon*

© 2013 Revised and translated edition by Leuven University Press / Presses Universitaires de Louvain / Universitaire Pers Leuven. Minderbroedersstraat 4, B-3000 Leuven (Belgium)

First edition published 2013
Reprint published 2021

Original title: *Josquin des Prez en zijn muzikale nalatenschap*
© 2011 Dutch language edition by Uitgeverij Verloren, Hilversum

ISBN 978 94 6270 285 1
D / 2013 / 1869 / 8
NUR: 662

Design: *Venti catteruzzi*
(venticaratteruzzi.com)

For Eric Jas

Contents

Preface

After Ottaviano Petrucci in Venice had founded the first-ever music publishing house in 1501, successfully publishing a couple of editions of secular songs and sacred motets, he decided, the following year, to add Mass compositions to his catalogue. It is significant that the first book was given the title *Misse Josquin*. Apparently, the reputation of Josquin des Prez at the beginning of the sixteenth century was already so established that Petrucci deemed it sufficient merely to mention his name. That his judgement was sound is borne out by the fact that a second collection of Masses appeared three years later with the title *Missarum Josquin Liber secundus*, followed by yet another in 1514, the *Missarum Josquin Liber tertius*.

This book, the result of an interest in Josquin des Prez spanning over forty years, seeks to bring the reader closer to the composer, and to provide an insight into his musical legacy. Every work included in the recent new edition of his complete works is here briefly described, so the early music lover may regard this book as an introductory guide to the composer. For musicians wanting to perform Josquin's music, the scoring and voice ranges of each work is given, as well as the number of the surviving sources, since this serves as an indicator of its popularity in the sixteenth century.

The editions of Josquin's works
When Albert Smijers was commissioned to publish the works of Josquin des Prez by the Royal Society for Music History of The Netherlands, in 1919, no-one suspected it would take half a century to complete the task. At his death, in 1957, Smijers had made accessible 20 Masses, 3 Mass sections, 70 motets and 34 secular compositions. Responsible for the completion of the edition, Myroslaw Antonowycz – assisted by myself from 1965 – added 4 Mass movements, 38 motets and 34 secular works. But it would be premature to assume that with this, the oeuvre of Josquin had now been fully explored.

During the 1971 Josquin Festival-Conference in New York, 450 years after the composer's death, the decision was taken by an international team of musicologists to start work on the *New Josquin Edition*. The first of 30 volumes appeared in 1989 and the last will appear in a few years' time. The *NJE*'s structure differs in many respects from the first edition. The oeuvre as a whole is presented in 28 volumes on clear organising principles (see Appendix A). An overview of the sources (vol. 1) and a selection of facsimiles (vol. 2) complete the edition. Each of the 28 volumes of music has a separate and comprehensive critical commentary, in which all known sources of the compositions are carefully evaluated.

The *New Josquin Edition* is referred to in this book as the *NJE*. Italian and Latin quotations are translated or summarised. Poems in French and Italian are quoted in the original language and followed by a translation. The numbering of the psalms follows the Vulgate (used in the fifteenth and sixteenth centuries), that of the Septuagint is given in parentheses. The translations of biblical texts are based on the Douai-Reims Bible version of 1582/1609.

In Part II, titles are followed by their number in the *NJE*. The number before the dot indicates the volume, and the one after the dot indicates the number of the composition in that volume. Doubtful works are marked with an asterisk. For works that have not yet appeared in the new edition, the *NJE* number is followed by a reference to the old Josquin edition (Mi = Missen; Ww = Wereldlijke werken). Manuscript sources are referred to by the name of a city followed by their siglum, and the libraries where they are kept are identified in the list of manuscript sigla.

I should like to express my gratitude to my partner, Marianne Hund, for carefully checking chapters 7–9 and for her thought-provoking remarks on some of the works considered. I am also indebted to Odile Noël for her meticulous revision of my own translation of these chapters as well as for proofreading the whole book, and to Paul Shannon for adding a number of relevant details while translating chapters 1–6. The process of revision has also benefited from suggestions made by the anonymous readers for Leuven University Press. Last but not least, I am most grateful to Carlo Fiore, who graciously offered to provide the design and professional layout for this book.

Willem Elders, Saint-André d'Olérargues, December 2012

Bibliographical abbreviations and manuscript sigla

Bibliographical abbreviations

AcM   Acta Musicologica

Blackburn   *'Uno gentile et subtile ingenio.' Studies in Renaissance Music in Honour of Bonnie J. Blackburn*, edd. M. Jennifer Bloxam, Gioia Filocamo, & Leofranc Holford-Strevens (Turnhout 2009)

EM   Early Music

Fallows   David Fallows, *Josquin* (Turnhout 2009)

JAMS   Journal of the American Musicological Society

JM   The Journal of Musicology

JosqComp   *The Josquin Companion*, ed. Richard Sherr (Oxford 2000)

Mf   Die Musikforschung

MGG2   *Die Musik in Geschichte und Gegenwart*, 2nd edition (Kassel 1999–2007), Personenteil

Miller   *Heinrich Glarean Dodecachordon*. Translation, Transcription and Critical Commentary by Clement A. Miller. Musicological Studies and Documents 6 (American Institute of Musicology 1965), 2 vols.

NGD2   *The New Grove Dictionary of Music and Musicians*, 2nd edition (2001)

NJE   *New Josquin Edition*

Osthoff   Helmuth Osthoff, *Josquin Desprez* (Tutzing 1962-1965)

ProcM   *Josquin and the Sublime. Proceedings of the International Josquin Symposium at Roosevelt Academy*, Middelburg 2009, edd. Albert Clement and Eric Jas (Turnhout 2011)

ProcNY   *Josquin des Prez, Proceedings of the International Josquin Festival-Conference* ... New York 1971, ed. Edward E. Lowinsky in collaboration with Bonnie J. Blackburn (London 1976)

ProcU   *Proceedings of the International Josquin Symposium Utrecht 1986*, ed. Willem Elders in collaboration with Frits de Haen (Utrecht 1991)

TVNM   Tijdschrift van de (Koninklijke) Vereniging voor Nederlandse Muziekge-schiedenis.

	Manuscript sigla
Augsburg 142a	Staats- und Stadtbibliothek, Ms. 2° 142a
Barcelona 454	Biblioteca Central, Ms. 454
Basel F.IX.25	Öffentliche Bibliothek der Universität, Ms. F.IX.25
Berlin 7	Geheimes Staatsarchiv Preussischer Kulturbesitz, Ms. XX. HA StUB Königsberg Nr. 7
Berlin 40021	Staatsbibliothek Preussischer Kulturbesitz, Ms. Mus. 40021
Bologna Q20	Museo Internazionale e Biblioteca della Musica, Ms. Q20
Bologna R142	Museo Internazionale e Biblioteca della Musica, Ms. R142
Brussels 228	Bibliothèque Royale, Ms. 228
Brussels 9126	Bibliothèque Royale, Ms. 9126
Cambrai 18	Médiathèque Municipale, Ms. 18
Cambrai 125-128	Médiathèque Municipale, Mss. 125-128
Cividale 59	Museo Archeologico Nazionale, Ms. LIX
Florence II.I.232	Biblioteca Nazionale Centrale, Ms. II.I.232
Florence Magl. 178	Biblioteca Nazionale Centrale, Ms. Magliabechi XIX.178
Florence 2439	Biblioteca del Conservatorio di Musica Luigi Cherubini, Ms. Basevi 2439
Florence 2442	Biblioteca del Conservatorio di Musica Luigi Cherubini, Ms. Basevi 2442
Herdringen 9820	Schloss Fürstenberg, Bibliothek, Ms. 9820
Jena 3	Thüringer Universitäts- und Landesbibliothek, Ms. 3
Kassel 38	Murhard'sche Bibliothek der Stadt Kassel und Landesbibliothek, Mss. 4° Mus. 38/1-6
London 35087	British Library, Department of Manuscripts, Ms. Additional 35087
London 8 G.VII	British Library, Department of Manuscripts, Ms. Royal 8 G.VII
Paris 12744	Bibliothèque Nationale, Ms. Fonds Français 12744
Piacenza (3)	Archivio del Duomo, Fondo Musicale, Mss. s.s. (3)
Rome 2856	Biblioteca Casanatense, Ms. 2856
Saint Gall 461	Stiftsbibliothek, Ms. 461
Segovia s.s.	Archivo Capitular de la Catedral, Ms. s.s.
Seville 5-I-43	Catedral Metropolitana, Biblioteca Capitular y Colombina, Ms. 5-I-43
Toledo 9	Biblioteca Capitular de la Catedral Metropolitana, Ms. B.9
Verona 218	Biblioteca Capitolare, Ms. CCXVIII
Verona 761	Biblioteca Capitolare, Ms. DCCXI
Vienna 15941	Österreichische Nationalbibliothek, Musiksammlung, Ms. Mus. 15941
Zwickau 78/2	Ratsschulbibliothek, Ms. LXXVIII,2

Manuscripts from the Cappella Giulia and Cappella Sistina belong to the collections of the Biblioteca Apostolica Vaticana in Vatican City.

PLATE 1: Putative portrait of Josquin des Prez,
ca. 1485, attributed to Leonardo da Vinci.
Milan, Pinacoteca Ambrosiana.

PART I – *Josquin and his cultural environment*

It could be called a twist of fate that neither the year, nor the place of birth of the greatest composer of the Renaissance is known. After Josquin des Prez died in Condé-sur-l'Escaut (nowadays Northern France) on 27 August 1521, it took until the end of the twentieth century before it was discovered that his actual name was 'Jossequin Lebloitte, dit Desprez'.[1] Little is known about the life of the man who, by many contemporaries, was considered the 'princeps musicorum', and who was courted by the great of the world to work as a singer or composer in their service. A brief outline of his life follows, to the extent that it can be determined from the documents found to date.

Jossequin is the diminutive of Josse (Judocus in Latin), a very popular name in the fifteenth and sixteenth centuries. Des Prez is a name that had already been adopted by Josquin's grandfather. Archival documents suggest that he was from the region east of Tournai. That Josquin must, as is now assumed, have been born around 1455 seems to be confirmed by a poem that Serafino dall'Aquila wrote for him. Its dedication reads: "Ad Jusquino suo compagno musico dascanio" (for his companion Josquin, Ascanio's musician) (see p. 34). Since Serafino himself was born in 1466, the young poet's 'companion' cannot have been much more than a dozen years his senior.

After being a choirboy or altar boy at St. Géry's in Cambrai, Josquin's name is found again between 1475 and 1478 as a singer in the chapel of René of Anjou in Aix-en-Provence. Although no archival documents are known for the years 1478–1483, it is possible that Josquin remained in the service of René until the latter's death in 1480. When Anjou and Provence were then absorbed by Louis XI into the kingdom of France, he may, together with René's other singers, have joined the chapel of the

---

1   Lora Matthews and Paul Merkley, 'Iudochus de Picardia and Jossequin Lebloitte dit Desprez: The Names of the Singer(s)', in *JM* 16 (1998), 200–226. For further bibliographical references regarding Josquin's biography, see Patrick Macey in *NGD2*, vol. 13, sections 1–9, at 220–229.

French court, in the Sainte-Chapelle in Paris. From this period perhaps comes one of his early motets, *Misericordias domini*. But another scenario is possible. Two documents show that the composer was in the service of the House of Sforza in Milan in the 1480s. According to the first, dated 1484, he belonged to the household of Cardinal Ascanio Sforza; the second, from 1489, calls him 'cantorem duchalem', indicating that he was, at least in name, in the service of the young Duke Giangaleazzo.

In 1483 he travelled to Condé-sur-l'Escaut to claim his part of the inheritance left by his apparently childless uncle, Gilles Lebloitte dit Desprez, and his aunt Jaque Banestonne. During the same visit to the town he received four 'los' of wine from the chapter of Notre Dame. And documents in the archives of Troyes state that during meetings with some singers in 1499 and 1501 he was also offered wine, including clairet (wine mixed with honey and aromatic spices).[2]

In the retinue of Cardinal Ascanio Sforza, Josquin travelled to Rome. There he became a member of the Papal Chapel, first of Innocent VIII then of Alexander VI, from 1489 to at least the early part of 1495. During restoration work of the singers' gallery of the Sistine Chapel (Fig. 1), in 1997, a *graffito* of the name 'Josquin' emerged (Fig. 2).[3]

FIGURE 1: Interior of the Sistine Chapel in the Vatican in Josquin's time with the singers' gallery (after an engraving from 1899 by G. Tognetti).

---

2   See Rob Wegman, 'Ockeghem, Brumel, Josquin: New Documents in Troyes', in *EM* 36 (2008), 203–217.

3   Klaus Pietschmann, 'Ein Graffito von Josquin Desprez auf der Cantoria der Sixtinischen Kapelle', in *Mf* 52 (1999), 204–207.

FIGURE 2: Graffito with Josquin's name on the wall of the singers' gallery in the Sistine Chapel.

According to an anecdote recorded in 1547 by the Swiss theorist Heinrich Glarean, Josquin was at the French Court at some time during the reign of Louis XII (1498–1515). His instrumental fanfare *Vive le roy* was probably composed during his stay there. It is not inconceivable that the composer's next move, to Ferrara in 1503, was occasioned, in part, by the meetings that took place between Louis XII and Ercole d'Este in 1499 and 1502. Whether he had stayed at the court of the Estes earlier in his career cannot be proved, but some indications make it plausible. After the assassination of Galeazzo Maria Sforza in December 1476, his brother Ascanio, the future cardinal, was exiled from Milan. In 1480 he enjoyed, together with a retinue consisting of no fewer than two hundred people, the hospitality of Ercole d'Este. That Josquin may have left Milan with Ascanio can be inferred both from the document of 1484 stating that he was in his service, and from the attribution of one of his most brilliant secular songs, *El grillo*: in its only source the composer is identified as 'Josquin d'Ascanio'. His *Missa Hercules Dux Ferrarie* was composed possibly during this stay at the request of Ascanio in honour of the Duke, in gratitude for his hospitality. 13 September 1480 was the forty-seventh anniversary of Ercole's knighthood, conferred on him by Emperor Sigismund at the age of only two. In Josquin's imposing Mass for the Duke, the underlying motif is heard forty-seven times.[4] If the 'Hercules' Mass indeed dates from this time – though Josquin could also have written it in Paris by commission of Ascanio – the fact that the Duke ignored the following advice of his courtier Gian de Artiganova in 1502 and offered Josquin the post of Maestro di Cappella would be unsurprising:

... To me he [Heinrich Isaac] seems very well suited to serve Your Excellency, much more so than Josquin, because he gets along well with his colleagues, and will compose new works more often.

4   See Willem Elders, 'New Light on the Dating of Josquin's *Hercules* Mass', in *TVNM* 48 (1998), 112–149.

It is true that Josquin composes better, but he composes when he wants to, and not when someone else wants him to, and he is asking 200 ducats in salary while Isaac will come for 120. But Your Excellency will see fit to decide …

It was quite probably the plague outbreak in Ferrara in 1504 that caused the speedy end to Josquin's stay in the city. Later the same year he already found himself in Condé, where he was appointed canon, probably at the instigation of Philip the Fair. In his capacity as provost, Josquin was in charge there of a large establishment that included a dean, a treasurer, twenty-five canons, eighteen chaplains, six vicars and six choristers. From this town the composer may have maintained contact with the court of Margaret of Austria in Mechlin. A letter of 1519 survives in which the regent asks Josquin to recommend Jehan Lommel be appointed dean at Condé. Both Margaret and Charles V were in possession of some of his songs. About the last years of Josquin's life hardly anything is known.

At Josquin's death, his will showed that he had bequeathed his house and property to the Church. From the proceeds, a so-called *Salve* service – a devotional service in honour of the Virgin Mary – was to be held on Marian feast days. His will also stipulated that his motet *Pater noster – Ave Maria* (see below, Fig. 35) be sung in an annual procession on the anniversary of his death, when the singers, having reached the marketplace, stood before the statue of the Virgin set into the facade of his house. His tombstone read:

Chy gist Sire Josse depres	Here lies Master Josse Despres,
Prevost de cheens fut jadis	Who was formerly provost of this place.
Priez Dieu pour les trepassés	Pray to God for the deceased,
Qui leur donne son paradis	That He give them His paradise.
Trepassa l'an 1521 le 27 d'aoust	He died in the year 1521 on 27 August.
Spes mea semper fuisti	You have always been my hope.

Four young composers wrote dirges in his memory. Two of them, Benedictus Appenzeller and Nicolas Gombert, chose the same text, *Musae Jovis*. In this poem, by the Nijmegen humanist Gerardus Avidius, Apollo says that Josquin was dear to Jupiter and triumphs in the heavenly host. The elegy by Hieronymus Vinders, *O mors inevitabilis*, has the following text:

O mors inevitabilis,	Oh inevitable death,
Mors amara, mors crudelis,	Bitter death, cruel death,
Josquin des Pres dum necasti,	By killing Josquin de Pres
Illum nobis abstulisti,	You have taken him from us,
Qui suam per harmoniam	Him, who with his harmony
Illustravit ecclesiam.	Has given lustre to the Church.
Propterea tu musice dic:	Say now with music:
Requiescat in pace.	"May he rest in peace."

This motet is set for seven voices as a sign of mourning (see for example Genesis 50:10, "and he observed seven days' mourning for his father") and based on the introit *Requiem eternam* from the liturgy of the dead. Right from the beginning, the composer imitates the tolling of funeral bells in the lower voices. Lastly, in one of the choirbooks of St. Peter's in Leiden is a six-voice *Requiem* attributed to Josquin. Its composer, however, was Jean Richafort, who wrote it in commemoration of Josquin. The Mass is based on the *cantus firmus* "Circumdederunt me gemitus mortis" (The sighs of Death surround me) that Josquin used in his chanson *Nimphes, nappés*, and quotes several times appropriately from another of Josquin's chansons: "C'est douleur non pareille" (No pain is equal [to mine]) (see p. 216).

Josquin's personality

Although knowing little about someone's life makes it difficult to describe his personality, some of the documents relating to Josquin, along with his music, still conjure up a fairly concrete picture. In the first place, this is one of a composer who knew his worth. The letter quoted above to Ercole d'Este in particular, referring to Josquin's desired salary for the post of Maestro di Cappella in Ferrara, gives the impression that he was a good businessman.[5]

More important, however, is to examine the secret of his genius.[6] This is undoubtedly explained by the synthesis of constructional skills unmatched in his time and a high degree of musical expressiveness. The first aspect is reflected in his complete mastery of contemporary compositional techniques, which he employs to achieve great feats of complexity. Sometimes this is seen in musical constructions that are determined by a number. It may perhaps be concluded that Josquin had a talent for mathematics, which may be why the late sixteenth-century south-Netherlander mathematician Simon Stevin, in chapter 4 of his *Van de Spiegeling der Singkonst* (Reflection on the Art of Singing), calls "Josquin du Pres" as well as "his Master Jan Ockegens the discoverers and first founders ... of the song that is used today." Like Josquin, Ockeghem was a composer who enjoyed demonstrating his extraordinary mastery of counterpoint, as in, for example, his *Missa Prolationum*. He was praised in this respect by numerous theorists after his death.

What filters through from many of his compositions for the Church, though, is that Josquin must have been above all a pious man, with a strong feeling for the mystical element in worship. Using the musical rhetoric of his time, he rarely failed to underline in a prayer to God or the Virgin Mary the moments of most importance to him. This could be through melodic or harmonic means, or through text repetition. His *Illibata dei virgo* (see pp. 84 and 179), which has rightly been called a musical self-portrait, is an excellent example. It is the interaction displayed in

---

5   John Kmetz, 'Josquin the Businessman', in *Josquin. International Conference New Directions in Josquin Scholarship, Princeton University 1999*, Conference Packet, 78–84.

6   Glarean uses the term 'ingenium' (see p. 37). In a comprehensive essay, Paula Higgins enters at length into the meaning of the word "genius" in the context of the scholarly reception of Josquin, proposing "a renewed sensitivity to the imbrication of mythologies of musical genius in music historiographies." See 'The Apotheosis of Josquin des Prez and Other Mythologies of Musical Genius', in *JAMS* 57 (2004), 443–510, at 510.

this motet between a unique structure and a musical and emotional tension that explains why Josquin can be labelled a forerunner of Johann Sebastian Bach.

Josquin's patrons
In Josquin's time, freelance musicians and composers hardly if ever existed. For their livelihood they sought an appointment with the church authorities or a monarch. Thus it appears that Josquin worked in the same institutions as had his two greatest predecessors, Guillaume Dufay and Johannes Ockeghem, before him. These were the Papal Chapel and the French court. The exact nature of the relationship between a composer and his patron is seldom or never revealed in the documents. We may nevertheless assume that artists were generally treated with respect. During his visit to Ferrara in 1437, Dufay received twenty gold ducats from Nicolò d'Este, whose son Leonello transferred a similar amount, six years later, to Dufay's account at the Borromei Bank in Bruges. And after Ockeghem returned from a diplomatic mission to Spain in 1470, Louis XI paid him as much as £275 in expenses.

In the following brief biographical notes on those assumed to have employed Josquin for various periods of time, some very differing personalities appear. Obviously, we can only guess what Josquin himself thought about his patrons. But if, as suggested by his sacred music, a belief in God determined his attitude to life, it seems likely that his employment by those Church leaders who surrendered more to their worldly inclinations than to worship would not have been free of deep disappointment. The patrons closest to him in temperament may have been René of Anjou, Louis XI, and Ercole d'Este. If the impressive motets *Virgo salutiferi* and *Miserere mei, deus*, composed during his stay at the court of Ercole d'Este in 1503–1504, are any guide, Josquin must have found in the Duke of Ferrara, especially, a man after his own heart.

Josquin's probable first employer, Duke René of Anjou and Lorraine, the last sovereign of Provence and titular King of Naples, Sicily and Jerusalem (1409–1480), was already a legend in his own time (Fig. 3). Nicknamed 'le bon Roy', he was one of the most archetypal patrons of the late Middle Ages. In his residences in Aix-en-Provence and Tarascon, a cosmopolitan culture flourished. He commissioned Nicolas Froment to paint the triptych *Mary in the Burning Bush* for the Carmelites in Aix (Aix-en-Provence, St. Sauveur's Cathedral), and his own writings comprise the allegorical *Cuers du Livre d'Amours Éspris*. His rich library included illuminated masterpieces such as the *Livre des Tournois*, which contains miniatures of parades and tournaments and the swearing of the oath.

The highly politically gifted Louis XI, who reigned from 1461 to 1483, created the modern monarchy in France (Fig. 4). A very religious person, he tried through patronage to prolong his life, which was dominated by conflict. So, two years before his death he commissioned Jean Bourdichon to paint 50 prayer rolls at his palace of Plessis-lès-Tours.[7] On three of these, held by angels, was the first verse of Psalm 88 (89): "Misericordias domini in eternum cantabo" (I will sing of the Lord's mercy for ever). Josquin wrote a motet that begins with this verse (see p. 143). Johannes

---

7   See Patrick Macey, 'Josquin's *Misericordias Domini* and Louis XI', in *EM* 19 (1991), 163–177.

Ockeghem, who had been employed by his predecessor Charles VII, remained a chapel member until Louis' death, in 1483.

Ascanio Sforza (1455–1505) was the fifth of six sons of Francesco Sforza, Duke of Milan, and Bianca Maria Visconti. Destined for a career in the Church, he enjoyed a classical education. In 1477, along with three of his brothers, he was banned from the city of Milan for his part in the murder of their eldest brother, Galeazzo Maria. From 1480 to 1482 he enjoyed the hospitality of Ercole d'Este in Ferrara. After being elevated to cardinal in 1484, he twice reached the final round of papal elections (Fig. 5). In Rome, he managed to gather a large fortune; music was an important form of entertainment at his court. Contemporaries described him as a diplomat rather than a man of religion.

The election of Innocent VIII (1484–1492) in a sense ushered in a low point in the history of the Papacy. A man without higher education, he was primarily interested in political matters, and he committed to a war against the Turks. As the first pontiff openly to acknowledge his illegitimate children, he counts as one of the most undignified popes of the Renaissance. The Belvedere, a villa in the Tuscan style (Fig. 6), was built during his reign just north of the Vatican Palace. He is the only pope whose tomb, constructed by Antonio del Pollaiuolo, was transferred (in 1619) from the old Basilica of St. Peter's to the new one.

Alexander VI (1492–1503) acquired the tiara by bribery after the death of Pope Innocent. From the House of Borgia, he combined skill with debauchery, and entered history as the Holy See's antichrist. Between 1492 and 1495 he had Pinturicchio decorate the Borgia apartments with scenes from lives of the saints, but secular elements such as Sibyls and Sciences are also the subjects of a number of frescoes. His son Cesare inflicted on Rome a reign of terror, but it remains uncertain whether he envisaged a secularisation of the Papal States. Alexander's daughter Lucrezia's third marriage, in 1501, was to Alfonso d'Este, son of Ercole I of Ferrara.

FIGURE 3: Medallion with René d'Anjou. Translation of the inscription: "Renatus, by the grace of God, King of Jerusalem and Sicily, etcetera".

FIGURE 4: Medal by Francesco da Laurana with the portrait of Louis XI, "King of the French".

Ercole I d'Este, Duke of Ferrara from 1471 to 1505, acquired great political power through his marriage to Eleanora of Aragon, daughter of the King of Naples (Fig. 7). As a patron of literature, music and art, he first engaged the Flemish composer Johannes Martini, and later Jacob Obrecht and Josquin. He also provided hospitality to Ludovico Ariosto, one of the greatest epic poets of the Italian Renaissance, whose *Orlando furioso* served to glorify the Estes. Ercole's eldest daughter, the musical Isabella, who married Francesco Gonzaga, had a riddle canon by Ockeghem inlayed in her study at the ducal palace in Mantua. Leonardo da Vinci made a portrait of her.

Louis XII, son of Charles, Duke of Orléans, ruled France between 1498–1515. In 1498 he married the twentyone-year-old Anne of Brittany, widow of his childless predecessor Charles VIII. Louis was more interested in foreign than domestic politics. In 1499 he conquered Milan, and through his alliance with Ferdinand the Catholic of Aragon managed also to occupy Naples for a while. By adding a red-brick wing to Blois, the medieval castle of his father, he created the 'Versailles of the Renaissance' (Fig. 8).

FIGURE 5: Portrait of Cardinal Ascanio Sforza by an unknown master. Florence, Uffizi.

FIGURE 6: Rome in the time of Innocentius VIII and Alexander VI. Woodcut in the *Cosmographia universalis* of Sebastian Münster (Basel 1550). The Belvedere, built under Innocentius VIII, is visible in the upper right corner.

FIGURE 7: Portrait of Ercole d'Este by Ercole de'Roberti (between 1482 and 1496); copy by Dosso Dossi (ca. 1480-1542). Modena, Galleria Estense.

FIGURE 8: Equestrian statue of Louis XII above the entry of the west front of his chateau in Blois.

IOSQVINVS PRATENSIS.

FIGURE 9: Woodcut with the portrait of Josquin des Prez in Petrus Opmeer, *Opus chronographicum orbis universi* (Antwerp 1611), vol. I, p. 440.

Portraits

The image most often reproduced of any Renaissance composer is the small woodcut with the caption "Josquinus Pratensis" (Fig. 9). The accompanying text states that it was taken from a painted portrait of the composer. This was originally owned by a certain Petrus Jacobi, who was cantor and organist at St. Gudula in Brussels and who died in 1568. According to his will, the portrait was to become a side panel of a triptych whose central panel would show his patron saint, St. Peter, and the other side panel Jacobi himself. The altarpiece was to be placed next to his tomb in one of the side chapels of the church. It was destroyed during the iconoclasm of 1579–1585.[8]

The woodcut was included in a historical work by Petrus Opmeer, *Opus chronographicum orbis universi*, which was published in Antwerp in 1611, though the text had already been completed in 1569. It includes short biographies of the most celebrated men in history, such as popes, emperors, kings and artists. Each is depicted in a woodcut. Josquin is described as, among other things, one of the greatest figures in the history of music after Pythagoras and Guido of Arezzo. The text mentions that

---

8   Barbara Haggh, 'Josquin's Portrait: New Evidence', in *From Ciconia to Sweelinck. Donum natalicium Willem Elders*, edd. Albert Clement and Eric Jas (Amsterdam 1994), 91–110.

Josquin was originally portrayed "honestâ sane facie ac blandis oculis" (with a very distinguished expression and charming eyes). But how faithfully does the woodcut reproduce the original? A comparison of the portraits of others such as Erasmus, Thomas More, Leo X and Leonardo da Vinci with the originals after which the woodcuts were made, shows the technical competence of the 'portraitist' to be unsatisfactory.[9]

Modern literature on Josquin also mentions a few other possible portraits from his time. One is the *Portrait of a Musician* in the Pinacoteca Ambrosiana in Milan, which is believed to have been painted by Leonardo da Vinci around 1485 (Plate I, see p. 15). It represents a young man getting on for thirty who holds in his hand a piece of parchment with a few musical notes derived perhaps from a composition. In the past it was suggested to be a portrait of Franchinus Gaffurius, who was appointed Maestro di Cappella of Milan Cathedral in 1484. Because Gaffurius' reputation, however, rests more on his theoretical treatises than on his compositions, one would expect the painter to have portrayed him as a 'teacher' – which is not unusual in the sixteenth century – rather than as a musician. And since Leonardo belonged at this time to the same ducal court as Josquin, having started working for the Sforzas of Milan in 1482, the two men certainly knew each other.

The panel is unfortunately in a frail condition. In a restoration undertaken in 1905 the yellow ochre of the parchment leaf was evidently removed too drastically, so that some of the notes and words were lost. Nevertheless, a recent X-ray of the panel taken at the Opificio delle Pietre Dure in Florence has revealed six hidden letters in the undercoat, just above the nail of the right index finger. In a recent article it has been argued that these letters can best be read as JOSQIN.[10]

---

9   Willem Elders, 'Who Was Josquin', in *ProcU*, 1–14, at 1–3.

10 Walter Testolin, 'Did Leonardo Paint Josquin? New Light on the "Musician" in the Ambrosiana', in *ProcM*, 211–213.

Josquin was the first composer in the history of Western music not to have been forgotten after his death. References to the composer are not only very numerous but also very varied.[1] A bibliography of titles containing his name, put together by Carlo Fiore, lists more than 1100 items up to the year 2000. The anthology included in this chapter is preceded by a brief, general discussion.

For more than half a century after his death, we find numerous remarkable tributes to Josquin's fame. Several are worth mentioning here. In his *Ragionamenti accademici* [...] *sopra alcuni luoghi difficili di Dante* (Venice 1567) the Florentine humanist Cosimo Bartoli devotes the third chapter to musicians before 1545, and makes a striking comparison between visual artists and composers:

> It is known that Ockeghem was, as it were, the first in his days to rediscover music when it was almost extinguished, just as Donatello in his time breathed new life into sculpture. It can be said of our Josquin, Ockeghem's pupil, that in music he was a natural prodigy, just as our own Michelangelo Buonarroti has been in architecture, painting, and sculpture. For just as no-one until now has rivalled Josquin as a composer, so Michelangelo still stands lonely at the summit of all those who have practised his arts. Both have opened the eyes of all those who rejoice in these arts or who will rejoice in the future.[2]

1　See, among others, Jessie Ann Owens, 'How Josquin Became Josquin: Reflections on Historiography and Reception', in *Music in Renaissance Cities and Courts: Studies in Honor of Lewis Lockwood*, edd. Eadem and Anthony M. Cummings (Warren, MI, 1997), 271–280; Honey Meconi, 'Josquin and Musical Reputation', in *Essays on Music and Culture in Honor of Herbert Kellman*, ed. Barbara Haggh (Paris 2001), 280–297; and Jesse Rodin, 'When Josquin Became Josquin', in *AcM* 81 (2009), 23–38.

2　*Ragionamenti* ..., f. 35v.

We also come across his name in literary works such as *Pantagruel* by François Rabelais (1532) and the *Livre des meslanges* by Pierre de Ronsard (1560). Perhaps one of the most remarkable instances of the persistence of Josquin's fame is found in the Portuguese writer António Prestes. He published seven plays in Lisbon in 1587, three of which mention Josquin. In the comedy *The jealous wife*, the woman is so paranoid that she will not allow her husband to visit the barber alone; instead, the barber must come to him. When asked by his client not to cut too much hair off, the barber reassures him that he knows his trade: "Direy como diz josquin/señor, la so fa re mi/porque ja sou perro velho" (Sir, as Josquin once said, *La sol fa re mi*, for I am an old dog at this).[3] Could the composer have wished for anything wittier, more than sixty years after his death, than this pun – 'Lascia fare mi' means 'leave it to me' – on the theme of his *Missa La sol fa re mi*?

In Germany it was Martin Luther who sang the praises of Josquin's music. In his *Zwelffte predig von Doctor Luthers historien* (1540), the theologian Johannes Mathesius described how highly the great Church reformer praised Josquin. Apparently Luther had a habit of singing during and after meals. In an after-dinner speech on 1 January 1537, he was said to have called Josquin "der noten meister". Luther makes clear that he is referring to Josquin's acclaimed craftsmanship by comparing him to other composers, who he said composed music in the straitjacket of compositional rules. Nor was this Luther's only hymn of praise. Some five years earlier he likened the Holy Gospel and the law to Josquin and *fincken gesang*. Thus he credited Josquin's music with divine, evangelical revelation: his method of composition was not bound by rules, like 'Finck Song' – referring perhaps to the music of Josquin's German contemporary Heinrich Finck, in which he apparently sought divine inspiration in vain.

The respect Luther showed for Josquin was not without consequences for the longevity of his music in (Lutheran) Germany. Many of Josquin's compositions are preserved in German manuscripts and prints, in particular psalm motets, Masses, and chansons furnished with new spiritual texts. Many are also 'changelings', for the posthumous fame of Josquin meant that his music was held up as a model, and this inspired many a composer to write works in the style of the older master. Consequently, the history of Western music knows hardly another oeuvre about which so many questions must be raised. In this regard, Josquin can be mentioned in the same breath as, for example, Rembrandt. Of the 325 works that carry Josquin's name in fifteenth- and sixteenth-century sources, more than half are wrongly or doubtfully attributed. Evidently this was already known in the sixteenth century, because the German music publisher Georg Forster wrote in 1540, "I recall a certain eminent man saying that, now Josquin is dead, he is producing more compositions than when he was still alive."[4]

The influence of Josquin in Germany reaches well into the baroque, detectable even in the music of Bach himself. The latter, in his capacity as director of the library of the Thomaskirche in Leipzig, had in his care what is now manuscript 49 in the University Library, which includes Josquin's *Pange lingua* Mass. The structure of

---

3   After Robert Stevenson, 'Josquin in the Music of Spain and Portugal', in *ProcNY*, 227–246, at 236.

4   *Selectissimarum mutetarum … tomus primus* (Nuremberg 1540), Preface.

the counterpoint at "Gratias agimus tibi" in the Gloria of this Mass is clearly related to that of the same passage in Bach's *B*-minor Mass.[5]

Josquin's name inspired the imagination in Italy even more than in Germany. That his fame was sometimes disadvantageous to his colleagues is clear not only in the case of Isaac (see Chapter 1), but also that of Adrian Willaert. An anecdote recorded by the Italian music theorist Gioseffo Zarlino about the Flemish composer speaks volumes: Willaert was still young but becoming wildly popular in Italy. In July 1515, during a visit to the Papal Chapel in Rome, he heard his six-voice motet *Verbum bonum et suave*. The singers believed it to be by Josquin, but when they learned that the composer was actually the young Willaert, they apparently refused to keep it in their repertoire.

In 1514, an anonymous artist used intarsia to inlay the famous proportion canon in the Agnus dei from Josquin's *Missa L'homme armé super voces musicales* in the back of a choir stall in the Basilica of San Sisto in Piacenza. He replaced the Agnus dei text by a Latin distich that can be translated as follows: "This [i.e. Josquin's] well-known talent has brought all the arts to life and the whole world rejoices in eternal song." (See below, Fig. 17)[6]

The citations below are listed as chronologically as possible within each section. They consist of fragments of prose and poetry, and the judgements of music theorists, publishers and historians. Lastly, an account is given of composers that have implemented technical procedures first used by Josquin, or who have paid him homage by reworking some of his musical material.

Writers

In 1510, Paolo Cortese published *De cardinalatu libri tres*, an encyclopaedic treatise on correct behaviour for cardinals, intended primarily for the young Cardinal Giovanni de' Medici, the future Pope Leo X. His pronouncements include how a cardinal was supposed to encourage the development of music. In the second book, he says "Josquin the Frenchman stood out among many, because more learning was added by him to the sacrificial kinds of song [i.e. polyphonic Masses] than is wont to be added by the unskilled zeal of recent musicians."[7]

A few years later, the Italian nobleman and writer Baldesar Castiglione (1478–1529) – Raphael's portrait of him hangs in the Louvre – mentioned Josquin in Book II of his famous *Libro del Cortegiano* (The Book of the Courtier). This work was published in Venice in 1528 with a print run of 1030 copies. Referring probably to an incident at the court of Urbino in 1507, one of the participants in the discussion, a certain Frederico, says:

5   Willem Elders, 'Kompositionsverfahren in der Musik der alten Niederländer und die Kunst J.S. Bachs', in *Beiträge zur Bach Forschung* 6 (1987), 110–134, at 111–113.

6   Jaap van Benthem, 'Einige Musikintarsien des frühen 16. Jahrhunderts in Piacenza und Josquins Proportionskanon Agnus dei', in *TVNM* 24 (1974), 97–111, at 99.

7   After Andrew Kirkman, *The Cultural Life of the Early Polyphonic Mass: Medieval Context to Modern Revival* (Cambridge 2010), 29.

You must not say that women are completely irrational, signor Gaspare, even if sometimes they fall in love more by someone else's judgement than by their own. For there are very often noble men and wise men who do the same, and, if the truth were told, you yourself and all of us frequently, and at this very moment, rely more on the opinion of others than on our own. And to prove this, consider that not so long ago, when certain verses were presented here as being by Sannazaro, everyone thought they were extremely fine and praised them to the skies; then when it was established that they were by someone else their reputation sank immediately and they seemed quite mediocre. Then again, when a motet was sung in the presence of the Duchess, it pleased no one and was considered worthless, until it became known that it had been composed by Josquin des Près.[8]

Of a clearly anecdotal nature is the tale related by the German humanist and collector of aphorisms Johannes Manlius in his *Locorum communium collectanea* (Basel 1562), p. 542:

When Josquin was living at Cambrai [sic] and someone wanted to apply ornaments in his music which he had not composed, he walked into the choir and sharply berated him in front of the others, saying: 'You ass, why do you add ornamentation? If it had pleased me, I would have inserted it myself. If you wish to amend properly composed songs, make your own, but leave mine unamended!'[9]

This anecdote shows that Josquin strove for such perfection in his compositions that further intervention was redundant.

Although many references to Josquin can be found in the writings of music historians after the sixteenth century, we must wait until the twentieth century before writers had got to know him well enough to pay him much attention. The novelist Theun de Vries, for example, published *Het Motet voor de Kardinaal* (The Motet for the Cardinal) in 1960, based on the documents about Josquin that were then available. The protagonist, a student of Josquin called Wolf – there were in fact several sixteenth-century composers that went by the Latin name 'Lupus' – relates his life story. As a young man in Milan in the 1480s, Wolf describes what Josquin meant to him:

Josquin became my star. The singers in the choir taught me to read and write, music as well as words; they taught me what is meant by a psalm, a motet, a Mass, and along the way acquainted me also with the most frivolous dance songs, pivas, saltarellas and barzellettas. But Josquin taught me how to twist and turn one of these melodies until it became suitable for a hymn to the Holy Virgin, or a penitential psalm. In the very first Easter Mass I sang, I was astonished when I realised that the Alleluia contained the tune of a hunting song I had learned years before from some Italian archers: *Iamo alla caccia, su alla caccia! / Su su su su, ognun se spaccia!* I quickly got used to such discoveries and quick-wittedness, because I saw that my master Josquin only used them to stimulate his musical imagination; he seized music wherever he could, whether from Gregorian or Ambrosian chant, from the bagpipe tunes of the *pifferari* or rattle rhymes of the children on the street – he captured it, and

---

8   *The Book of the Courtier* (Harmondworth, Middlesex R1980), 144–145.
9   After Rob Wegman, ' "And Josquin Laughed" … Josquin and the Composer's Anecdote in the Sixteenth Century', in *JM* 17 (1999), 319–357, at 322.

once caught, it was digested like base lead and iron in the fire of his musical soul to emerge as pure gold ... and this was truly more profitable than all the chrysopoeia of the alchemists.[10]

The fictional travelogue *Magister X* by Belgian radio host Johan van Cauwenberge, about a Flemish polyphonist, pays tribute to the many anonymous composers of the Low Countries around 1500. Great masters like Josquin are also mentioned:

> Josquin lived from the patronage of princes, but his nature was anything but obsequious. That he was allowed to leave France, was actually a sign of appreciation from King Louis. What happened was this: the master was supposed to write a song to which the king, with his frail voice, could sing along. Josquin accepted the challenge, though he was aware that the king did not know a note of music. When the time came for music at dinner the next day, Josquin presented a new composition to the monarch. He had given him a part that, as befitted a royal voice, consisted of a single note. For this King Louis rewarded Josquin with a generous gift and promised to grant him all his wishes.[11]

The source of this story is an anecdote told by Heinrich Glarean in 1547, in which the composer was not named. But in 1636 he was identified as Josquin by the French music theorist Marin Mersenne (1588–1648). Glarean speaks of Louis XII; even so, it is much more likely to have been his predecessor Louis XI, whom Josquin had also served for a short time. The piece in question, *Guillaume se va chauffer* (NJE *28.17), is of doubtful authenticity, however.

Poets
Although we find Josquin named amongst older colleagues in earlier poems, Jean Molinet, chronicler to the House of Burgundy, was the first to put him in the limelight. On the death of Ockeghem, in 1497, he wrote the lament *Nymphes des bois*, which mentions four composers:

Acoutrez vous d'habits de deuil:	Dress yourselves in clothes of mourning:
Josquin, Piersson, Brumel, Compere,	Josquin, La Rue, Brumel, Compère,
Et plourez grosses larmes d'oeil:	And weep great tears from your eyes:
Perdu avez vostre bon pere.	You have lost your good father.

Serafino dall' Aquila (1466–1500), poet and musician, wrote a sonnet with the following dedication: *Ad Jusquino suo compagno musico dascanio* (To Josquin, his companion, Ascanio's musician).[12] Though not printed until 1502, it was probably written, as mentioned in Chapter 1, in the 1480s, when both men were in the service of Cardinal Ascanio Sforza, either in Milan or in Rome:

10   (Amsterdam 1962; ⁷2002), 42.

11   (Peer 1996), p. 25.

12   Quoted after Edward E. Lowinsky, 'Ascanio Sforza's Life: A Key to Josquin's Biography and an Aid to the Chronology of his Works', in *ProcNY*, 31–75, at 56.

Jusquin, non dir che'l ciel sia crudo et empio	Josquin, don't say the heavens are cruel and [merciless
Ché te adornò de sì sublime ingegno,	That gave you genius so sublime.
E se alcun veste ben, lassa lo sdegno	And if someone is well dressed, do not mind,
Che di ciò gaude alcun buffone o scempio.	For this is the privilege of buffoons and fools.
Da quel ch'io te dirrò prendi l'exempio:	Take your example from these, I pray:
L'argento e l'or, che da se stesso è degno,	Silver and gold that bear their value in [themselves
Se monstra nudo, e sol si veste el legno	Appear unclothed; but wood is overlaid
Quando se adorna alcun teatro o tempio.	When stage or temple are bedecked.
El favor di costor vien presto manco	The favour to those others lent fades fast;
E mille volte el dì, sia pur giocondo,	A thousand times a day, however pleasant,
Se muta el stato lor de nero in bianco.	Their status turns from white to black.
Ma chi ha virtù, gire a suo modo el mondo,	But [he] who has talent may wander through [the world in his own way;
Come om che nòta et ha la zucca al fianco,	Like the swimmer wrapped in a vest of cork:
Mettil socto acque, pur non teme el fondo.	Put him under water, yet he fears not drowning.

By likening his talent to the swimmer's life jacket, and to precious metals rather than to wood, it seems that Serafino intended to give encouragement to Josquin, who was perhaps slightly depressed from what he felt was a lack of recognition. At the time the poem was written this may have been true, since Josquin's international reputation only began to manifest itself around 1500.

The poem *La plainte du désiré* by Jean Lemaire de Belges (1473–ca.1525) dates from the start of the sixteenth century and was published in 1509. This Walloon poet and chronicler was most celebrated in his time for a prose romance about Troy. In the poem, he addresses Josquin directly:

Ung grave accent, musicque larmoiable,	A mournful sound, plaintive music,
Est bien seant a ce dueil piteable,	is well suited to join
Pour parfounir noz lamentations.	our lamentations to this pitiful grief.
A toy, Josquin, en prière amiable	To you, Josquin, the deceased addresses
Le deffunct mande estre tant serviable	his amicable petition as to enable
Qu'on puist chanter sa complaincte louable	the lament in his honour to be sung
Sur tes motetz et compositions.	to your motets and compositions.
Fais doncq ung chant ainsi que de tenebres,	Thus make a song in black notation,
Sans mignotise et sans point d'illecebres,	without finery and any attraction,
Remply de deuil en ses proportions:	in proportions that befit our sadness.
Comme on faisoit es grans pompes funebres	Like the way it was done during the mystery [plays
Jadis a Rome, où aux festes celebres	in ancient Rome, where, at the famous
D'Isis, querant par troux et par latebres	Isis feasts, they pretended to look for her [deceased husband
Son mary mort, aumoins par fictions.	in every nook and cranny.

The lament is on the death of Louis of Luxembourg, in 1503. Related to Charles VIII and one of the most famous knights of the French court of Louis XII, he was one of the leading generals in the French invasions of Milan in 1499 and 1500. The word "proportions" probably refers to the particular form of rhythmic notation that Josquin had used in his *Déploration de Johan. Okeghem* (see p. 210), which was notated exclusively in black notes. It is not known whether Josquin responded to Lemaire's appeal.

A remarkable tribute to Josquin is by Teofilo Folengo (1491–1544) in Book XX of his *Baldus*, a long poem composed in hexameters published in the year of Josquin's death (and reprinted in Amsterdam in 1692). After predicting a glorious golden era of the music of Josquin and his successors, he says that God, listening to his compositions, will open to him the gates of Heaven. The poet goes on to list eight Masses, four motets and a chanson (here in italics):

> Josquini quoniam cantus frifolabitis illos,
> Quos Deus auscultans coelum monstrabit apertum.
> Missa *super voces Musarum, lassaque far mi,*
> Missa *super sextum, Fortunam,* missaque *musque,*
> Missaque *de Domina, sine nomine, Duxque Ferrarie.*
> Partibus in senis cantabitur illa *Beata,*
> *Huc me sidereo, se congé, Praeter,* et illud
> Compositum *Miserere,* Duca rogitante Ferrara.

These Masses are published in the *NJE* as *Missa L'homme armé super voces musicales, Missa La sol fa re mi, Missa L'homme armé sexti toni, Missa Fortuna desperata, Missa Une mousse de Biscaye* and *Missa De beata virgine* (known in some sources as *Missa de domina*). The six-voice motet *Beata* probably refers to *O virgo prudentissima,* since it is based on the *cantus firmus* "Beata mater". The other pieces are *Huc me sydereo, Se congié prens, Preter rerum seriem* and *Miserere mei, deus.*

A related poem, *Dum vastos Adriae fluctus,* also in hexameters, was set to music by Jacquet of Mantua and published as a motet in 1554. The author is unknown, but he takes several phrases from the classical poet Virgil, who also had connections to Mantua. After the introductory lines, describing the observations of Bacchus by the Adriatic Sea, the poet continues:

> Josquini antiquos, Musae, memoremus amores,
> Quorum iussa facit magni regnator Olympi
> Aeternam *praeter seriem* et moderamina *rerum,*
> Dum *stabat mater* miserans natumque decoris
> *Inviolata* manens lacrimis plorabat iniquo
> Iudicio extinctum. *Salve,* o sanctissima, *salve*
> *Regina* et tu summe Deus *miserere* quotannis
> Cui vitulo et certis cumulabo altaria donis.
> Dixerat. Argutae referebant omnia cannae
> Mincius et liquidis annuit amnis aquis.

The pieces named (two of which appear also in Folengo's poem) are published in the *NJE* as *Preter rerum seriem, Stabat mater, Inviolata, integra et casta es,* the four-voice *Salve regina,* and *Miserere mei, deus.* Jacquet apparently uses thematic material from Josquin's motets when they are mentioned in the text.

After the middle of the sixteenth century, Josquin as the composer of choice for poetic tributes begins to be supplanted by Orlando di Lasso. In 1576, a collection of his chansons was published in Paris with a sonnet by Jean Mégnier that begins by calling Josquin "Le bon pere de la Musique", and ends with

Josquin aura la Palme ayant esté premier:	Josquin will bear the palm, having been the first;
Willaert le Myrte aura: Cyprian le Laurier:	Willaert will have the myrtle; Cypriano the laurel;
Orlande emportera les trois comme le maistre.	Orlando, as the master, will earn all three.

In his poetry collection *Achtendertig Componisten* (Thirty-eight Composers) from 1987, Jozef Eyckmans, placing Josquin second in his chronology between Philippe de Vitry and Monteverdi, evokes in some abstract and hermetic lines a "resinous, sacred song". In the same year, Guus Wakelkamp, in *De stad is een jongen*, recalls the time of his childhood when he was a choirboy:

In hoge kathedralen zong ik eens uw lied	In high cathedrals once I sang your song
ver van mijzelf en dicht bij God.	Far from myself and close to God.
Nu voel ik mij verlaten. Ik ben in alle staten,	Now I feel bereft, and desperate
want ik vind u niet.	Not to find you.
De muziek geeft mij de vrede niet,	The music does not grant me any peace,
noch de herinnering aan vervlogen jaren.	Nor the memory of years far gone.
Niets van die gewijde dag kon ik bewaren.	Of that sacred day nothing could be kept.
In hoge kathedralen zong ik eens uw lied.	In high cathedrals once I sang your song.

Lastly, inspired by the text of the motet *Illibata dei virgo* (see p. 180), the Dutch poetess Maria van Daalen dedicated to Josquin the following acrostic in the form of a hendecasyllabic sonnet, which is first published in this book:

Joy of songs, high find of love's harmony and
Order of this world, where in cascades of tones
Strength piety evokes: her name will prevail.
Queen of heaven, bring forth the Son of Man! For life
Unifies design; its weaving voices count
Inviolate rhythm of breath abundant, strive
Nimbly climbing for canonic verses, mount
Day and night, outline the stars' eternal trail;
El grillo's persistent choice: to sing, condones
Superior moves that save embellishment,
Proclaims its heat, its now – such a simple drive
Reins in human passion. Honey of its sound
Eternally, make all our tongues to hive
Zealous, in ears and hearts, your call sublime: Hail!

Music theorists

The first music theorists to explore Josquin's music were the Italians Franchinus Gaffurius in 1496 and 1508, Pietro Aaron in 1516 and 1529, and Giovanni Spataro in 1521 and 1531. The latter states in his *Tractato di musica* "ho trovato Josquim despret, optimo de li compositori del tempo nostro ..." (I have found Josquin, the best composer of our time ...). In Germany, the first treatise to name Josquin was that of Andreas Ornitoparchus from 1517; Sebald Heyden followed in 1540 with *De arte canendi* (On the Art of Singing), which, though it contains numerous examples from Josquin's oeuvre, does not actually name him.

FIGURE 10: Glarean. Drawing by Hans Holbein the Younger in the margin of Chapter 50 of the Basel copy from 1515 of Erasmus' *Praise of Folly* (Stultitiae laus).

By far the most important theoretical work concerning Josquin was *Dodecachordon* (1547) by Heinrich Glarean, a Swiss humanist influenced by Erasmus, who later became his friend (Fig. 10). Not only does he discuss a large number of works, but in Chapter 24 of Book III is also a long eulogy, which includes the following:

> Moreover, although his genius [*ingenium*] is indescribable and we can be amazed at it more than we can treat it worthily, it also seems that not only in genius should he be placed above others, but also in carefulness of his emendations. For those who knew him say that he published his works after much deliberation and with manifold corrections; neither did he release a song to the public

unless he had kept it to himself for some years, the opposite of what Jacob Obrecht appears to have done, as we have previously said.[13]

The title of Glarean's treatise refers to the theory of the twelve modes, which he himself developed by adding four modes to the medieval eight. This is the basis of another passage from the same eulogy:

> If the knowledge of twelve modes and of a true musical system had fallen to the lot of this man, considering his natural genius and the acuteness of intellect through which he became esteemed, nature could have produced nothing more august, nothing more magnificent in this art. His talent was so versatile in every way, so equipped by a natural acumen and vigor, that there was nothing in this field which he could not do.[14]

Yet it should not be overlooked that this passage concludes with the following critical observation:

> But in many instances [Josquin] lacked a proper measure and a judgement based on knowledge and thus in some places in his songs he did not fully restrain as he ought to have, the impetuosity of a lively talent, although this ordinary fault may be condoned because of the otherwise incomparable gifts of the man.[15]

In contrast to Glarean's expert commentary are the assertions by Adrianus Petit Coclico in his *Compendium musices* of 1552. This musician was born in Flanders, emigrated to Germany, and claimed he was a pupil of Josquin, though there is no documentary evidence to support this. Nevertheless, he says in the introduction to the second part of his book:

> My teacher Josquin ... never gave a lecture on music or wrote a theoretical work, and yet he was able in a short time to form complete musicians, because he did not keep back his pupils with long and useless instructions, but taught them the rules in a few words, through practical application in the course of singing.[16]

In the last chapter, dealing with the rules of composition, Coclico refers to his teacher saying that composers who make no use of counterpoint "wish to fly without wings."

Exactly 25 years later, the blind Spanish organist Francisco de Salinas wrote in his *De musica* (pp. 288–289):

> Aristotle in his Problems [book XIX, paragraph 5], inquiring why we tend to listen with greater pleasure to a song that we already know than to one that is unknown to us, among other reasons

---

13 After Miller, vol. 2, 265.

14 *Ibidem*, 264.

15 For still other criticisms, see Rob Wegman, ' "And Josquin Laughed" ...', 356.

16 After Albert Smijers, 'Josquin des Prez', in *Proceedings of the Musical Association* 53 (1926-27), 95–116, at 105.

gives these: that when we know what is sung, it is more obvious that the singer is performing what the composer intended; just as the familiar attracts the eye with more pleasure, so also the familiar is sweeter to the ear than the unfamiliar. Furthermore, when a familiar song is heard, we more pleasurably perceive in its sounds the various modes which the good writer of music uses. Wherefore, those highly celebrated motets of Josquin des Prez, *Inviolata*, *Benedicta es coelorum regina*, and *Preter rerum seriem*, are held in greater esteem than those of which he himself was entirely the composer, since to the songs that have been used for centuries in the church and are familiar to all, the intertwining of many parts was added.[17]

Also of interest is the reference to Josquin by Cesare Monteverdi in defence of his elder brother Claudio. After the latter had been criticised by Artusi, a polemist from Bologna, for ending pieces in a different mode from the one he had begun in, Cesare retorted, in the preface to his brother's *Scherzi musicali* of 1607, that Claudio was not alone: "Would not Josquin be an ignoramus for having begun his Mass on "Faisant regrets" in the sixth mode and finished it in the second?"[18]

Finally, Andrea Adami, maestro of the Sistine Chapel, of which Josquin had also been a member, published in 1711 a treatise containing regulations for the singers: in a lengthy description of Josquin, he mentions that his name is engraved in the choir of the chapel (see above, Fig. 2), and says, "His works show that he was an extraordinarily intelligent composer, who applied the rules exactly, and with much lively inventiveness, and was gifted with a lot of aptitude for the compositional art of his time ..."[19]

Music publishers

Music publishers, too, joined the ranks of those expressing admiration for Josquin's talents. Below are the words of four of them, by way of a sample.

The German publisher Hans Ott, who did not have a printing press at his disposal, had the two parts of his *Novum opus musicum* printed by Hieronymus Formschneider in Nuremberg in 1537–1538. In the Latin dedication of the first part to King Ferdinand I, he writes, "All will easily recognize JOSQUIN as the most celebrated hero of the art of music, for he possesses something that is truly divine and inimitable." When he published Josquin's motet *Miserere mei, deus* a year later, he commented:

> I beg whether anyone can listen so carelessly as not to be moved in his whole spirit and whole intellect towards contemplating the message of the Prophet more carefully, since the melodies conform to the feelings of one who is burdened by the magnitude of his sins and [since] the very deliberate repetition [of the prayer "Miserere mei, deus"] by which [the sinner] begs for mercy, does not permit the soul either to reflect idly or to fail to be moved toward hope and assurance.[20]

---

17   After Stevenson, 'Josquin in the Music of Spain and Portugal', 236–237.

18   After Oliver Strunk, *Source Readings in Music History* (New York 1950), 412.

19   See Carlo Fiore, *Josquin des Prez* (Palermo 2003), 147.

20   After Stephanie P. Schlagel, 'A Credible (Mis)Attribution to Josquin in Hans Ott's *Novum et insigne opus musicum*. Contemporary Perceptions, Modern Conceptions, and the Case of *Veni sancte Spiritus*', in *TVNM* 56 (2006), 97–126, at 117.

Johannes Petreius, also in Nuremberg, published the second volume of *Kurzweiliger gu-ter frischer teutscher Liedlein*. In the introduction, Georg Forster writes that his book is particularly suitable for "schlechten singern" (ordinary singers), who will do them more justice than they would "a precious work by Josquin or another celebrated composer."

In 1545, Tylman Susato published his famous *Septiesme livre* in Antwerp. In the dedication to the "tres honnorable & vertueulx seigneur" Lazarus Doucher, he writes, among other things, that the book contains chansons by the late 'Iosquin des Pres' of blessed memory, "in his time most excellent & highly eminent in musical knowledge."[21] He continues, "I wanted to begin to print these works so that everybody may have a perpetual memorial, which he well deserved."

Ten years later, the Parisians Adrian le Roy and Robert Ballard published a book of four-, five- and six-voice motets by Josquin. From the outset, the title proclaims the composer to be "praestantissimus" – the most superior. This book has a long Latin dedication to the Parisian magistrate Jacques Aubry, whom Le Roy wishes to reward, for his magnanimity and benevolence, by republishing works of the man that can be called the father of music, just as Homer is the father of poetry.

> This man had the ideal forms [he uses the Platonic term 'ideas'] of all modulationes and cantus [i.e. the harmonic and melodic aspects of music] as though imprinted or etched upon his mind. No combination of sounds, whether low or high, subtle and refined or popular and crowd-pleasing, slow or swift, thin and bare or full and complex, no combination can be imagined which he did not both attempt and accomplish. And (something which you particularly value) he added to sometimes laughable music such a quality of majesty that the most learned of Germans [probably Glarean] would call him the divine and inimitable hero of this discipline.[22]

Even though this praise may be called pompous, it makes clear that, at least in cultivated French musical circles of the mid-sixteenth century, Josquin was still regarded as a model.

Music historians

When the first books on general music history began to appear in England in the 1770s, the authors did not hide their admiration for the quality of Josquin's music. Examples of his music began to appear again for the first time in the histories by Charles Burney and John Hawkins, showing that they had both studied Josquin's music in depth. In his *General History of Music* (1776–1789), Burney writes:

> Indeed the laws and difficulties of Canon, Fugue, Augmentation, Diminution, Reversion, and almost every other species of learned contrivance allowable in ecclesiastical compositions for

---

21   After Bonnie Blackburn, 'Josquin's Chansons: Ignored and Lost Sources', in *JAMS* 29 (1976), 30–76, at 54.

22   After Jeremy Noble, 'Another *Regina celi* Attributed to Josquin', in *From Ciconia to Sweelinck: Donum natalicium Willem Elders*, edd. Albert Clement and Eric Jas (Amsterdam – Atlanta 1994), 145–152, at 146.

voices, were never so well observed, or happily vanquished, as by Josquin; who may justly be called the father of modern harmony, and the inventor of almost every ingenious contexture of its constituent parts, near a hundred years before the time of Palestrina, Orlando di Lasso, Tallis, or Bird...[23]

After considering his Mass compositions, motets and secular works, Burney concludes with some general observations: "Indeed, I have never seen, among all his productions that I have scored, a single movement which is not stamped with some mark of the great master."[24]

In Germany, Johann Nikolaus Forkel followed in the footsteps of his English colleagues in the second volume of his *Allgemeine Geschichte der Musik* of 1801, which also came with numerous music examples and no fewer than 65 pages devoted to the composer: "Josquin – as far as all facts recounted about him allow us to conclude – was without question a true genius, even from time to time perhaps in the same sense that one is accustomed to in our own times."[25] But although he emphasizes the extraordinary fame of the composer, Forkel, still under the spell of eighteenth-century philosophy on music, is more reserved than his English colleagues.

After winning a gold medal in Amsterdam in 1826 for his essay *Die Verdienste der Niederländer um die Tonkunst* (The Contributions of the Netherlanders to Music), Raphael Kiesewetter wrote in his general history of music, eight years later, "Without a doubt, Josquin was one of the greatest musical geniuses of all time."[26]

The third volume of the *Geschichte der Musik* by August Wilhelm Ambros, which appeared in Leipzig in 1868, is a milestone in the historiography of Josquin. Pages 203–236 are witness to such a depth of knowledge that musicologists today still make reference to his work. His understanding undoubtedly rests on the fact that he transcribed much of Josquin's music into modern score. His conclusion is striking: "Josquin underwent an artistic growth like no-one before him, and after him only a few (p. 209)."

We end this brief overview with two publications from the twentieth century. The first major monograph on the composer, written by Helmuth Osthoff, appeared in 1962–1965. In the first volume of *Josquin Desprez*, the author explores, among other things, the composer's personality and the many testimonies to Josquin's posthumous fame. Regarding his personality, Osthoff writes:

Josquin is the first great composer to whose personality anecdotes became attached, and none thereof proved to be more tenacious than the famous story of how he once made the French king fulfil his promise of remuneration. Even after more than one hundred years, it circulated in Europe as a unique example of how a famous and brilliant musician behaved towards a monarch (p. 81).

---

23   Vol. 2, 485; (R/1935), 735.

24   *Ibidem*, 509; (R/1935), 751.

25   After Andrew Kirkman, 'From Humanism to Enlightenment: Reinventing Josquin', in *JM* 17 (1999), 441–458, at 446.

26   *Geschichte der europäisch-abendländischen oder unsrer heutigen Musik* (Leipzig 1834), 57.

The American musicologist Richard Taruskin devotes the fourteenth chapter of the first volume of *The Oxford History of Western Music* (2005) to the composer. Drawing on Osthoff, he writes:

> Josquin was the first composer to interest his contemporaries and (especially) his posterity as a personality. He was the subject of gossip and anecdote, and the picture that emerges again resembles the popular conception of Beethoven: a cantankerous, arrogant, distracted sort of man, difficult in social intercourse but excused by grace of his transcendent gift. Josquin, like Beethoven, was looked upon with awe as one marked off from others by divine inspiration – a status formerly reserved for prophets and saints (p. 548).

Composers
Josquin's *Missa De beata virgine* (NJE 3.3) had a strong influence on later composers: Jacques Arcadelt (ca. 1505–1568) and composers linked to the Vatican in the first half of the sixteenth century, such as Johannes Bonnevin and Vincent Misonne, all reworked material from the Mass into new settings of the same name.[27] Lupus Hellinck (ca. 1495–1541) and an anonymous Polish composer were both inspired in their *Missae Mater patris* by Josquin's eponymous Mass (NJE 10.1). But it was his *Missa Hercules Dux Ferrarie* (NJE 11.1) that had the most imitators. The theme of the Mass, ingeniously based on the solmisation tones *ut re mi fa sol la* (called a *soggetto cavato*; see p. 118), gave several later masters the idea of undertaking something similar. So by Hellinck we have the Masses *Hercules Dux Ferrarie* and *Carolus Imperator Romanorum Quintus*, by Jacquet of Mantua the Masses *Hercules Dux Ferrarie* and *Ferdinandus Dux Calabrie*, by Cipriano de Rore the Mass *Vivat felix Hercules*, by the Spaniard Bartolomé de Escobedo the Mass *Philippus Rex Hispanie*, and by Philippe Rogier the Mass *Philippus secundus Rex Hispanie*. In each of these Masses, the theme on which the five parts are based is formed from solmisation notes corresponding to the vowels in the title. Five Masses, notably that of Robert de Févin, are also known to be indebted to Josquin's Mass on the solmisation syllables *La–sol–fa–re–mi* (NJE 11.2).

The extent to which Josquin's music inspired imitation is even clearer from parody Masses than in the case of the *soggetto cavato* technique. The technique of parody is the reuse of pre-existing polyphonic material in a new composition. The composer divided his model into a number of segments, which were placed at key moments in the new Mass and separated by longer or shorter interpolations. The beginning of the model will normally be heard at the start of each Mass section, and in the longer Mass sections, certain thematic groups may be used more than once. In many cases, it is clearly not only musical quality that underlies the choice of model, but also a desire to pay tribute to an older master, and to get to know his works better through imitation.

Here follows a list of motets and chansons, together with the composer(s) that used material from these works for a parody Mass.

---

27   See Rob van Haarlem, 'The *Missa De beata virgine* by Josquin Used as a Model for the Mass of the Same Name by Arcadelt', in *TVNM* 25 (1975), 33–37.

Absalon fili mi (NJE *14.1) – an anonymous composer

Ave Maria (NJE 23.6) – Antoine de Févin, Daser and an anonymous composer

Benedicta es, celorum regina (NJE 23.13) – Celliers de Hesdin, Morales, Palestrina, Merulo, La Hèle, De Monte and Köler

Inviolata, integra et casta es (NJE 24.4) – Daser and an anonymous composer (Verdelot?)

Memor esto verbi tui (NJE 17.14) – an anonymous composer

Mente tota (NJE 25.14, V. pars) – Antoine de Févin and Willaert

Miserere mei, deus (NJE 18.3) – Parvus

Missus est Gabriel angelus (NJE 20.7) – Moulu

O intemerata virgo (NJE 25.14, III. pars) – Hellinck and Forestier

Preter rerum seriem (NJE 24.11) – Le Maistre, Daser, De Rore, La Hèle, Spongopeus and an anonymous composer

Qui habitat in adjutorio altissimi (NJE 18.7) – Daser

Stabat mater (NJE 25.9) – Vinders and an anonymous composer

Baisiez moy (NJE 28.4) – Forestier

En l'ombre d'ung buissonnet (NJE 27.7) – Carpentras

Le villain jaloux (NJE 28.22) – Robert de Févin

It appears that Antoine Brumel, Antoine de Févin and his brother Robert, all contemporaries of Josquin, were the first composers to choose his works as a starting point for their own. Those that followed came from all over Europe, and included both minor composers and famous masters such as Giovanni da Palestrina and Philippe de Monte. And the Masses of George de la Hèle, for example, published in Antwerpen in 1578, more than sixty years after their models were composed, show that Josquin's music remained long influential.

Benedicta es and *Preter rerum seriem*, both for six voices, became the best known motets. They served not only as models for a number of Masses, but, as we see with Orlando di Lasso, also for settings of the *Magnificat*. The Spaniard Diego Ortiz quoted several melodic fragments from *Benedicta es* in a seven-voice setting, as did Jean de Castro in a tricinium and Claude Le Jeune in a five-part instrumental fantasy. The Christmas motet *Preter rerum seriem* resurfaces in motets by the Portuguese composer Vincente Lusitano, and in Germany by Sethus Calvisius, cantor at St. Thomas' Church in Leipzig. On the famous *Ave Maria* not only were three parody Masses composed, but several composers, including Ludwig Senfl in a six-voice motet, also incorporated material from it into new settings of the text. The same can be said of the five-voice psalm *Miserere mei, deus*. The recurring ostinato-like refrain "Miserere mei, deus", which is repeated after each verse, inspired over twenty later composers to a more or less similar procedure insofar as they chose this motto as a starting point for a setting of the same psalm or a motet based on another text.[28]

As for Josquin's four-part chansons *Adieu mes amours*, *Bergerette savoysienne* and *Mille regretz*, we find quotes from one or more voices in the eponymous Masses by Jacob Obrecht, Brumel and Cristóbal de Morales. Brumel also applied Josquin's

---

28   See Patrick Macey, *Josquin's Miserere mei deus: Context, Structure and Influence* (Ph. D. diss. University of California at Berkeley, 1985), 151f.

double-canon technique from his chanson NJE *28.13 in his *Missa A l'ombre d'ung buissonet*. Petrus Roselli's *Missa Baisez moy*, which actually is a 'Quodlibet' Mass, uses in Kyrie II material from Josquin's three-voice *Quant je vous voye*, and in the Sanctus from the canonic *Baisez moy*. Finally, manuscripts in Berlin and Jena from around 1500 each contain an anonymous Mass incorporating fragments from *Bergerette savoysienne*.

Another phenomenon is the addition of newly-composed voices to a work of Josquin. An extra voice is to be found, for example, in *Miserere mei, deus*, the last Agnus dei of the *Missa L'homme armé super voces musicales*, and the *Stabat mater*. In the last motet, there were even two musicians, one in England and one in Bohemia, that composed a sixth voice, independently of each other. To the four-voice motets *Ave Maria* (NJE 23.6) and *O bone et ducissime Jesu* (NJE 21.9) two new voices were added, and Jean Guyot went so far as to add six additional voices to the six-voice *Benedicta es*. This also happened frequently with the chansons. For instance, the double canon *Baisez moy* (NJE 28.4) survives in a version consisting of three two-part canons. It cannot be said, though, that Josquin's compositions were in any way improved by these additions. Rather, we get the feeling that the above-mentioned statement by Glarean on Josquin's sense of perfection, and the incident that is supposed to have happened in Cambrai, speak volumes in this regard.

Josquin also turns out to have been a 'standard' for a few composers in the twentieth century. In a letter to Roland Holst in 1928 about his book *Shelley* (Een afscheid) (Shelley (a Farewell)), Matthijs Vermeulen sees himself, as an idealistic composer, placed in a dilemma, because of the barrier that separates him from "what for our predecessors was a safe and heavenly wonderland":

> In music, I can still experience the capacity for hearing – that wonderland – as a possible reality of every moment, because Genius, which we are doubtful of, has caused that wonderland beauty to be realised with human and superhuman excellence, an automatic excellence that, even on the greyest of days, cannot be unpicked. (I am thinking of e.g. Mozart and Josquin des Près.)[29]

Also in the 1920s, Dimitri Shostakovich had regular contact with Alexander Glazunov during his studies at the Saint Petersburg Conservatoire. In his memoirs dictated to Solomon Volkov and published in 1979, Shostakovich writes:

> Glazunov's erudition in music history was outstanding for those days. He knew, as few others did, the wonderful music of the great contrapuntalists of the Flemish and Italian schools. It's only nowadays that everyone is so educated, and no one doubts the genius and viability of fifteenth- and sixteenth-century music. But in those days, let us be frank, the picture was completely different; that music was hidden beneath seven seals. Even Rimsky-Korsakov felt that music began with Mozart ... Glazunov delighted in Josquin des Prés, Orlando di Lasso, Palestrina, and Gabrieli, and willy-nilly, I began to find delight in them too, even though

---

29   See Ton Braas, *Door het geweld van zijn verlangen. Een biografie van Matthijs Vermeulen* (Amsterdam 1997), 306.

at first I thought their music difficult and boring. It was also very interesting to listen how Glazunov evaluated this music, for he never limited himself to general delight, he truly knew and loved these composers. And it seemed to us that he could always distinguish between the general 'style of the era', and the individual composer's insights, the truly marvellous example of musical genius.[30]

Of the seventy or so admirers of Josquin's music that have 'spoken' in this chapter, composers, significantly, form the largest group. It is they, after all, more than writers and poets, more than music theorists and music historians, who had the wherewithal to find their way to the core of his work and appreciate the talent of its creator. Unlike, for example, publishers, who may have had a commercial interest in publishing Josquin, composers had other motives for their fascination. For them, 'borrowing' musical material or following certain compositional principles was inherent to their deep respect for the man they all regarded as the *primus inter pares*.

---

30   Solomon Volkov (ed.), *Testimony: The Memoirs of Dmitri Shostakovich* (London 1979), 44.

Josquin's reputation and the quality of his music explain why his work is preserved in a large number of sources. Scrutinising their distribution, it is clear that we are concerned with a composer whose music was performed in most European countries.

The sources fall into four categories:
- Manuscripts, the earliest of which date from the 1480s
- Printed editions, which appear from the beginning of the sixteenth century
- Manuscripts and printed editions of instrumental arrangements
- Handwritten or printed music theory treatises

Manuscripts
More than for the monophonic music of the Middle Ages, which had a long oral tradition, notation was a prerequisite for the survival of composed polyphonic music. Until the invention of the printing of polyphonic music in the years 1498–1501, the manuscript was the only medium for the dissemination of this musical heritage. As a rule, manuscripts were produced in so-called scriptoria, and, as is inherent in any handicraft, they differed from each other in both appearance and content. In size they also varied considerably. Placed on a large lectern where the whole choir could sing from it, a church choirbook could measure as much as 60 × 43 cm. The voices of the composition were notated above and beside each other on the verso and recto sides of the folios. In the realm of secular music the format was always much smaller. For example, French *chansonniers* from the second half of the fifteenth and early sixteenth centuries, often gems of calligraphy, measure on average only 20 × 14 cm. 'Partbooks' – separate books for each voice – also remained on the small side.

It is not uncommon for a manuscript to consist of sections that did not initially belong together. When these were later bound into one volume, the larger pages were trimmed, which could lead to the partial or complete loss of a composer's name, since it was generally written in the top margin at the start of a composition.

In contrast to parchment manuscripts, many paper manuscripts have suffered from so-called bleed-through. This is a process, especially disastrous for black note-heads, whereby iron contained in the ink reacts with carbon monoxide from the atmosphere and digests the paper. Modern restoration techniques can halt this process, as in the case of Codex 15 from the Sistine Chapel, which contains Josquin's famous *Illibata dei virgo*.

Manuscripts including Josquin's authentic and dubious works can be found today in the following locations. The number of manuscripts per town, if more than one, is given in parentheses. (Note that partbooks originally belonging together have sometimes become separated, so may now be found in more than one library.)

AUSTRIA – Vienna (11)

BELGIUM – Brussels (7), Tournai

CZECH REPUBLIC – Brno (2), Hradec Králové (7), Prague, Rokycany

DENMARK – Copenhagen (3)

ENGLAND – Cambridge, London (8)

FRANCE – Cambrai (3), Paris (7)

GERMANY – Augsburg, Berlin (12), Dresden (12), Eisenach, Erlangen, Frankfurt am Main, Gotha, Greifswald, Halle, Hamburg, Heilbronn (2), Herdringen (3), Iserlohn, Jena (6), Kassel (2), Leipzig (3), Munich (20), Nuremberg, Regensburg (15), Rostock (5), Stuttgart (3), Ulm (2), Weimar, Wittenberg, Wolfenbüttel (2), Zwickau (10)

HUNGARY – Budapest (6)

ITALY – Bergamo, Bologna (11), Casale Monferrato (2), Cividale del Friuli, Cortona, Florence (15), Milan (3), Modena (6), Padua, Perugia, Piacenza, Rocca di Mezzo, Rome (5), Siena, Treviso, Vatican City (28), Verona (5)

NETHERLANDS – Amsterdam, Leiden (4), Utrecht (2)

POLAND – Gdańsk, Kraków (3), Poznań, Warsaw, Wrocław (2)

PORTUGAL – Braga, Coimbra

SCOTLAND – Edinburgh

SPAIN – Barcelona (4), Madrid, Saragossa, Segovia, Seville (2), Tarazona, Toledo (10), Valladolid (4)

SWEDEN – Uppsala (4)

SWITZERLAND – Basel (9), Saint Gall (4), Sion

USA – Buffalo, New Haven, Washington

In total, 314 manuscripts are known, of which 284 contain one to five works, 26 contain six to ten, and 4 contain eleven or more. A similar inventory of the works of Jacob Obrecht generates just 110 manuscripts. Of these, 27 contain only the *Passio*, which, although attributed to him in nine late sources, is regarded as very doubtful due to the fact that three other composers are associated with it in the earlier manuscripts. We can conclude therefore that, though Obrecht was second only to Josquin in the eyes of many of his contemporaries, the latter's reputation is clearly reflected in the much greater number of sources of his music. Nevertheless, it is good to remember that these numbers are only relative. If we take printed music as a reference, the survival rate of publications that have come down to us (which would probably have had print runs of about a hundred copies or more) was seldom more than three to ten percent. This means that the over 300 manuscripts containing works by Josquin must represent only a small fraction of those that existed in the sixteenth century.

The great loss of manuscripts produced five centuries ago was caused by fire, wars and revolutions (Fig. 11). They could also be destroyed as a result of changing musical interests. Thus, in the University of Amsterdam Toonkunst Collection are fragments of two motets by Josquin among several folios of a sixteenth-century choirbook that had been reused to strengthen the binding of another volume (Fig. 12). The manuscripts that have best stood the test of time are the richly decorated choirbooks, often illuminated with miniatures. This group includes those produced by a 'school' of scribes headed by Petrus Alamire (Peter van den Hove) in Mechlin and Brussels, which made manuscripts for Emperor Maximilian I, his daughter Margaret of Austria and his son Philip the Fair, Emperor Charles V, Emanuel I (King of Portugal), Henry VIII (King of England), Pope Leo X, Frederick III the Wise (Elector of Saxony), Pompejus Occo (an Amsterdam banker), and the Fugger family (Augsburg bankers).

FIGURE 11: *O intemerata virgo* (Pars III of NJE 25.14). Milan, Archivio della Veneranda Fabbrica del Duomo, Librone 4, f. 104'. The codex was seriously damaged by fire in 1906.

FIGURE 12: Fragment of the motet *Memor esto verbi tui* in the University library in Amsterdam, Bijzondere Collecties, Toonkunstcollectie, Ms. V A 1.

Manuscripts for practical music making were much more vulnerable than luxury manuscripts. This can be seen clearly when compositions were written out in partbooks. Incomplete sets of such manuscripts – and this also applies to printed editions – are numerous. A typical example is a soprano partbook from a set of four or five that was copied around 1550 in Wittenberg, now privately owned in Utrecht. It contains two psalm motets by Josquin that are fully preserved in other sources (see below, Fig. 32). This is not the case, though, with the motet *Ave mundi spes Maria*, found in a set of three books in the Austrian National Library, which has lost its soprano partbook, nor with the chanson *Tant vous aimme* in a set of three books in the Library of the Florence Conservatoire, which lacks the bass. Both works have been published in the *NJE* with a reconstruction of the missing voice.

A few comments should be added to the overview of manuscript distribution given above. Josquin's music cannot be said to have been performed in a particular place just because a manuscript is found there today. Thus the Kraków manuscripts are of German provenance and, before the Second World War, were to be found in the Prussian State Library in Berlin. Three of the manuscripts in the Austrian National Library in Vienna were once owned by the Fugger family in Augsburg. The manuscripts in Utrecht come from Wittenberg, in Germany, and Lerma, in Spain. Nor is the current location of a manuscript indicative of where Josquin worked. For though he is not known ever to have set a foot in Germany, over a third of the manuscripts are found there today, more than in any other country. This is undoubtedly due to the fact that Luther sang the praises of Josquin's music in the 1530s, inspiring a veritable 'Josquin Renaissance'. Anyone expecting Josquin's homeland to be richly endowed would be disappointed: only ten manuscripts are preserved there, probably due in part to the French Revolution, which caused the destruction of much church property. Italy stands in distinct contrast to France, particularly since a third of his surviving works there are found in the Vatican Library. This is a direct result of Josquin's activities at the Sistine Chapel in the years 1489–1495 or later. Finally, Spanish manuscripts are witness to the intensive political and cultural contacts between the Southern Netherlands and Spain, both then countries of the Habsburg Empire: in Toledo are found manuscripts dating from the period 1520–1555 that, together, contain 22 different compositions by Josquin. Among other manuscripts in Spain, now lost, the following can be mentioned. The library of Germaine de Foix, the second wife of King Ferdinand II of Aragon, contained a book with twenty Masses attributed to Josquin that, in 1538, was bequeathed to the cloister of San Miguel de los Reyes. And from 1602, in the reign of Philip III, dates an inventory of the Escorial Library listing, among other manuscripts with works by Josquin, a parchment codex with ten Masses "de Jusquin".[1]

Printed editions

Even more than to the diffusion of his works in manuscript, Josquin owes his great significance for the history of Western music to the fact that the printing of polyphonic music was developed some twenty years after his compositions first began to circulate. For, interestingly enough, it appears that music publishers named the composer more consistently than music scribes, and this led to the affirmation of Josquin's international reputation. Below are listed the most important publishers of his works.

ITALY – Andrea Antico (Rome/Venice); Giacomo Giunta, Giovanni Giacomo Pasoti & Valerio Dorico (Rome); Ottaviano Petrucci (Venice/Fossombrone)

GERMANY – Johann Berg & Ulrich Neuber (Nuremberg); Christian Egenolff (Frankfurt am Main); Hieronymus Formschneider (Nuremberg); Sigismund Grimm & Marcus Wirsung (Augsburg); Melchior Kriesstein (Augsburg); Johannes Petreius (Nuremberg); Georg

---

1   See, respectively, RISM B XV (2005), 375, and Edmond vander Straeten, *La musique aux Pays-Bas avant le XIXᵉ siècle*, 8 vols. (Brussels 1867-88), vol. 8, 365–383.

Rhaw (Wittenberg); Peter Schöffer (Mainz)
BELGIUM – Pierre Phalèse & Jean Bellère (Antwerp); Tielman Susato (Antwerp)
FRANCE – Pierre Attaingnant (Paris); Nicolas Chemin & Claude Goudimel (Paris); Adrian
Le Roy & Robert Ballard (Paris)

The first printer of polyphonic music was Petrucci. He settled in Venice in 1498 and acquired a privilege from the city authorities granting him a monopoly on printed music for 20 years. From the outset in 1501, his first edition, a collection of three- and four-part secular works entitled *Harmonice Musices Odhecaton A*, included eight pieces from Josquin's hand (Fig. 13); and the opening piece in each of Petrucci's four earliest motet collections is also by him. His first edition of Masses in 1502 – as immediately evident in the title *Misse Josquin* – is devoted entirely to the composer. It was reprinted fourteen years later as *Liber primus Missarum Josquin*, because two further volumes had meanwhile appeared. Petrucci published a total of 17 Masses, 8 Mass movements, 32 motets and 24 secular works by Josquin.

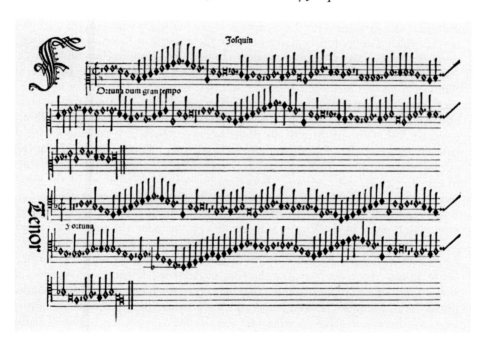

FIGURE 13: Superius and tenor voice parts of *Fortuna dun gran tempo*. Petrucci, *Harmonice Musices Odhecaton A* (Venice 1501), f. 80'.

The publications of Antico in the period 1516–1521 also date from Josquin's lifetime and include 3 Masses, 10 motets and 8 chansons. Although the Masses were previously published by Petrucci, Antico was the first printer of seven motets and six chansons. For *Recordare, virgo mater*, *La belle se siet*, and *Si j'eusse Marion*, Antico is actually the only source. Between 1526 and 1529, Giunta and his associates published only reprints of earlier editions by Petrucci. A book dating from 1522 comprises ten Masses by eight different composers, including two by Josquin, copied (with errors) from Antico's edition of 1516. It would seem, then, that Petrucci's editions had sold out by this time. In total, over 90 of Josquin's works were published by one or more Italian printers.

In Germany, between 1513 and 1591, almost 60 works attributed to Josquin appeared in 42 publications. The earliest edition, containing three chansons, was Schöffer's *Quinquagena carminum*, of which only the tenor partbook survives; this was in fact a pirated reprint of Petrucci's *Canti B numero cinquanta* of 1502/1503. Seven years later, Grimm & Wirsung published six of Josquin's most famous motets in *Liber selectarum cantionum*, commissioned by Matthaeus Lang, Archbishop of Salzburg. This is a very exceptional music print in the format of a small choirbook (44.5 × 28.5 cm); with voices below and opposite each other on facing pages, it differed from the usual oblong partbook format, which measured generally no more than about 17 × 25 cm. Sixteen copies of this book have been preserved; they show small variations from each other, indicating that it had gone through one or more reprints. From about 1535 a new generation of German music printers began to publish prolifically. Most interesting are the psalm motets, which played a central role in Protestant worship. With the exception of the psalm *De profundis clamavi* (NJE 15.13) from the liturgy for the dead, which in Germany is only found in manuscript sources, all the psalm settings come down to us in one or more German prints.

In Belgium, Josquin's music was first published in 1544 by Susato. This was the chanson *N'esse pas ung grant desplaisir*, which was reprinted the following year in the famous *Septiesme livre*. This volume starts with 24 chansons for five or six voices, all attributed to Josquin, including his lament on the death of Ockeghem – though Josquin's authorship of three of the pieces has been rejected. It concludes with the laments on the death of Josquin mentioned in Chapter 1. Four years later, Susato also published the chanson *Mille regretz*, which had already been printed by Attaingnant in Paris in 1533. In 1590 and 1609, about a century after it was composed, the middle section of the popular *Benedicta es* was printed by Phalèse in a book of duets.

In France, the first publisher of Josquin was Attaingnant. His twelfth book of motets in honour of the Virgin Mary, from 1535, included the five-voice *Salve regina*. In 1549 appeared *Trente sixiesme livre contenant xxx chansons tres musicales ... Le tout de feu Josquin des prez*. Twenty-three of these chansons were taken straight out of Susato's *Septiesme livre*, and the same question mark therefore hangs over the authenticity of a number of them. Shortly afterwards Chemin & Goudimel published the famous motets *Benedicta es* and *Stabat mater*, but of this edition only the soprano partbook survives. A milestone was reached in 1555 when Le Roy & Ballard for the first time devoted a book of 15 motets entirely to Josquin. Even though three of these works were misattributed, the dedication of the book to the Parisian magistrate Jacques Aubry makes amply clear the respect the publishers had for the composer: "... the best thing we could do was ... to uncover the 'monuments' of the man that enriched music more than any other ..." (see p. 40). Unfortunately, the tenor and bass partbooks of this print are lost. In their collections of songs published in the 1560s and later, we again come across many pieces by Josquin.

How does the number of printed editions of Josquin's music relate to the number of manuscripts? The probability of losing all copies of a sixteenth-century music print must be considered very small, so the number of manuscripts of music by Josquin was at least three times greater than the hundred or more prints. But when we consider that some 100 copies of each print would probably have circulated, the picture becomes very different. The total number then increases to about ten thousand copies. Moreover, dissemination of a music print was not confined to its country of origin, as the widespread distribution of extant copies shows. There is, for example, mention in an old inventory in the Moses and Aaron Church in Amsterdam, of a copy of Petrucci's edition of Obrecht Masses that has not survived. Similarly, it would seem certain that the musicians in Spain that arranged sections of Josquin's Masses for keyboard or plucked string instrument would have used Petrucci's editions rather than manuscripts, which were generally in choirbook format, but not a single copy of these prints has yet turned up there.

Among music printers of Josquin, Petrucci was the most productive with 24 publications, including reprints under his own name. Because of the number of compositions he published and because of the great care he took – aided perhaps by his editor Petrus Castellanus – he was of the greatest significance for the promulgation of Josquin's music.

Finally, with regard to repertory, it does not appear that any Masses were printed in Belgium or France; and in Italy the five- and six-voice chansons were absent, no doubt because singers were not sufficiently familiar with the French language. (In the three- and four-part chansons, we see that the texts are either omitted or contain spelling mistakes and corruptions.) In German speaking countries, sources include several chansons supplied with a Latin or even a German text.

Instrumental arrangements

The status of Josquin in the music of the sixteenth century can also be gauged by the large number of arrangements of his vocal compositions for keyboard, lute or other plucked stringed instrument. Among approximately 235 such arrangements in manuscripts and printed editions are found Mass sections, motets and secular works. They were always written in a tablature notation – a combination of notes, letters and/or rhythmic signs – that was specific to the country and/or intended instrument. Compositions transmitted in tablature are called intabulations.

The artistic significance of the intabulations is highly variable. On the one hand are straightforward transcriptions, usually for organ, that follow the model almost literally, and on the other, imaginative arrangements that add a new dimension to the original concept. Here too, the widespread dissemination of Josquin's music is evidenced by the number of countries in which this repertory originated.

Between the earliest print from Venice in 1507 and the last from Lauingen in 1594, we can count over 50 editions containing at least one work by Josquin. Most of these publications name the arranger, as shown below:

BELGIUM – Pierre de Teghi (in publications by Pierre Phalèse)

FRANCE – Grégoire Brayssing, Albert de Rippe

GERMANY – Nicolaus Ammerbach, Benedict de Drusina, Hans Gerle, Simon Gintzler, Wolffen Heckel, Hans Newsidler, Melchior Newsidler, Sebastian Ochsenkun, Jakob Paix

HUNGARY – Valentin Bakfark

ITALY – Melchiore de Barberiis, Franciscus Bossinensis, Girolamo Cavazzoni, Francesco da Milano, Francesco Spinacino

PORTUGAL – Gonzalo de Baena

SPAIN – Antonio de Cabeçon, Miguel de Fuenllana, Alonso Mudarra, Luys de Narváez, Diego Pisador, Enriquez de Valderrábano, Luis Venegas de Henestrosa.

Intabulations of Josquin's compositions are also found in handwritten form, and these tablatures are named after the musician that assembled the collection. The following names are known:

GERMANY – Leonhard Kleber, Jorg Wiltzell
ITALY – Vincenzo Capirola (Fig. 14)
POLAND – Jan of Lublin
SWITZERLAND – Clemens Hör, Hans Kotter, Fridolin Sicher

Like the number of sources of an original composition, the number of intabulations of each composition can also be an indication of its popularity. With 28 intabulations the motet *Benedicta es, celorum regina* bears away the palm, followed by *Stabat mater* with 19. Of both the *Pater noster* and parts of the *Missa De beata virgine* 15 arrangements are known, and 14 of the chanson *Mille regretz*.

An exceptional situation arises in two Spanish sources in tablature, both for vihuela, the Spanish lute: Fuenllana's *Orphenica lyra* of 1554 and Valderrábano's *Libro de musica de vihuela* of 1546. Each contains a piece attributed to Josquin not known in its original vocal form. They are verse 6 from a *Magnificat quarti toni* (see p. 149) and the motet *Obsecro te, domina* (see p. 179).

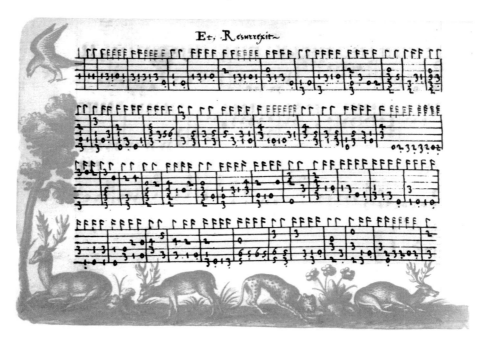

FIGURE 14: Section of the *Credo* of the *Missa L'homme armé sexti toni* in an arrangement for lute by Vincenzo Capirola. Chicago, Newberry Library, Case Ms.VM 140.C25, f. 53'.

Music theory treatises

There are fourteen theoretical treatises known from the sixteenth century and two from the seventeenth century where one or more compositions of Josquin are partially or fully recorded. Eleven of them were published in printed form, the remaining five in manuscript. The printed treatises in particular would clearly have enjoyed widespread dissemination, therefore the compositional examples included could have been widely studied. Here follow some remarks on the most important among them.

The earliest titles are by the German theorist Sebald Heyden. He published two books on the art of singing (*De arte canendi ...*) in Nuremberg in 1537 and 1540, each consisting of two parts, with together over 100 examples from polyphonic compositions. Josquin is represented by over 30 works, more than any other composer.

With the appearance, in 1547, of Glarean's *Dodecachordon* (see p. 37), Josquin's high international standing was again confirmed. Among the 30 composers represented in this disquisition on the twelve modes, he takes by far the most important place with 29 works. What makes Glarean particularly striking is the fact that he, unlike the authors or compilers of most other theoretical treatises, reproduced also entire compositions. These include eight motets and three chansons by Josquin. *Comment peult avoir joye* (NJE 28.7) is supplied with the Latin text "O Jesu fili David", and the two other chansons are without text.

In the treatises of Heinrich Faber (Nuremberg 1550), Johann Zanger (Leipzig 1554) and Hermann Finck (Wittenberg 1556), best regarded as books on general music theory, Josquin remains the most frequently cited composer. In the case of Zanger, it is interesting that the title of his book suggests that he used examples taken from compositions he had sung when a chorister in the chapel choir of Ferdinand I, in Vienna, between 1527 and 1536.

A somewhat exceptional example of 'Josquin as model' is found in Gregorio Fabro's *Musices practicae erotematum* (The question of practical music), printed in Basel in 1553. This is the only theoretical treatise that contains the complete five-voice *Stabat mater* (see p. 173). The author says he records this motet to illustrate the use of ligatures – these are groups of two or more notes whose duration generally depend on their position in the group. The tenor of the motet is a melody from the chanson *Comme femme desconfortée* by Binchois, the note values of which have been lengthened fourfold, and which displays many complex ligatures.

Ten years later, Ambrosius Wilfflingseder published a treatise in Nuremberg with almost the same title (*Erotemata musices practicae*), which contains ten examples taken from Josquin's compositions. The last music theory treatise of the sixteenth century, *Compendium musicae* (Augsburg 1591) by Adam Gumpelzhaimer, appears to have been a bestseller: it was reprinted no less than fourteen times, the last in 1681. However, we find there only a couple of pieces by Josquin. The seventeenth-century treatises by Johann Corvinus, in Copenhagen, and Marin Mersenne, in Paris, likewise cite only one chanson by him, the doubtful *Guillaume se va chauffer* (NJE *28.17).

The five handwritten theoretical treatises are now in Berlin, Hof, Stuttgart, Zwickau, and London. They date from the second half of the sixteenth century and together contain fewer than 30 examples, some no more than as a brief excerpt.

The manuscripts in Berlin, Hof and Zwickau include works by Heinrich Faber (see above). Three of them contain the second *Agnus dei* of the Mass *L'homme armé super voces musicales* (NJE 6.3), which takes the form of a proportion canon (see p. 80). This canon is also found in six of the above printed tracts, making it one of the most cited examples of Josquin's compositional skill.

We should bear in mind that the purpose of the music examples from Josquin's oeuvre in these writings was primarily to educate the sixteenth-century musician. Since the theorists drew their examples, almost without exception, from earlier printed editions like those of Petrucci and Formschneider, or from other colleagues like Glarean or Fabro, their treatises rarely contain useful information about the original version of a composition. Finally, it is notable that nearly all the treatises were written in Latin, and that the area of propagation was mainly German-speaking lands.

In the history of Western music, more works have been wrongly attributed to Josquin than to any other composer. As mentioned in the Preface, the question of authorship is the reason for the significant differences in content between the old and the new editions of his works. Thus, 45 titles in the Smijers edition have been omitted from the *NJE* because the editors were of the opinion that they are not from Josquin's pen. On the other hand, the *NJE* includes 24 compositions, mostly chansons, that are not found in the earlier edition, though the authenticity of 14 of these is not yet secure.

It would be unfair to criticise Smijers for a lack of expertise. He was a pioneer, travelling half of Europe in the 1920s to compile a catalogue of all the manuscripts and prints that contained the works of Josquin, a Herculean task that could scarcely be completed satisfactorily by one person. Only in the 1970s, after musicologists at the University of Illinois at Urbana had begun to set up a microfilm archive of all manuscripts from 1400 to 1550 containing polyphony, together with a complete inventory of their contents, could the dissemination of Josquin's music in Europe be better charted. This project, which took many years, brought to light a great number of new Josquin sources.

The issue of authenticity in the case of Josquin is thornier than with any other composer. His compositional activity over nearly half a century shows different phases of development: while his earliest works display elements in common with Dufay (*d.*1474) and Ockeghem (*d.*1497), his late works point the way towards Palestrina (*d.*1594). But especially problematic are the numerous compositions the sources ascribe to both Josquin and one or more of his contemporaries. This was the focus of a project at the Festival of Early Music in Utrecht in 1986. Four concerts of music by Josquin and those contemporaries with whom he was most confused, Antoine Brumel, Jean Mouton, Pierre de la Rue and Philippe Verdelot, were accompanied by an international symposium that considered a number of compositions bearing multiple attributions. A particularly complex example is the *Magnificat quarti toni* ascribed in the sources to Alexander Agricola, Brumel, La Rue, as well as Josquin, but published as genuine in the *NJE* (NJE 20.3).[1] Sixteenth-century music theorists also struggled with the problem of authenticity. We read, for example, in a homage by Cornelius Grapheus (also known as Scribonius) to the Portuguese composer and diplomat Damiano de Gois, that his music could be mistaken for that of Josquin – a nice compliment perhaps, though the couple of pieces by Gois that have come down to us suggest the author may have been exaggerating. When we note, however, that even Glarean, one of the greatest sixteenth-century connoisseurs of Josquin, sometimes had doubts, the issue comes into sharper focus. In his *Dodecachordon* of 1547, he reproduced the duet "Per illud ave" from the six-voice *Benedicta es, celorum regina*, with the remark, "And it is by the French Jean Mouton. Some ascribe it to Josquin ..."[2] Glarean was misinformed, which is now clear not only from the compositional style, but also from no fewer than 30 attributions to Josquin in the sources. The evidence to the contrary is found in a single mid-sixteenth-century manuscript with the attribution "Jusquin alii Muton".

The 45 works printed in the first edition, but not in the *NJE*, consist of 2 Masses, 14 motets on texts from the Old Testament, 9 motets on texts from the New Testament, 6 motets in honour of Jesus Christ and the Virgin Mary, 2 motets on mixed texts and 12 chansons for four, five and six voices. Here follows a discussion of a few of these works.

MISSA DA PACEM

Although Smijers was aware of the conflicting attributions of the work – four sources ascribe it to Josquin, the remaining two to Noel Bauldeweyn and Jean Mouton – he accepted it as authentic because it "shows a strong stylistic relationship with other compositions by Josquin" (Introduction, p. XIX). However, he ignored the fact that the sources bearing Josquin's name are peripheral and all date from after about 1540, whereas the manuscript with the attribution to Bauldeweyn was produced in Flanders in the years 1516–1518. Bauldeweyn's authorship is confirmed by a sixteenth-century inventory of polyphonic music from Neuburg.[3] In addition, the fact that the counterpoint is much less transparent than in Josquin's other Masses weakens the argument of stylistic similarity.

CELI ENARRANT GLORIAM DEI and LEVAVI OCULOS MEOS

As we have seen in Chapter 2, the great popularity of Josquin's psalm-motets in Germany is due to Luther's admiration for the composer. All but four of the 52 settings attributed to him survive in German sources. Some we know only from German manuscripts or printed editions. This is the case with Ps. 18 (19), *Celi enarrant gloriam dei*, and Ps. 120 (121), *Levavi oculos meos*, with all four sources dating from after about 1535. But a thorough analysis of the two compositions has revealed that they are prototypes of the *imitatio Josquini*.[4] The composer, whoever he may

---

1   The symposium papers and discussions were published in *ProcU*.

2   After Miller, vol. 2, 263.

3   See the hand-written entry regarding this document made by Edgar H. Sparks in a copy of his book *The Music of Noel Bauldeweyn* (New York 1972), 70–96. (Personal communication by Patrick Macey.)

4   Patrick Macey, '*Celi enarrant*: An Inauthentic Psalm Motet Attributed to Josquin', in *ProcU*, 25–44, and Macey, 'Josquin as Classic: *Qui habitat, Memor esto*, and Two Imitations Unmasked', in *Journal of the Royal Musical Association* 118 (1993), 1–43.

have been, not only tried to imitate the style of Josquin's psalm-motets as closely as possible, but even borrowed long passages, with minor modifications, from his most famous settings. For example, the first fifteen measures of the first part of *Celi enarrant* are inspired by the beginning of *Miserere mei, deus* (NJE 18.3), and the first fourteen measures of the third part by the opening of *Fama malum* (NJE 28.15), one of Josquin's motets on a text by Virgil (see Exx. 1a and 1b, and Fig. 42 on p. 200). *Levavi oculos* contains a number of measures that derive from *Qui habitat in adjutorio altissimi* (NJE 18.7). The two psalm-motet models survive in eight and ten German sources, respectively, indicating that they must have been very well known there.

NUNC DIMITTIS SERVUM TUUM

This motet, based on Simeon's hymn of praise in Luke 2:29–32, is found in two Italian manuscripts, of which Bologna Q20 names Josquin. Once again, we find here imitation of his style and adoption of motivic material. When we compare the beginning and end of *Nunc dimittis* with the parallel passages in *Memor esto verbi tui* (NJE 17.14), the degree of similarity is immediately apparent. Because it must be considered extremely unlikely that Josquin, through lack of inspiration, would have fallen back on an earlier work, it appears that Italy also had imitators of his music. This case may perhaps have been motivated by a textual similarity, the first line of each text consisting of two words and four syllables.[5]

AVE CHRISTE IMMOLATE and SANCTA MATER, ISTUD AGAS

Two of the motets in honour of Jesus Christ and the Virgin Mary in the old edition were included through ignorance of other attributions. *Ave Christe immolate* appears in two earlier sources with a slightly different opening line, "Ave caro Christi cara" instead of "Ave Christe immolate", and an attribution to Noel Bauldeweyn – the composer we encountered in connection with the *Missa Da pacem*.[6] Before the discovery of the concordant manuscripts, the motet was widely praised. Helmuth Osthoff (see p. 41) said, among other things, that it has "einen Grad von Schönheit und Ausdruckshaftigkeit, der in der Literatur immer wieder zu Recht betont worden ist" (such a degree of beauty and expressiveness that it has always been justly emphasized in the literature) (vol. 2, 96). This citation indicates in short why, ever since the first modern edition by Franz Commer in about 1850, it had been regarded as a 'real Josquin'.

The situation is somewhat different in the case of the Marian motet *Sancta mater, istud agas*. This survives only in Spanish manuscripts, and carries the name of Josquin in Barcelona 454. However, three other manuscripts have surfaced with an attribution to Francisco de Peñalosa, a contemporary of Josquin linked to the court of Aragon. It is striking that the text of the motet consists of the four stanzas of the *Stabat mater* that are missing from Josquin's famous setting of the sequence (NJE 25.9), a work that became known in Spain shortly after it was composed. It is therefore possible that the copyist of the Barcelona manuscript believed that *Sancta mater, istud agas* was a later addition by Josquin himself, perhaps intended for the

5   See Macey, 'Josquin as Classic ...', 28–41, and NJE *20.8, Critical Commentary, 87–89.
6   Sparks, *The Music of Noel Bauldeweyn*, 98–103.

feast of 'Nuestra Señora de la Soledad'.[7] The origin of this feast, which commemorates the loneliness of Mary on Holy Saturday, originated with Juana of Castile. After the sudden death of her husband Philip the Fair in 1506, she could indeed be compared with the inconsolable woman in Binchois' chanson *Comme femme desconfortée*, on which Josquin's *Stabat mater* is based (see p. 174).

CUEURS DESOLEZ

The last example of a work that has been excluded from the *NJE* is the six-voice chanson *Cueurs desolez*. This time there is no conflict of attribution, but rather a single source that ascribes a number of works to Josquin for no apparent reason; some of these do little to honour his reputation. The source in question is Attaingnant's *Trente sixiesme livre* of 1549, an edition that draws primarily on a collection by Susato that appeared four years earlier in Antwerp (see p. 52). Two of the remaining seven chansons are, according to other sources, by Pierre de la Rue, so there is some cause for doubt about *Cueurs desolez*. The incorporation of the Gregorian *cantus firmus* "Plorans ploravit in nocte" does not entail, as is usual with Josquin, any special procedure. The two top parts have nearly the same range, which is also unusual in Josquin, and the harmonic rhythm is faster than in his authentic laments. Lastly, there occur a few awkward discords and inept parallel fifths.[8]

Doubtful works

Unlike the old edition, the *NJE* makes a distinction between genuine works and those of which it is difficult to determine Josquin's authorship with certainty, but which also cannot easily be brushed aside as spurious. These *opera dubia*, about 40 in number, are identified by an asterisk before the NJE number. Here are a few examples.

ABSALON FILI MI (NJE *14.1)

Volume 14 of the *NJE* opens with the motet *Absalon fili mi*, a four-voice setting of excerpts from 2 Samuel 18:33, Genesis 37:35 and Job 7:16 which, taken together, form David's lament on the death of his son Absalom. About this motet Ambros wrote:

> Here Josquin ... reveals himself a Seelenmaler [a painter depicting the soul] of a subtlety and depth of feeling of which his predecessors had no idea, and which hardly any of his successors would attain (Vol. 3, 230).

Before appearing in the *NJE*, the work had already been published four times under Josquin's name and once as an *opus dubium* in the *Opera omnia* of Pierre de la Rue. Though it survives anonymously in its oldest source, London 8 G.VII, it is attributed to Josquin in two German prints from 1540 and 1559, and in an arrangement for lute from 1558. The authenticity question caused lively debate. Some have rightly pointed out that certain stylistic elements are more typical of La Rue than of Josquin. But after

---

7   See NJE *25.8, Critical Commentary, 82–84.

8   See Lawrence F. Bernstein, 'Chansons for Five and Six Voices', in *JosqComp*, 393–422, at 414–417.

weighing the arguments for and against, the editor of Volume 14 decided to include the work as an *opus dubium*, partly because the extremely low ranges and the downward modulation around the circle of fifths brand *Absalon fili mi* as an exceptional work that has no counterpart in the oeuvre of either Josquin or La Rue.

EXAMPLE 1a

EXAMPLE 1b

QUI HABITAT IN ADJUTORIO ALTISSIMI (NJE *18.8)

Besides the four-voice setting of the psalm *Qui habitat* (NJE 18.7), Volume 18 contains a 24-voice canon on verses 1–8 of the same psalm. This motet is preserved only posthumously in four German sources. Partly because the attributions in Lutheran Germany are quite often unreliable, this setting is spurious in the eyes of some musicologists. But, like *Absalon fili mi*, we are dealing with music that is quite unique in the repertoire of the first half of the sixteenth century, and cannot be compared with the work of any other composer. Considering that the structure of the canon in relation to the text hides a deep symbolic meaning (see p. 90), Josquin would indeed be its most likely architect – reason enough to include it in the *NJE*.

OBSECRO TE, DOMINA (NJE *24.8)

The publication of this Marian motet is exceptional for two reasons: because the *NJE* presents the first modern edition, and because this edition consists of a vocal reconstruction. *Obsecro te, domina* is known only in an arrangement by Enriquez de Valderrábano for two vihuelas, in *Silva de sirenas*, a collection of lute music printed in Valladolid in 1547. Since Valderrábano names Josquin in as many as thirteen other authentic pieces in this collection, we can assume that he chose his music carefully. It must originally have been a vocal composition, because, among other things, fragments of text are printed under the tablature. They are a free paraphrase of the opening of a long medieval prayer to the Virgin Mary for protection against sudden death. Performances of the reconstruction, for example by the Calmus Ensemble during the 2009 Josquin Festival in Middelburg, have shown the music to possess great power of expression. Though an attempt was made, in the five-voice reconstruction, to adhere as much as possible to the later style of Josquin, it would have been unwise to have included this motet in the edition without an asterisk.

EL GRILLO (NJE *28.12) and IN TE, DOMINE, SPERAVI (NJE *28.18)

The editor of Volume 28 of the *NJE*, David Fallows, and the *NJE*'s General Editor had differing opinions over whether these two songs should be provided with an asterisk. Petrucci published them both in his *Frottole libro primo* of 1504 and its reprint as by 'IOSQUIN DASCANIO'. The frottola was the most common poetic form in Italy around 1500. Although it had always been assumed that this attribution could be explained by Josquin's employment in the service of Ascanio Sforza (see p. 23) and the authenticity of *El grillo* had never been questioned, the contrapuntal quality of the altus part of *In te, domine, speravi* did not stand up to scrutiny, and this piece was therefore omitted from the old edition. Regardless of the fact that *El grillo* is one of the most brilliant songs of the late fifteenth century, that Josquin signed it using gematria (see p. 94), and that no other work by a composer called Iosquin Dascanio has come to light, the altus of NJE *28.18 was, for Fallows, sufficient reason to publish both works only as *opera dubia*: "This kind of heterophony between two voices cannot be found in any other work ascribed to Josquin with any plausibility."[9] The editor himself, however, suggested that this voice could be a later addition, and

---

9   See NJE *28.18, Critical Commentary, 255.

in fact the piece is shown as being for three voices in the index of the incomplete 'Tschudi Liederbuch'. The general editor urged in vain that the altus part be omitted, and four years later Fallows acknowledged in his monograph on Josquin that it would indeed have been better to have done so (p. 208, fn. 43). In short, there is no need to doubt Josquin's authorship of NJE *28.12 and *28.18.

Chronology
The authenticity of a composition can often only be considered in the light of its stylistic characteristics, especially in the case of conflicting attributions. The question the musicologist must then try to answer is whether the style corresponds to that of authentic works of Josquin from roughly the same period. This throws up a new problem, that of the chronology of Josquin's works. Since only a handful of pieces can be dated from historical evidence, the compilation of a chronology of his oeuvre as a whole is one of the most challenging tasks facing Josquin scholars. This is partly because the compositional techniques by which the style of a Renaissance composition is largely determined formed the basis of a 'language' shared by many composers, and could be employed unchanged for decades. Thus, examples of paraphrase and imitation are found from 1450 until the late sixteenth century. Nor does the use of a compositional technique that would have been regarded as old-fashioned after 1500 place a work in the fifteenth century: as Richard Sherr rightly put it regarding Josquin's motet *Illibata dei virgo*, "Being archaic is not the same thing as being old."[10] We are therefore almost always dependent on the dating of the sources. This can, however, give us no more than a so-called *terminus ante quem*, the time before which a piece must have been composed.

Although a number of works have been assigned a plausible period of composition on the basis of the sources, many others survive only in sources that are posthumous or suspiciously late. Assuming that Josquin produced his first compositions at the age of about twenty, he would have had to wait at least 25 years before his music began to appear in print, in 1501. The handwritten record is not much better, with less than ten percent of the surviving manuscripts dating from the fifteenth century.

That the year of publication of a printed edition can be misleading for dating the music is also clear from the three books of Masses published by Petrucci (see p. 51). All five Masses in the first book, from 1502, demonstrate, in one way or another, the extraordinary craftsmanship of the composer, and can thus be dated with reasonable certainty to the last decade of the fifteenth century. Petrucci's choice was undoubtedly motivated by rational considerations, for with this, the first edition devoted to a single composer, he inevitably threw himself into a commercial venture. Consequently, some of the Masses published only in 1514, with the third book, predate those in the first book.

Mention should also be made of a problematic situation in the scholarly literature on Josquin. Previously it was assumed that 'biscantor Juschinus de Frantia', in a list of singers on the payroll of Milan Cathedral in 1459, referred to Josquin. But when

---

10   '*Illibata dei virgo nutrix* and Josquin's Roman Style', in *JAMS* 41 (1988), 434–464, at 436.

this biscantor regained his true identity, in 1998 (see fn. 1, p. 17), Josquin's lifespan lost about fifteen years, and the dating of some of his works in the older literature became obsolete.

Assuming he was active as a composer for about 45 years, we can distinguish three periods of about the same length: 1) from 1475 to 1489, the year he entered the Sistine Chapel; 2) from 1489 to 1504, when he returned from Ferrara to Northern France; 3) from 1504 to 1521, the year he died. The probable period into which each of his compositions falls will be indicated, where possible, in Chapters 7–9.

The monodic, diatonic vocal music called Gregorian chant originated in the Middle East. It was a source of inspiration to composers from the beginning of polyphony until well into the sixteenth century. Josquin was no exception, quite the reverse: four of his Masses, six Mass movements, twenty-five motets and five chansons are indebted to one or more chants from this repertoire. One frequently quoted liturgical chant is Credo I from the modern Solesmes chant editions, fragments of which recur in most of Josquin's settings of the text.

Gregorian chant can rightly be called a European heritage. Familiarity with chant was a requirement for every singer of Josquin's time, because it formed the basis of music in Christian worship. Every choirboy was therefore trained in the singing of these often beautiful melodies. Those that went on to become composers undoubtedly knew many chants by heart. At first transmitted orally, Gregorian chant then developed local written traditions, so that there was never uniformity across Western Europe. The sequence *Inviolata* in the Ambrosian liturgy of Milan, for example, was slightly different in Rome. But even within religious institutions such as large churches or monasteries, a single chant could contain melodic variants which might later be reflected in polyphonic compositions. In the case of composers from France and the Southern Netherlands who worked for part of their lives in Italy, tracing the original melodic form of a chant they quote in their music is often a difficult task.

The extent to which we can determine how faithfully the composer adopted his 'model' depends also on the technique he employed: the melody could be quoted unchanged in long note values, or these notes be used as a basis of a 'new' melody. The latter technique is called paraphrase, the adaptation by means of interpolation and ornamentation, merging original and new notes into a homogeneous melody. This proved an ideal medium for combining old and new musical material, and left its stamp on polyphony for nearly two hundred years. The inventiveness of the composer thereby allowed an almost infinite variety of melodic expression, in which the underlying liturgical chant was sacrosanct but did not have to lead to repetition.

Josquin reworked Gregorian chant in many ways. Sometimes, if the chant is repeated, he quotes the melody first in long notes then in shorter values, and sometimes in two-voice canon. The text of the chant in such cases usually differs from that of the motet or chanson in which it is used. In three of his Masses, the original text is omitted altogether. In the motets on the same text as the chant, on the other hand, the original melody can be changed into a two-voice canon or split between different voices, either in long note values or paraphrased. Although the complete chant is generally used, in some motets Josquin quotes only a single phrase. The five chants below illustrate different approaches.

AVE MARIS STELLA

The seven-verse hymn "Ave maris stella", in praise of the Virgin Mary as the "star of the sea", was one of the most popular liturgical songs in Western Europe. It was set to at least eight different melodies. In the Roman liturgy of Josquin's time, a first-mode version, probably of Cistercian origin, was sung at the Vespers of many Marian feasts. This is the first phrase (Ex. 2):

EXAMPLE 2

The lowest voice of the three-voice chanson *A la mort* ((NJE 27.1) quotes the melody twice at different pitches (Fig. 15). The unique source gives the text of the fourth verse, "Monstra te esse matrem" (Show that you are a mother). Why the composer chose this verse becomes clear from reading the French text of the upper voices:

A la mort on prioit à l'heure:	At the very hour of death, one prayed:
Je te requiers de cueur contrit,	"I ask of you with a contrite heart,
Dame des cieulx, rends mon esprit	Lady of Heaven, to set my soul
Devant ton filz et me sequeure.	Before your Son, and save me."

Josquin's name also appears against the fourth verse (NJE 23.9) of a complete setting of the same hymn found in Cappella Sistina 15. The odd verses were sung in plainchant and the even verses, the first of which was written by Guillaume Dufay in the 1430s, in polyphony. On paper, Josquin's setting is for three voices (altus, tenor and bassus), but he quotes the hymn melody, with a small interpolation between the third and fourth notes, as a canon between tenor and superius (Ex. 3).

One of Josquin's Masses is also based on the hymn. All four parts quote liberally from the beautiful plainchant. Here is the opening of the top voice (Ex. 4).

Finally there is the four-voice setting of the complete hymn, NJE 23.8. It is clear how innovative the opening is (see Ex. 5) from the first eleven measures. The leap of a fifth on "Hail" is repeated ten times, and at least two voices mark the start of each verse. The hymn melody is reused again and again, but monotony is avoided by every manner of variation and paraphrase. In the seventh and last strophe, the opening takes on the following shape (Ex. 6).

FIGURE 15: Tenor and bassus voice parts of the chanson *A la mort*. Florence, Biblioteca del Conservatorio di Musica, Ms. Basevi 2439 ('Basevi Codex'), f. 80ᵛ.

EXAMPLE 3

EXAMPLE 4

EXAMPLE 5

EXAMPLE 5 (continued)

EXAMPLE 6

AVE MARIA

Another Marian chant used several times by Josquin was the well-known "Ave Maria", Gabriel's greeting to the Virgin Mary (Ex. 7).

The antiphon appears in no fewer than five motets, which seem to represent every phase of his compositional development. The early *Ave Maria* (NJE 23.4) quotes the opening phrase in each of the voices but abandons the melody at the words "benedicta tu".

Missus est Gabriel angelus (NJE 20.7) combines two antiphons that borrow from Luke 1:26–28. "Ave Maria" is used first in the bassus at m. 40, then in the tenor (m. 42), superius (m. 44) and altus (m. 46). The way the composer handles the melody in the top voice is a particularly good illustration of his creativity: a short, familiar phrase is transformed into one of twice the range (Ex. 8).

In contrast, the lowest voice of *O bone et dulcis domine Jesu* (NJE 21.8) quotes the melody literally. The two upper voices of this motet carry a devotional text unknown elsewhere, against the tenor with "Pater noster" and the bassus that quotes first the "Ave Maria", then the antiphon "Benedicta tu in mulieribus" (see also p. 162). The surviving plainchant sources suggest that Josquin adopted these melodies without changing a single note.

A truly spectacular use of the antiphon is in the five-voice *Virgo salutiferi* (NJE 25.13). In this three-partite motet the opening phrase of the antiphon appears in strict canon in each part, always at the same pitch. This happens in the first part in long note values, which distinguishes the melody from the other voices. In the second part, the note values are reduced, and in the third part reduced again so that there is now time for the whole antiphon: this produces a stretto effect. In the first part, the middle voice enters with the antiphon only after 40 measures and, three measures later, the canonic superius reaches its highest note in m. 50. This has a similar effect as the chorale in the opening chorus of Bach's *Saint Matthew Passion*, and was the first time such a procedure was used.

The fifth and almost certainly last time that Josquin cited the "Ave Maria" was in his six-voice double motet *Pater noster – Ave Maria* (NJE 20.9). In contrast with *O bone et dulcis domine Jesu*, he combines the Gregorian melodies sequentially rather than simultaneously. As in *Virgo salutiferi*, they form a canon, this time in two tenor voices at the unison. The quotation from the antiphon is limited to the words "Ave Maria". But Josquin would not have been Josquin if he had left it at that. Previously, the sixth note of the melody had always been flattened (as *b*flat instead of *b*), following the so-called *fa supra la* rule, but this time, in measures 6 (= m. 126 in the second part) and 9 (=129), we hear a chord with a major third: embedded in a passage of minor chords, this produces a subtle but surprising effect that lends lustre to the harmony (Ex. 9).

EXAMPLE 7

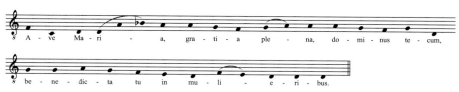

EXAMPLE 8

EXAMPLE 9

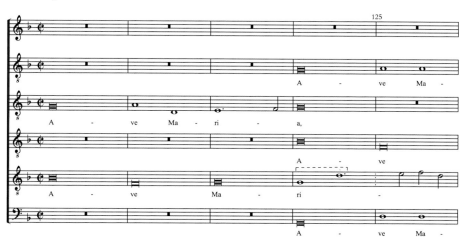

EXAMPLE 9 (continued)

SALVE REGINA

Of the four great Marian antiphons – *Alma redemptoris mater, Ave regina celorum, Regina celi* and *Salve Regina* – Josquin set the last one twice. The earlier work, NJE 25.4, shows again his complete mastery of canon technique. Two canonic pairs are formed by the two upper and the two lower voices. The bassus, the first voice to enter, is followed half a measure later by the tenor a fourth higher; the altus and the superius then repeat this pattern from m. 2 (Ex. 10). The upper voice pair, especially, cannot fail to enrapture the listener familiar with the Gregorian melody it paraphrases.

The second setting, NJE 25.5, is for five voices. This motet consists of three parts and is on a larger scale. The tenor, the middle voice, sings the first four notes of the antiphon repeatedly. The symbolic meaning is discussed in the next chapter. Just as in NJE 25.4, the whole motet is impregnated with the Gregorian melody, heard mostly in the superius, but also fragmentarily in the other voices. So at the start of the third part, the bassus carries the most prominent notes of the antiphon in the chords of "Et Jesum, benedictum".

EXAMPLE 10

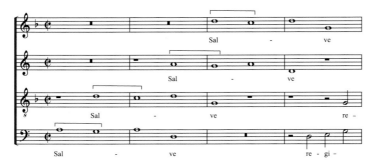

INVIOLATA

This popular twelfth-century sequence was sung at Candlemas, on the 2nd of February. It has five couplets, the last consisting of three invocations and a closing verse. The version that Josquin adopted is very similar to the one in use at the Basilica of Our Lady in Tongeren. NJE 24.4 is a five-voice setting of the sequence in three parts. The Gregorian melody starts in the first tenor and is answered quickly by the second tenor a fifth higher. A third voice also sometimes joins in, as in the third part, which opens with the three invocations, "O benigna, O regina, O Maria", forming a motif of three dense chords in the middle voices (Ex. 11).

The second setting of the sequence, NJE *24.5, is very different. The Gregorian melody no longer functions as the structural basis for the other voices, but is placed, clearly audible, in the top voice, while figurative counterpoint sounds in the lower voices. From m. 27, when the first tenor enters with a freely composed *cantus firmus*, the twelve-voice motet unfolds in a richness of sound. The next chapter will consider the symbolic aspects of these two works.

EXAMPLE 11

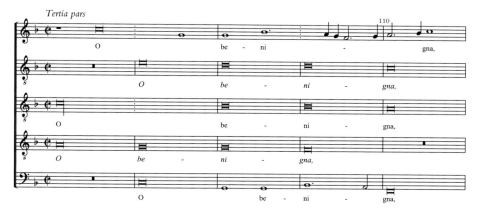

REQUIEM ETERNAM

The last example of Josquin's creativity is the incorporation of the introit from the funeral Mass in compositions he wrote on the decease of Johannes Ockeghem and Jacob Obrecht (see also p. 84–85). The text begins with "Requiem eternam dona eis domine" (Eternal rest grant unto them, O Lord). In the five-voice chanson *Nymphes des bois* (see p. 33 and Fig. 43 on p. 211), Josquin writes the introit melody in the tenor in long note values, at the same pitch as his model. The 'Medici Codex' of 1518 gives, however, a warning: "Pour eviter noyse et debas Prenez ung demy ton plus bas" (To avoid argument and debate, take [the melody] down a semitone). It turns out, in other words, that the introit fits with the other voices only when transposed. This transposition gives the melody, originally in the 5th mode, a new modal character, that of the 3rd, whereby the semitone shifts from between the third and fourth notes in the scale to between the first and second. The 3rd mode was associated in the Middle Ages with grief, which gives this lament a deeper dimension.

Absolve, quesumus, domine makes use of the same *cantus firmus*. Again quoted in long notes, the melody is worked this time into a two-voice canon, the two tenors singing a fifth apart. The dense six-voice texture intensifies the melancholy character of the music.

In Josquin's time, the functions of worship and of music within worship were interwoven. Sacred music derived from worship (in the most comprehensive sense) its own terms of reference; that is, it had its place in an existing system of understanding and belief, a system that, for the composer, was an existential reality. Central were an omnipresent God, hell as the final home of the damned after the Last Judgement, and the Virgin Mary in the role of mediator between heaven and earth. It is not easy for anyone outside this reality to understand the essential character of many of Josquin's works and the symbolic meaning that he sometimes put to them.

Esoteric and symbolic structures have been found in much greater variety in Josquin's compositions than in those of his contemporaries. In the works of music theorists one finds an occasional passing comment, as when Glarean spoke of the "riddle of the sphinx" in relation to a canon rubric in one of Josquin's Masses (see p. [119]); otherwise, they were silent on this aspect of his music. Nevertheless, the techniques illustrated in this chapter show unequivocally that the warning of the Parisian master builder Jean Mignot (d. ca. 1410) was still valid: "ars sine scientia nihil est" (Art without science is nothing).[1] Josquin might also have adopted Leonardo da Vinci's well-known dictum, "la pittura [i.e. la musica] è cosa mentale" – painting, i.e. music is a matter of the mind.

Cantus prius factus

The *cantus prius factus* is one of the most important structural elements in the music of the fifteenth and sixteenth centuries. The term seems to have been first used by Franco of Cologne about 1260, and means, literally, 'the already composed melody'. The melody that served as the starting point for a new composition was generally

---

1   Quotation attributed to the Parisian architect Jean Mignot; see James S. Ackerman, 'Gothic Theory of Architecture at the Cathedral of Milan', in *The Art Bulletin* 31 (1949), 84–111.

borrowed from chant, but secular songs were also often used, especially in an abstract context. For example, in Josquin's five-voice *Stabat mater* (NJE 25.9), the middle voice is derived from the tenor of the popular three-part chanson *Comme femme desconfortée*, which has a unique attribution to Binchois in the Mellon Chansonnier, and was already some forty years old at the time. The notes of the chanson were augmented fourfold to accommodate the much longer text of the medieval sequence.

The text of the chanson relates the complaint of a woman inconsolable in love who has given up all hope of life, and longs night and day for death. The composer clearly associated it with the image of the Virgin Mary at the foot of the crucified Christ, one of the commonest themes of late medieval and Renaissance art. But it is also clear that the relationship between chanson and motet is meant to be purely symbolic, because the chanson melody is in the middle of the texture and so stretched out as to be unrecognizable to the listener (see also below).

We find a similar sort of symbolism in the five-voice *Nymphes des bois* (NJE 29.18; see also below), where the 'parent melody' was a Gregorian chant and the new composition was on a French text. The chanson was probably written shortly after the death of Ockeghem in 1497. Jean Molinet's text mentions not only the deceased but also Josquin and three of his contemporaries (see p. 33). As we have seen in Chapter 5, the *cantus prius factus* is taken from the introit of the Funeral Mass, but sung a semitone lower in the 3rd mode instead of the 5th, because the former was associated in the Middle Ages with grief. Josquin also pays homage to Ockeghem by making a reference to his *Missa Cujusvis toni*: the opening motif in the superius quotes from the Kyrie of the Mass (see Fig. 43 on p. 211); and the 'Medici Codex', reflecting undoubtedly the original version, lacks clefs, like the Mass. Unlike the Mass though, which can be sung 'in whatever key one wants', the motet remains in the Phrygian mode.

Josquin's prayer for Jacob Obrecht (*d.*1505), *Absolve, quesumus, domine* (NJE 26.1; see also below), is based on the same introit. Obrecht too had used it in the lament *Mille quingentis*,[2] written for his father Willem Obrecht, a trumpeter, who had died in 1488. *Absolve* is for six voices. The second altus and second tenor carry the introit melody canonically in long notes. The other four voices begin with two consecutive rising fourths, a fairly common motif in Josquin's compositions, but only here does it open a composition in full imitation. This is no coincidence. The same head-motif is found in the Credo of Obrecht's *Missa Fortuna desperata*, based on the chanson, ascribed to Antoine Busnois, about the goddess Fortuna, bringer of (mis)fortune. After Josquin, in 1504, had fled Ferrara because of the increasing threat of plague, which broke out in July 1503, his place at the Este court was taken by Obrecht, who soon after became infected and died, probably in July 1505. The adoption of a motif from the *Fortuna* Mass is of course highly symbolic. By juxtaposing the goddess with the Almighty Father ("Patrem omnipotentem"), Josquin expresses the hope that He save the late composer's soul.[3]

---

2   *New Obrecht Edition*, vol. 16, no. 16.

3   See also Willem Elders, 'Josquin's *Absolve, quesumus, domine*: A Tribute to Obrecht?', in *TVNM* 37 (1987), 14–24.

Soggetto ostinato

Since the first centuries of Christianity, the path to heaven had been depicted as a ladder (*scala regni celesti*). In early Christian art, the motif often appears as Jacob's Ladder (Genesis 28:12) or the Ladder of Virtue. In his *Divine Comedy*, Dante wrote, "Within the crystal ... I saw ... a ladder set up, so far above, my eyes could not follow it" (*Paradiso* 21:25–30). According to the theologian Fulgentius of Ruspe (ca. 465–ca. 530), Mary herself had "become a ladder to heaven, since God through her descended to earth, and men through her may ascend to heaven."[4] Ten centuries later, the motif still played an important role both in theological writings and in art. Domenico Benivieni published a study in Florence in 1472 entitled *La scala della vita spirituale sopra il nome di Maria* (The ladder of spiritual life upon the name of Mary). Leonardo da Vinci and Michelangelo painted stairways in the *Adoration of the Magi* (Uffizi Gallery, Florence) and the *Madonna of the Stairs* (Casa Buonarroti, Florence) respectively.

Composers also used this symbolism. *Scala musicalis* was a term used for the Guidonian Gamut (all the notes in the hexachord system), which may have inspired Josquin in the construction of his four-voice motet *Ut Phebi radiis* (NJE 25.10). Here a stepwise motif is repeated continually, ascending and descending. The tenor and bassus are constructed from the six solmisation syllables of the hexachord, *ut re mi fa sol la*. In the first section, the bassus sings a *pes ascendens* beginning on *c*, imitated one measure later by the tenor a fourth higher: *ut, ut–re, ut–re–mi*, etc. until the whole hexachord is included. In the second section, the tenor sings a *pes descendens* on *d'* with *la, la–sol, la–sol–fa*, etc., which the bassus imitates a fourth lower. These groups of syllables are each separated by an eight-measure rest.

The text of the motet, in part extremely cryptic, consists of two strophes of seven hexameters each (see p. 181–182). The central theme of the first section is the Virgin Mary, who "rules over all that exists"; the second focuses on Jesus Christ, who was born of Mary. For an interpretation of the two lower voices we only have to recall Fulgentius' allegory: the rising hexachord symbolises the prayer to Mary and the falling hexachord the descent of God to earth through her.

Another remarkable example of ostinato is found in the five-voice motet *Domine, dominus noster* (NJE *16.4, published as doubtful because it survives only in posthumous sources). The text, from Psalm 8, is an expression of someone staring in wonder at the night sky and singing of the fullness of God's creation. The second tenor limits himself to the start of verse 1: "Domine, dominus noster" (Lord, our Lord), on an eight-note motif preceded by an eight-measure rest. The motif is sung five times during the motet, with note values in the proportions 2:3:4:5:6. Thus the last iteration lasts 24 measures, preceded by a 24-measure rest. *Psalmorum selectorum ... liber primus* (Nuremberg 1553) prints the rubric "Crescite et multiplicamini" (Be fruitful and multiply; Genesis 1:22) which reveals the deeper meaning of the musical construction, namely God's creation of all the earth.

---

4   See Gerd Heinz-Mohr, *Lexikon der Symbole. Bilder und Zeichen der christlichen Kunst* (Düsseldorf – Cologne 1976), 185–186.

Special forms of notation
Two works of Josquin are transmitted completely in black notation, *Absolve, quesumus, domine* and *Nymphes des bois* (see Fig. 43 on p. 211). This was exceptional, since by 1500 all notes longer than a semiminim (minim, semibreve, breve, longa and maxima) were normally 'white'. The only other piece from Josquin's time to have been notated in black notes was the seven-voice *Proh dolor*, thought by some musicologists to be also by him. It survives only anonymously in Brussels 228 and was written on the death of Emperor Maximilian in 1519. There can be no doubt, therefore, that black notation symbolized mourning. The number 7, as in the seven voices of *Proh dolor*, was also associated with mourning because of certain passages in the Bible, for instance Judith 16:23–24: "She died, and was buried with her husband in Bethulia. And all the people mourned for seven days." We shall return to *Absolve* and *Nymphes* later.

Several later works of Josquin use the antiquated time signature 'O2' in certain passages of a single voice, meaning modus perfectus, or the ternary division of the longa. These passages, found in the *Masses L'homme armé sexti toni* (NJE 6.2) and *Pange lingua* (NJE 4.3), and in the motets *Ave nobilissima creatura* (NJE 23.11), *Huc me sydereo* (NJE 21.5) and *Preter rerum seriem* (NJE 24.11), are, without exception, concerned with Jesus Christ. Examples are the second Agnus dei of the *Missa Pange lingua* (Lamb of God, who takest away the sins of the world ...) and the start of *Preter rerum seriem* (Beyond the order of nature / A virgin mother gave birth / To a man who is God). The circle, being a figure without beginning, middle and end, has been universally accepted in Christian iconography as a symbol for God. The addition of the number 2 could refer to Christ as the second person of the Trinity, or to His dual nature, both human and divine.[5]

In the Gloria of the *Missa De beata virgine* (NJE 3.3), m. 144–153, Josquin introduces a triple rhythm using black notation, which must be a symbolic reflection of the text at this point, "Qui tollis peccata mundi" (Who takes away the sins of the world).

The last articles of the Credo concern the Holy Spirit. At the text "Qui cum patre et filio simul adoratur" (Who together with the Father and the Son is adored) in the same Mass, the superius has an extraordinary series of nine black breves, in three groups of three. The resulting triplets contrast rhythmically with the four lower voices. One could hardly wish for a clearer reference to the Trinity.

Mode and musica ficta
Mode is a row of eight notes which determines the character of the melody and harmony according to the position of the two semitones. *Musica ficta* refers in polyphonic music before 1600 to the generally un-notated sharpening or flattening of certain notes, according to contemporary usage. Modern editions print these sharps and flats above instead of before the note. Flat signs do occasionally occur, but their absence in other sources can leave the composer's intention ambiguous. *Ficta* was

---

5   See Willem Elders, 'The Symbolism of Reconciliation in Agnus Dei Settings of Josquin des
     Prez', in *The Blood of Jesus and the Doctrine of Reconciliation in the Works of Johann Sebastian
     Bach*, ed. Albert Clement (Amsterdam 1995), 49-62.

applied to make dissonant intervals consonant and to change the modal character of a composition. Here follow some illustrations.

In m. 133 of the *Stabat mater*, at the words "Fac me tecum plangere" (Let me weep with you), the major sonority changes suddenly to a minor one. While this is an example of word painting, the harmonic mutation in *O admirabile commercium* (NJE 21.7a) at "commercium" in m. 19 is more symbolic, and can be explained by the "wondrous exchange" in the antiphon text, when Christ, through his birth, took on mortal form (Ex. 12).

EXAMPLE 12

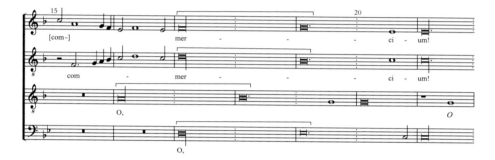

The Marian motet *Virgo salutiferi* (NJE 25.12) is in three parts. It is based on a poem by the Ferrarese court poet Ercole Strozzi, which was published in Venice in 1513 by Aldus Manutius with the title *Ad gloriosam virginem*. Two of the five voices (superius and tenor) sing the famous antiphon *Ave Maria* (see p. 68–69) in canon at the octave, in each section in proportionally reduced note values. At the word "Maria" the melody reaches its highest note, e^2 flat, supported in the first and third parts by a chord on *C*, giving a fairly consonant effect. But in the second part there is a surprise in the bassus (see Ex. 13, m. 145). Lowering the *A* to *A* flat eliminates the dissonance, but leads to a weak melody *d–A* flat (m. 144–145). This 'tritone' was tolerated by contemporary music theory when it avoided an illegal vertical interval such as the diminished fifth here. It seems obvious that Josquin made this change in consideration of the text of the other voices, "conciliare genus", referring to the appeal to Mary to expurgate the sin of the First Mother (Eve) and to reconcile the human race with God. This reconciliation is given a deeper meaning by the modal 'manipulation', since "genus" was also used by music theorists to mean "mode".[6]

Inviolata, integra et casta es (NJE 24.4) is another five-voice motet in three parts; this time the two tenors sing the Gregorian sequence of the same name in canon, the first in *F* with a *b* flat signature and the second a fifth higher in *C* without. The three other voices are freely composed in *F*, which results sometimes in modal–harmonic 'conflicts', diminished fifths that must be corrected with an accidental. The explanation for Josquin's decision to contravene the accepted principle of identical canonic voices must be sought in the text.

---

6   See Willem Elders, 'On the Sublime in Josquin's Marian Motets', in *ProcM*, 7-26, at 14–16.

EXAMPLE 13

The sequence *Inviolata* finds its origin in the doctrine of Mary's 'immaculate conception' in the womb of her mother Anne. The position that she alone of all mortals was
free from any stain of original sin, i.e. she was conceived without lust, was defended
notably by the Franciscan friar Duns Scotus (ca. 1266–1308). It had however been a
matter of long-standing controversy, denied by, among others, the Dominicans, including Thomas Aquinas. Since the text of Josquin's famous *Ave Maria* (NJE 23.6)
likewise alludes to the Virgin's conception, it is tempting to assume that he also knew
of this debate. From the start of the fifteenth century onwards one finds paintings of
the 'Virgin of the Immaculate Conception' with attributes such as the sun and moon,
a lily, and a rose without thorns. In 1475, the feast was instituted by Sixtus IV for the
Roman Church, who ordered Leonardo of Nogarola to formulate the texts of a new
Mass and Office (December 8). So it should not come as a surprise that composers also
made contributions, as Pierre de la Rue did with his *Missa Conceptio tua*. Considering that of all of Josquin's motets in which Gregorian chant is quoted in canon at the
fourth or the fifth, only *Inviolata* presents such a remarkable 'clustering' of diminished fifths needing correction, we may suppose that Josquin was inspired to hide in
his motet a series of perfect intervals to illustrate Mary's freedom from sin.[7]

Canon
A canon consists of a leading voice (the *dux*) followed by another voice with the
same musical material (the *comes*). The theorist Johannes Tinctoris described the
technique in his dictionary of musical terms of ca. 1475 as follows: "The sameness
of the voice parts in a composition as to the value, name, shape, and sometimes even
the place [on the staff] of its notes and rests."[8] Although the great majority of can-

---

7   See Willem Elders, 'Perfect Fifths and the Blessed Virgin's Immaculate Conception: On *Ficta* in
     Josquin's five-part *Inviolata*', in *Blackburn*, 403-411.

8   "Fuga est identitas partium cantus quo ad valorem nomen formam et interdum quo ad locum
     notarum et pausarum suarum."

ons in the fifteenth and sixteenth centuries seem to have been written as technical exercises – the composer clearly wanting to display his technical skill – Josquin's generation in particular could use the technique for more erudite reasons. This is manifest either from an accompanying rubric, when it is a quotation from the Bible for example, or from the text of the composition in which the canon is employed. Tinctoris introduces a canon between the superius and altus in the Credo of his *Missa L'homme armé* at the words "Et incarnatus est de spiritu sancto ex Maria virgine" (And He was born through the Holy Spirit of the Virgin Mary). Since however this canon continues into the next section, it is not certain here that Tinctoris' intention was symbolic.[9]

Josquin's intention in the antiphon *Alma redemptoris mater* (NJE 23.1) is clearer. Here the same concept is expressed: "Tu que genuisti ... tuum sanctum genitorem": the tenor follows the altus after two measures with exactly the same melody, symbolizing the birth of the Creator from the mother.

The idea of 'issuing from' is also contained in the Credo verse "Et in spiritum sanctum, dominum et vivificantem; qui ex patre filioque procedit" (And [I believe] in the Holy Spirit, the Lord and giver of Life; who proceeds from the Father and from the Son). In his four-voice setting of the Mass movement NJE 13.2, based on what is regarded as the most famous chanson of the fifteenth-century, Hayne van Ghizeghem's *De tous biens playne*, Josquin gives a masterly example of canon symbolism. At that verse, the bassus is the only notated voice of the four, and carries in Cappella Sistina 41 the rubric "Duo in carne una" (They two shall be in one flesh; Matthew 19:5): two voices should sing the notated melody at the same pitch one measure apart, symbolizing the Holy Spirit issuing from the Father and the Son.

In the first part of the Sanctus of the *Missa L'homme armé sexti toni* (NJE 6.2), the two middle voices have a canon at the unison (Fig. 16) and in the Osanna the tenor and bassus a canon at the fifth. Four of the sources carry the rubric "Duo seraphim clamabant alter ad alterum" (Two seraphim cried out, the one calling to the other), which derives from Isaias 6:2–3: "Seraphim stabant super illud ... et clamabant alter ad alterum, et dicebant: Sanctus, sanctus, sanctus Dominus, Deus exercituum; plena est omnis terra gloria eius." The two voices of the canon therefore personify two seraphim who alternately intone a song of praise to the glory of God, the original text of which had been incorporated into the liturgy of the Mass. This image seems to extend to the six-voice Agnus dei III, where two pairs of voices in canon at the unison sing in endlessly repeating waves above the two lower voices in long notes.

The five-voice psalm motet *De profundis clamavi* (NJE 15.13) was probably written for the obsequies of a head of state of France or the Southern Netherlands. The canon between superius, altus and bassus 1 carries in Cappella Sistina 38 the rubric "Les trois estas sont assembles / Pour le soulas des trespasses" (The three estates are assembled to console the departed). Josquin undoubtedly wanted to symbolise the three estates (nobility, clergy and commoners) uniting in mourning at the death of their ruler.

---

9   For a study on the symbolism of canonic techniques see Willem Elders, 'Canon and Imitation as Musical Images of the Three Divine Persons', in Idem, *Symbolic Scores. Studies in the Music of the Renaissance* (Leiden – New York – Cologne 1994), 185–210.

FIGURE 16: Sanctus of *Missa L'homme armé sexti toni* with the two-voice canon. Vatican City, Biblioteca Apostolica Vaticana, Ms. Cappella Sistina 41, f. 33'-34.

A comparable but more profound example is found in the second Agnus dei of the *Missa L'homme armé super voces musicales* (NJE 6.3; see also below). This piece, only 33 measures long but with an exquisitely balanced melody, has become the most famous 'proportion canon' of the Renaissance. In this type of canon, the voices begin together but proceed differently according to their respective proportion signs. The canon was reproduced in several treatises (see p. 56). The painter Dosso Dossi used it to symbolise musical perfection in his *Allegory of Music* (Museo Horne, Florence, dated ca. 1524–34), inscribing it in the form of a triangle. In 1514 the canon was depicted on the back of a choir-stall in the Basilica of San Sisto in Piacenza with a fourth mensuration sign, allowing a four-voice performance (Fig. 17);[10] but the rubrics found in the musical sources ("Trinitas", "Tria in unum", "Sancta Trinitas salva me") leave no doubt that the piece was conceived for three voices. They also suggest, along with the differing rhythmic character of the three voices, that each voice symbolises one of the persons of the Trinity.

The earliest representations of the Trinity in art were abstract and therefore symbolic, probably because of the reluctance of the Church "to represent naturalistically the first person of the Trinity who, being unseen, was unknowable."[11] From Josquin's period comes a woodcut of a person with three heads, surround-

---

10   See Van Benthem, 'Einige Musikintarsien des frühen 16. Jahrhunderts ...'

11   James Hall, *Dictionary of Subjects and Symbols in Art* (New York 1974; R1979), p. 309. Examples are the equilateral triangle and the threefold circle, with or without inscription.

ed by the four creatures of Revelation 4:6–9 (Fig. 18). The most common representation of the Trinity, however, shows God the Father as an old man, holding before him the body of the dead Christ, or Christ on the cross, with the dove, a symbol of the Holy Spirit, placed above their heads. This representation has become known as the 'Throne of Mercy', a term coined by Luther in his translation of Hebrews 9:5, where it (*der Gnadenstuel*) is said to be given shade by the cherubim of glory. This theme is found in painting, sculpture and book illumination from the twelfth century onwards. Among the most famous examples are Masaccio's *Trinity* (Santa Maria Novella, Florence, ca. 1427), *The Trinity* by the Master of Flémalle (Städelsches Kunstinstitut, Frankfurt am Main, ca. 1430), and Albrecht Dürer's *Adoration of the Trinity* (Kunsthistorisches Museum, Vienna, 1511).

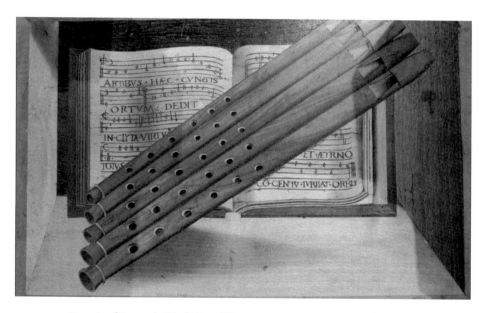

FIGURE 17: Intarsia of Agnus dei II of *Missa L'homme armé super voces musicales*. Piacenza, Basilica di San Sisto.

To return to the canon, we can suppose that the middle voice, beginning on *a*, personifies God the Father: it has the longest note values and thus functions as moderator. Beginning on *d* with shorter note values, the lowest voice – as in the Gregorian passion and Bach's Passions – personifies the Son. And beginning on *d'*, the highest voice represents the Holy Spirit: with a most lively rhythm, it calls to mind the rays of light in representations of Pentecost (Ex. 14). No other compositional procedure could have symbolized the Trinity better.

In the above examples, the number of canonic voices has been related to a rubric or to a central theme of the text. A symbolic interpretation could then be made. In the structure of other works, Josquin was inspired by numbers, influenced, as we shall see in the following section, by both Christian and Jewish thinking.

FIGURE 18: Woodcut
in a book of hours,
printed by Simon
Vostre (Paris 1524),
with the inscription
"The Father is God.
The Son is God. The
Holy Spirit is God.
The Father is not the
Son. The Son is not
the Holy Spirit. The
Holy Spirit is not the
Father."

EXAMPLE 14

Number symbolism

The study of numbers has been a regular branch of philosophy, theology, science and the arts since ancient times. Underlying fifteenth- and sixteenth-century music was usually Christian number symbolism, developed by Augustine and others after him, though its origins are many centuries older. Christian theorists were at pains to recognize a significant place in the cosmos not only for numbers but for their associated music. Thus St. Bonaventure wrote, "Nihil in universo est inordinatum" (Nothing in the universe is in disorder). Nicholas of Cusa developed this thought in his *De docta ignorantia* (On Learned Ignorance) of 1440:

> In creating the world, God used arithmetic, geometry, music, and likewise astronomy. (We ourselves also use these arts when we investigate the comparative relationships of objects, of elements, and of motions.) ... Through music He proportioned things in such a way that there is not more earth in earth than water in water, air in air, and fire in fire, so that no one element is altogether reducible to another. As a result, it happens that the world-machine cannot perish ... And when Eternal Wisdom ordained the elements, He used an inexpressible proportion.[12]

The 'arts' named by Cusanus made up the *quadrivium*, four of which had been taught since the sixth century as part of the seven *artes liberales* (liberal arts). The other three, grammar, rhetoric and dialectics, were known as the *trivium*.

Among the most important books on number symbolism from the sixteenth century are Luca Pacioli's *Summa de arithmetica* (A Treatise on Arithmetic) and Pietro Bongo's *De mystica numerorum significatione* (On the Mystical Meaning of Numbers; 1583). Pacioli's treatise had first been published in Venice in 1494 and remained, for half a century, the most comprehensive and most cited mathematical work in Italy. He was a friar, so it was to be expected that his number theories often involved mysticism. As Leo Olschki put it,

> Each number allows him the opportunity to cover [a wide range of material, from] the simplest observed phenomena in nature and in people, from natural history and cosmography, to theological dogmas and religious mysteries, in this way exploiting and uniting his powers of observation with erudition and piety.[13]

Fifteen years later, Pacioli's *De divina proportione* (The Golden Ratio) was published, whose title page claims it to be

> an indispensible work for every clear-minded and inquisitive person of intellect, in which each scholar of philosophy, perspective, painting, sculpture, architecture, music, and other mathematical disciplines will obtain very pleasant, subtle and admirable instruction, and will delight in diverse questions of most secret science.

---

12   Book II, chapter 13. Translation by Jasper Hopkins, *Nicholas of Cusa on Learned Ignorance: a Translation and an Appraisal of* De Docta Ignorantia (Minneapolis 1985), 99.

13   *Geschichte der neusprachlichen wissenschaftlichen Literatur* (Heidelberg 1918), vol. 1, p. 172.

It is surely significant that the author targeted musicians amongst his readership. Moreover, the close relationships between Italian composers and those from the Southern Netherlands would suggest that the latter were also acquainted with some of these number theories.

Josquin's interest in the use of numbers can first be demonstrated in his motet *Illibata dei virgo* (NJE 24.3). The bipartite text is a song of praise to Mary, "immaculate virgin and mother of God". The first part contains an acrostic that reveals the name of the composer in the spelling 'Josquin des Prez' (see p. 180). The motet is for five voices, the middle of which consists of an ostinato motif of three notes, repeated alternately at the pitches of d' and g. In the solmisation system the motif is sung *la-mi-la*, which, containing the same vowels, stands no doubt for the name 'Maria'. Heard 29 times, the number of *cantus firmus* notes is therefore 88 when the final note is added. This number can be explained with the help of Kabbala, the esoteric and mystical Jewish teaching of the thirteenth and subsequent centuries. An important aspect of Kabbala is gematria, a method of exegesis employed by medieval kabbalists in which letters are assigned numerical values. Applied to the Latin alphabet, the letter A has the value 1, B has the value 2, and so on. The letters I and J both take the number 9, and U and V both 20. The spelling of the name 'des Prez' in the acrostic thus yields:

$$
\begin{array}{ccc c cccc}
\text{d} & \text{e} & \text{s} & \quad & \text{P} & \text{r} & \text{e} & \text{z} \\
4 & 5 & 18 & & 15 & 17 & 5 & 24 & = 88
\end{array}
$$

The ostinato motif is heard in the first part only three times, 9 notes that we may suppose stand for the 'J' of Josquin. The sophisticated structure of the tenor portrays the composer in union, as it were, with the Virgin Mary, thereby transforming a song of praise into an intimate expression of devotion by a great singer and composer.[14]

Josquin also applied gematria in laments in honour of Johannes Ockeghem (*d.* 1497) and Jacob Obrecht (*d.* 1505). Each work ends with "Requiescat in pace" (May he rest in peace), and the composer leaves no doubt concerning the intended beneficiary of the prayer, setting it in *Nymphes des bois* (NJE 29.18) to 64 notes, the numerical value of Ockeghem's name (Ex. 15), and in *Absolve, quesumus, domine* (NJE 26.1) to 97 notes, the number with which Obrecht had identified himself in his motet *Parce domine* (Ex. 16).[15]

---

14   See Willem Elders, 'Das Symbol in der Musik von Josquin des Prez', in *AcM* 41 (1969), 164–185, at 179–180.

15   See Kees Vellekoop, 'Zusammenhänge zwischen Text und Zahl in der Kompositionsart Jacob Obrechts. Analyse der Motette *Parce domine*', in *TVNM* 20 (1967), 97–119. But see also Willem Elders, *Studien zur Symbolik in der Musik der alten Niederländer* (Bilthoven 1968), 137–138. The motet is published in the *New Obrecht Edition*, vol.16, no. 20.

EXAMPLE 15

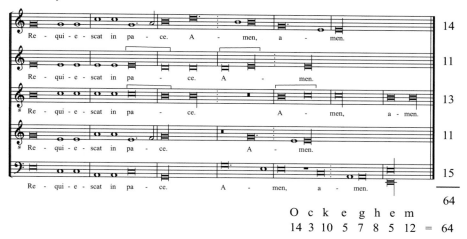

EXAMPLE 16

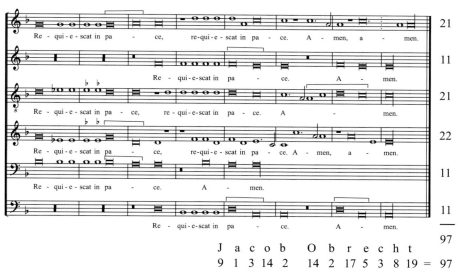

Similar to *Illibata dei virgo* is another Marian motet, the five-voice *Salve regina* (NJE 25.5), which is in three parts. Here too, the key to understanding the eso-teric structure of text and music lies again in an ostinato motif. The tenor consists exclusively of four breves on *la–sol–la–re*, the first notes of the antiphon *Salve regina*, once again starting alternately on *g¹* and *d¹*. Each presentation of the motif is preceded by a three-measure rest, and contains therefore the Marian number 7. It appears twelve times in the first part, four times in the second part, and eight in the third. These 12 double 'Salves' must surely be seen as a reference to the Woman of the Apocalypse (Revelation 12:1): "And a great sign appeared in heaven: A woman clothed with the sun, and the moon under her feet, and on her head a crown of twelve stars" (Fig. 19). A contemporary of Josquin, the Dutch painter Geertgen tot Sint Jans created a delicate representation of this text in his panel *The Glorification of Mary* (Museum Boymans-van Beuningen, Rotterdam). As in *Illibata dei virgo*, Josquin adds one or two notes at the end of each section, bringing the total number to 100. This number can be explained with the help of the rubric accompanying the tenor part, whose motif is written out only a few times in most sources: "Qui perseveraverit (usque in finem, hic) salvus erit" (He who endures to the end [singing the motif] will be saved; Matthew 10:22; Fig. 20). The composer must have conceived this device as a reference to the text in the third part of the motet, "Et Jesum, benedictum fructum ventris tui, nobis post hoc exilium ostende" (And, after this our exile, show us Jesus, the blessed fruit of your womb). In the Greek name for Christ, Χριστός, the initial letter resembles the Roman numeral X: the number 10, and therefore also the 10 × 10 tenor notes, refers to Jesus.

FIGURE 19: Albrecht Dürer, woodcut of the Woman of the Apocalypse (1498).

FIGURE 20: The five-voice *Salve regina* with the constantly repeated ostinato motif. Vatican City, Biblioteca Apostolica Vaticana, Ms. Cappella Sistina 24, f. 79ʹ-80.

The five-voice *Stabat mater* (NJE 25.9; see p. 173) also seems to be based on the number 100. Though the number of notes contained in the *cantus firmus* is not consistent over the 34 sources, the oldest, the 'Chigi Codex', produced in Flanders and now in the Vatican, has 50 notes in each half of the motet. In medieval symbolism, the number 100 was associated above all with eternal life, corresponding with the end of the motet:

Quando corpus morietur,	When my body shall die,
Fac, ut anime donetur	Grant that my soul is given
Paradisi gloria.	The glory of Paradise.
Amen.	Amen.

The tenor of Binchois' chanson, however, has only 95 notes, so Josquin seems to have manipulated the melody to achieve a certain number.[16]

The five-voice *Miserere mei, deus* (NJE 18.3) is anew based on an ostinato motif, this time the opening words of the psalm sung *recto tono*. Each of the nineteen verses of psalm 50 (51) is followed by the refrain "Miserere mei, deus", heard in all voices together with the ostinato, which gives the motet the character of a litany. The three parts contain seven, seven, and five verses, but Josquin inserts an additional refrain in the middle of verses 1 and 13, thereby increasing the number of statements to eight in the first two

---

16 See Willem Elders, 'A New Case of Number Symbolism in Josquin?', in *EM* 37 (2009), 21–26.

parts, or 21 times in total. These numbers correspond to the structure of the tenor: in the first part the motif descends stepwise over the octave $e'-e$, in the second part it ascends from $e-e'$, and in the third it descends again, from van $e'-a$. The insertion of the two extra refrains may also have sprung from another consideration. It is known from a sixteenth-century poem (see p. 35) that Josquin wrote this setting in 1503–1504 at the request of the seventy-year-old Duke Ercole d'Este, who possibly intended it to be sung at his funeral. He was a very pious man. In 1495–1497 he had corresponded with the Dominican preacher Girolamo Savonarola, who, just before he was burned at the stake in Florence in 1498, had written a meditation on this same psalm, the printed edition of which uses capital letters for each plea for mercy.[17] There can hardly be any doubt that this was the inspiration for the Duke's commission. Josquin had already used his name in the ostinato motif (see p. 117–119]) of his *Missa Hercules Dux Ferrarie* (NJE 11.1). The gematria value of Ercole's official title is 210 (10 x 21),[18] and thus made up of ten times the number of the "Miserere" statements, making it not unlikely that in the motet he assigned the Duke, figuratively speaking, the role of psalmist.

In the four-voice *Virgo prudentissima* (NJE 25.12), numbers play a more modest structural role. The motet ends with the words "pulchra ut luna, electa ut sol" (fair as the moon, resplendent as the sun), where "ut sol" is sung seven times as a rising fifth to the solmisation syllables *ut–sol*. The Marian number 7 is thus made audible (Ex. 17).

EXAMPLE 17

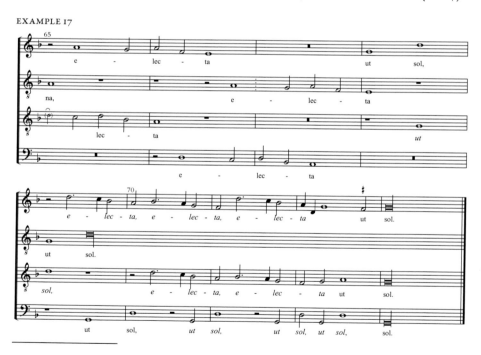

---

17   See Patrick Macey, 'Savonarola and the Sixteenth-Century Motet', in *JAMS* 36 (1983), 422–452, at 448–451, with a figure of the printed text from 1498.

18   H e r c u l e s   D u x   F e r r a r i e
     8 5 17 3 20 11   5 18   4 20 22   6 5 17 17 1   17 9 5   = 210

Similarly, in the five-voice *Obsecro te, domina* (NJE *24.8), the use of number is limited to a short phrase. The text, reconstructed from contemporary books of hours, speaks of the Virgin Mary being crowned by her only-begotten Son: "... quam filius tuus unigenitus coronavit". The twelvefold repetition of the motif on the word "coronavit" allows a connection to be made, like in *Salve regina* above, with the Woman of the Apocalypse: "... and on her head a crown of twelve stars" (Ex. 18).

EXAMPLE 18

The number 12 also lies behind *Inviolata, integra et casta es* (NJE *24.5). The motet has been published as doubtful because of its late transmission, and because many of the attributions by the scribe of Kassel 38 have proved unreliable, but it does contain stylistic elements that support Josquin's authorship. Its twelve voices must also have been inspired by the image of the Woman of the Apocalypse. This scoring, unusual before the sixteenth century, has been seen by some musicologists as another reason to doubt the attribution. Yet comparison can be made to the twelve-voice *Missa Ecce terre motus* by Antoine Brumel and the twelve-voice canon *Ista est speciosa* by Mathieu Gascongne, both contemporaries of Josquin. The *cantus firmus* lies in one of the middle voices and carries the text "O Maria, flos virginum" (O Mary, flower of maidenhood) with a melody in the image of a crown, serving as a symbol of ever-lasting life (Ex. 19):

EXAMPLE 19

Although the psalm-motet *Qui habitat in adjutorio altissimi* (NJE *18.8) has an asterisk indicating a doubtful composition, its profound symbolism is an argument for Josquin's authorship: no other composer of the period makes such prominent use of number symbolism. The work is imposing, though it seems not primarily intended for performance.[19] It is based on verses 1–8 of psalm 90 (91) and written canonically for 24 voices, in four choirs of six. From the start of the fourth canon, the other three six-voice canons are continued, so that the piece ends in real 24-voice counterpoint. The psalm text is a song affirming God's protection of the righteous. The 24 voices almost certainly personify the 24 Elders of Revelation,[20] which most commentators regard as the twelve Old Testament Patriarchs (the twelve sons of Jacob) and the twelve Apostles, representing the old and the new people of God. We can interpret the canonic structure further with the help of two passages in Revelation in which John expounds his vision:

> And behold there was a throne set in heaven, and upon the throne one sitting. And he that sat, was to the sight like the jasper and the sardine stone; and there was a rainbow round about the throne, in sight like unto an emerald. And round about the throne were four and twenty seats; and upon the seats four and twenty ancients sitting, clothed in white garments, and on their heads were crowns of gold ... And round about the throne were four living creatures, full of eyes before and behind. And the first living creature was like a lion: and the second living creature like a calf: and the third living creature, having the face, as it were, of a man: and the fourth living creature as like an eagle flying. And the four living creatures had each of them six wings (4:2–8) ... And when he had opened the book, the four living creatures, and the four and twenty ancients fell down before the Lamb, having every one of them harps, and golden vials full of odours ... And they sung a new canticle ... (5:8–9)

Each of the four canons has six voices, reflecting the six wings of each creature in the first passage. The second is undoubtedly the literary source for the many representations in medieval and Renaissance art of the Elders playing musical instruments. One of the finest of these may be found on the right-hand panel of Hans Memling's *Triptych of Saint John the Baptist and Saint John the Evangelist* (Sint-Jan Hospital Museum, Bruges). It shows Christ enthroned, with around

---

19   In the author's opinion, it forms part of a group of compositions that could be called *musica non exsequenda*; see Willem Elders, 'The Conception of *musica celestis* and Musical Composition', in Idem, *Symbolic Scores* ..., 211–258, at 223.

20   Edward E. Lowinsky, 'Ockeghem's Canon for Thirty-six Voices: An Essay in Musical Iconography', in *Essays in Musicology in Honor of Dragan Plamenac*, edd. Gustave Reese and Robert J. Snow (Pittsburg 1969), 157–180, at 179.

him the four six-winged creatures, creatures that had later been made symbols of the four Evangelists by the Church Fathers. Around them are the twenty-four Elders, each with a musical instrument. Their white robes recall the purification of the Elect through the blood of Christ the Mediator, and their crowns show that they reign eternally. The Elders are also mentioned by the music theorists Adam von Fulda and Gioseffo Zarlino as heavenly musicians next to God. The first verse of the psalm seems to support this interpretation: "He that dwelleth in the aid of the most High, shall abide under the protection of the God of Jacob." The concept of heavenly music was part of a long medieval tradition, in which even the animals praise God. Indeed, of all celestial beings, the four living creatures and twenty-four Elders are, in the vision of Saint John, nearest to God; in the vision of the composer, they are singing his motet, with its completely novel scoring, as the 'new canticle'.[21]

A Mass could also be based on numbers, as for example the *Missa L'homme armé super voces musicales* (NJE 6.3). If Ockeghem, as the theorists Zarlino (in 1571) and Ludovico Zacconi (in 1592) claimed, was indeed Josquin's teacher – and contemporary documents show that they at least met several times – it would not be surprising if the pupil had wanted to pay homage to his master while he was still alive. It is thought that the proportion canons of this Mass are references to Ockeghem's *Missa Prolationum*, and that the *L'homme armé* melody was expanded to 64 notes to represent Ockeghem's name,[22] just as in the prayer "Requiescat in pace" in his dirge *Nymphes des bois* (see above).

A remarkable passage in Josquin's oeuvre is found in the Benedictus of the Sanctus of his *Missa Pange lingua* (NJE 4.3), which is based on the hymn of that name sung at the feast of Corpus Christi. The word "Benedictus" is heard five times alternately by the bassus and the tenor alone, then a sixth time by both voices together (Ex. 20). This form of 'alternatim' is unique in the composer's oeuvre. One might suppose that Josquin had meant to symbolise the passion of Christ through his Five Wounds. As it appears though, it seems to have been inspired by the five blessings in the prayer "Unde et memores", said immediately after the consecration at the moment the singers start the Benedictus: the celebrant offers to God the sacrificed Victim (Christ), making the Sign of the Cross five times:

> Wherefore, O Lord, ... we offer unto Thy most excellent Majesty ... a pure † Victim, a holy † Victim, a spotless † Victim, the holy † Bread of eternal life, and the Chalice † of everlasting salvation.

---

21 See also Michael Zywietz, 'Fortdauerndes Mittelalter und Humanismus. Die 24stimmige kanonische Psalmmotette *Qui habitat in adiutorio Altissimi* von Josquin Desprez', in *Ars und Scientia im Mittelalter und in der Frühen Neuzeit*, edd. Cora Dietl and Dörte Helschinger (Tübingen 2002), 215–234.

22 See Dieter Heikamp, 'Zur Struktur der Messe *L'omme armé super voces musicales* von Josquin Desprez', in *Mf* 19 (1966), 121–141.

EXAMPLE 20

THE MISSA GAUDEAMUS

The symbolic meaning of numbers can go far beyond a simple game with letter-values, as is shown in the *Missa Gaudeamus* (NJE 4.2). This work is based on a mystical number series, the individual parts of which can be meaningfully interpreted, and which lead to the conclusion that the Mass was not composed for a Marian feast, as was formerly thought, but for All Saints (1 November).[23]

The Mass, in fact, belongs to the wide category of works of art that are determined in some way by the visions of St. John described in the Book of Revelation. These include mosaics in Roman basilicas, stained-glass windows in Romanesque and Gothic churches, book illustrations by the Limbourg brothers, tapestries by Jan Bondel and Nicolas Bataille in Angers, woodcuts by Albrecht Dürer and Lucas Cranach, and the altarpiece with the *Adoration of the Mystic Lamb* by Hubert and Jan van Eyck in Ghent. It can not be proved that Josquin ever had the opportunity to examine this magnificent altarpiece in St. Bavo's Church, but he must surely have been to the Cathedral of Milan, where a window by Stefano da Pandino depicted the Lamb of God.

Its *cantus prius factus* is the introit "Gaudeamus omnes in domino" (see p. 102). Even though the complete chant melody is used, the main structural element is its opening motif, which Josquin treats in a most unusual manner. It is heard 61 times in all, divided extremely irregularly between the movements of the Mass, implying the presence of a deliberate scheme.

The Kyrie has six statements of the motif. This number signifies the anticipation of salvation and refers, according to medieval belief, to the end of time: Christ's death took place on the sixth day, from the sixth hour. Mankind will therefore be saved through the number 6, and, by performing the six Works of Mercy, may be taken up into the multitude of the saints.

In the Gloria, the 'gaudeamus' motif is found at the beginning of all four voices. Thereafter it is repeated ten times in the tenor. When he interpreted the number 14,

---

23   For an excellent interpretation of mystical numbers in the Middle Ages, see Heinz Meyer, *Die Zahlenallegorese im Mittelalter. Methode und Gebrauch* (Munich 1975). A more detailed analysis of the numbers used in the Mass may be found in Willem Elders, 'Symbolism in the Sacred Music of Josquin', *JosqComp*, 531–568, at 549–558.

Gregory the Great thought in terms of the addition of the numbers 10 and 4, representing the Old Testament (from the Decalogue) and the New (from the four Gospels). The tenfold repeat of the motif in the tenor, always at the same pitch, seems to allude to the obligatory nature of the Ten Commandments. As is well-known, the Gloria begins with the Angelic Hymn from Luke's account of the birth of Christ (Luke 2:14). In the context of the feast of All Saints, the birth of Christ can surely be regarded as the moment He established His kingdom on earth. The number 14 in the Gloria, representing the establishment of the New Covenant, thus acts as a sequel to the number 6 in the Kyrie, representing salvation.

Though by far the largest movement of the Mass, the Credo uses the 'gaudeamus' motif only twice, at the very beginning in the tenor and superius. The number 2 represents salvation, because the Old Covenant was turned into the New through the blood of Christ. This interpretation can be traced back to St. Paul:

> For it is written that Abraham had two sons: the one by a bondwoman, and the other by a free woman. But he who was of the bondwoman, was born according to the flesh: but he of the free woman, was by promise. Which things are said by an allegory. For these are the two covenants (Galatians 4:22–24).

The believer also enters into a personal covenant with God the Father through the Son: "Credo in unum deo ... Et in unum dominum Jesum Christum" (I believe in one God, the Father Almighty ... And in one Lord Jesus Christ).

The superius of the Sanctus uses the motif three times in a high tessitura and long note values, reminiscent of the sound of a trumpet (see Ex. 23 below). At the same time, the motif appears once in the altus and then in the tenor. These numbers 3 and 2 signify faith in the Trinity and action in accordance with the command to love God as well as man. In the Osanna, the motif is heard seven times, which refers to Revelation 10:7: "But in the days of the voice of the seventh angel, when he shall begin to sound the trumpet, the mystery of God shall be finished," meaning "the all-embracing plan of God is to accomplish, through Christ, everlasting salvation and the total defeat of evil."[24]

The text of the Agnus dei is a prayer for eternal peace to the Lamb of God, a figure that takes a central place in many apocalyptic works of art. In more than one sense, this movement acts as a 'peroration' (Fig. 21). The 'gaudeamus' motifs are divided into two separate series. The four statements in the first Agnus dei clearly function as a symbol of the Cross of Salvation, for according to the theologian Honorius of Autun (*d.* ca. 1151), from the four strokes of the Roman numeral IIII the figure ÷ can be formed. An explanation of the 'gaudeamus' motifs of the final Agnus dei, as many as 23 in number, can also be found in Honorius: this is the number of Signs of the Cross the celebrant makes during de canon of the Mass, and refers to the Just in the Age of the Law (10) and in the Age of Grace (13).[25] It is therefore very probable that Josquin wrote his *Missa Gaudeamus* in the hope that he also would one day join the Elect.

---

24   *The Bible translated from the original texts*, Willibrord edition (Boxtel 1981), p. 1743.

25   Meyer, *Die Zahlenallegorese ...*, 153.

FIGURE 21: The final Agnus dei of *Missa Gaudeamus*. Cambrai, Médiathèque Municipale, Ms. 18, f. 96'-97.

Number symbolism could also play a role in secular works, though much less frequently. Its use in *El grillo* (NJE *28.12) is a nice example, and at the same time provides further proof that the work should have been published as an authentic work of Josquin (see p. 62). The first two sections each consist of 88 notes, which turns out, just as in *Illibata dei virgo* (see above), to be the gematria value of 'des Prez'. The next section repeats the first half of the opening section and has 44 notes. The last section has 97 notes, but ends with a cadence that existed at this time in two versions (Exx. 21a and 21b). Where more sources of a composition survive, it can be seen that scribes and publishers used the two versions interchangeably. The longer cadence would reflect the rhythm of the tenor in m. 36–37 and would bring the number of notes in this section to 99, i.e. the gematria value of 'Josquin'. Could it have been that, in this instance, the composer wanted to sign the *frottola* also with his forename?

The compositional procedures described in this chapter point to the existence of a symbolic language intelligible only to insiders. They show us a composer who wanted constantly to expand the horizons of his musical imagination. In this way, Josquin can be seen as an absolutely exceptional musician. Perhaps even more striking is that another musician of a similar disposition, Johann Sebastian Bach, would later create a body of work with many similarities, in this respect, to that of Josquin.

EXAMPLE 21a-b

PART II – *Josquin's musical legacy*

The eighteen Mass settings by Josquin that have been accepted in the *NJE* as authentic cover about 45 years of activity as a composer and demonstrate a high degree of stylistic diversity. While the two earliest Masses, *L'ami Baudichon* and *Une mousse de Biscaye*, betray the influence of Dufay and Ockeghem, it appears that Josquin, in his latest settings, was far ahead of his time. The determination of the chronological order is difficult not only because the dates of the sources are generally of little help, also because the composer poses, in most of his Masses, a different musical problem. The latter means that stylistic comparisons are bound to be limited. In addition, we can be quite sure that the bulk of Josquin's Masses was composed from the early 1480s onwards, when he had all current compositional devices at his disposal but never felt obliged to display them within one single composition. The differences between many of Josquin's Masses are therefore ones of conception rather than style or stylistic advancement. Even in his latest Mass setting, *Pange lingua*, the composer uses a conspicuous element that occurs already in his earliest Masses.[1]

The Masses will be commented on in order of publication in the *NJE*, and are classified according to the pre-existing material on which they are based or the composition technique used. The ten *NJE* volumes allocated to the Masses are subdivided as follows:

- Masses based on Gregorian chants
- Masses based on secular monophonic songs
- Masses based on secular polyphonic songs
- Mass based on a sacred polyphonic song
- Masses based on solmisation themes
- Canonic Masses

---

1 See Willem Elders, 'Which is Josquin's First Mass Based on a Gregorian Chant?', in *Littera NIGRO scripta manet. In honorem Jaromír Černy*, edd. Jan Bata, Jiři K. Kroupa, and Lenka Mráčková (Prague 2009), 59-70.

The majority of the Masses consist of five movements that set the so-called 'constant' or 'unchanging' texts of the *Ordinarium missae*, namely Kyrie, Gloria, Credo, Sanctus and Agnus dei.

Masses based on Gregorian chants

MISSA AVE MARIS STELLA (NJE 3.1)
The Mass survives, entirely or in part, in 20 sources: seven printed books and thirteen manuscripts. Furthermore, four sources contain arrangements for lute or organ of sections of the Mass. The scoring is for four voices with the following ranges: c'–g² (superius), d–b'flat (altus), f–g' (tenor), Bflat–e' (bassus). Length: 561 measures.

Of the medieval hymn on which the Mass is based, Josquin used the following first-mode version (Ex. 22):

EXAMPLE 22

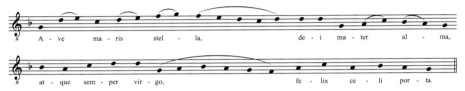

The wide dissemination of the hymn is reflected in the equally wide dissemination of the Mass. Its popularity is demonstrated by, among other things, the parchment manuscript 9126 of the Royal Library in Brussels, which was produced shortly after 1500 and where it appears at the opening. The Kyrie on f. 1v is illuminated with a miniature of the Holy Virgin (Fig. 22); f. 2r displays the portraits of Philip the Fair and Juana of Castile, the recipients of the manuscript.[2]

The composition probably dates from the years 1480–1490 and could have been written in Milan. The four short phrases of the hymn provide the frame for all five Mass movements and are elaborated upon in all voices. Josquin reinforces the cyclic form of the Mass by beginning the Kyrie and Agnus dei as well as the Gloria and Credo in the same manner. In the Sanctus, superius and tenor quote the chant's incipit in long notes, mainly longs and breves. The hymn melody in its entirety is sung only by the tenor in the Osanna. Since no more than three sections (Pleni sunt, Benedictus and Agnus II) are freely composed, the Mass is almost wholly permeated by the chant. Short motifs, whether repeated or not, alternate with free interpolations, literal quotations with richly embellished phrases. Even where Josquin presents the melody in its original form, he allows himself some licence. The degree to which the composer uses the same elements of his model in various ways finds expression, for example, in the canonic passages. Agnus I presents the hymn as a canon at the fourth between bassus and tenor, Agnus II likewise at the fourth between altus and supe-

---

2   For a reproduction in colour, see *NJE* vol. 2, 4-5.

rius, Agnus III at the octave between tenor and superius. In the central section of the Credo, brief homophonic passages at the words "et homo factus est" and "passus et sepultus est" underline the deeper significance of Christ's coming to earth and his death. In the article "Et resurrexit ..." (He rose again ...), the words "secundum scripturas" are set in *fauxbourdon*, pointing out by means of this traditional – but in Josquin's time already archaic – harmonic technique the visionary message of the Bible. Shortly afterwards, the long melisma on the words "non erit finis" denotes that there shall be no end to Christ's kingdom.

FIGURE 22: Superius and tenor voices of Kyrie I of *Missa Ave maris stella*. Brussels, Bibliothèque Royale, Ms. 9126, f. 1ʳ.

MISSA DE BEATA VIRGINE (NJE 3.3)

The Mass survives, entirely or in part, in no less than 54 sources: nine printed books and forty-five manuscripts. Furthermore, fifteen sources contain arrangements for lute or organ of sections of the Mass. The scoring of the Kyrie and Gloria is for four voices, while the Credo, Sanctus, and Agnus Dei are scored for five voices. The voice parts have a very variable range. For example, the range of the superius in the Kyrie and Gloria is from d^1-g^2, in the Sanctus and Agnus dei from f^1/g^1-g^2, but in the Credo from $g-e^2$. Length: 882 measures.

No other work by Josquin survives in so many sources and with so many attributions to its author as his Lady Mass. The great popularity of the Mass is proven by the fact that it features in manuscripts from nearly all Western European countries, four of them even opening with it. The parchment manuscript Guelferbytanus A Augusteus folio from the Herzog August Bibliothek in Wolfenbüttel, which dates from about 1520, is one example. On f. 1v, the Kyrie in this manuscript is illuminated with a miniature showing the annunciation of the angel Gabriel to the Holy Virgin (Fig. 23), and fol. 2r displays the portrait of Wilhelm IV, Duke of Bavaria and recipient of this particularly large manuscript (61 x 42 cm).

The cycle is composed of five individual Mass movements. Judging by their transmission, the Gloria and Credo were written before 1507, possibly in Condé; the Kyrie, Sanctus, and Agnus dei were added later. The earliest source containing the complete Mass, Cappella Sistina 45, is dated between 1511 and 1514. Unlike Josquin's other Masses based on Gregorian chants, each of the five movements of this Mass is built on a separate chant appropriate to that particular portion of the Ordinary. Originally, these chants were associated with a special feast of the Ecclesiastical year. Masses entitled *De beata virgine* were called votive Masses, and were intended to be sung on Saturdays. The tradition of these 'Lady Masses' no doubt contributed to the wide dissemination of Josquin's Mass setting. The melodies for the Kyrie and Gloria are those contained in Mass IX in the *Liber Usualis* (*in festis Beatae Mariae virginis*), for the Sanctus and Agnus dei those of Mass IV (*in festis duplicibus*). The Credo is based on the familiar Credo I. This design allows variation and contrast between the movements. Cyclic unity is sacrificed in favour of liturgical suitability. These aspects are also apparent in the composition techniques applied. For example, the four-voice Kyrie and Gloria are set in a predominantly imitative style, whereas the three five-voice movements each include a canon in the two tenor voices, in which the corresponding chant is quoted.

In the Gloria – for Glarean (*Dodecachordon*, 1547), this movement represented a highlight in the composer's oeuvre – we encounter the medieval practice of tropes: six short additions are made to the established liturgical texts in honour of Jesus Christ and the Virgin Mary. These include "Spiritus et alme orphanorum paraclite" (Spirit and generous protector of orphans) and "Ad Marie gloriam" (To the glory of Mary). These tropes were removed from the Missal in 1563 by the Council of Trent, and they have been erased in some of the manuscripts of the Mass. In the Credo there is a remarkable moment at the article "Qui cum patre et filio simul adoratur" (Who together with the Father and the Son is adored). These words are sung in the superius to nine notes (breves), grouped in three triplets, symbolizing the Holy Trinity.

FIGURE 23: Superius and bassus voices of Kyrie I of *Missa De beata virgine*.
Wolfenbüttel, Herzog August Bibliothek, Ms. Guelferbytanus A, f. 1'.

MISSA GAUDEAMUS (NJE 4.2)

The Mass survives, entirely or in part, in 16 sources: seven printed books and nine manuscripts. Furthermore, three sources contain arrangements for lute or organ of sections of the Mass. The scoring is for four voices with the following ranges: a–f² (superius), d–b¹flat (altus), c–a¹ (tenor), F–e¹ (bassus). Length: 768 measures.

This work was most likely composed when Josquin was employed at the Vatican. It was intended for the feast of All Saints, which had a long tradition at St. Peter's. No other Mass setting based on the introit 'Gaudeamus' is known. For edition in the

NJE, Cambrai 18, which has less errors than the other sources, served as the principal source. Its superius shows an unusual mensuration sign in the Sanctus (Ex. 23):

EXAMPLE 23

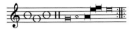

Since this same sign is found in the unrelated manuscript Basel F.IX.25, we may safely assume that it originated with the composer. A circle is the normal mensuration sign for a ternary metre; the three circles here reflect the threefold "Holy" in the text, and therefore symbolize the holiness of God.

The following example shows the introit for All Saints after a Northern-Italian manuscript from the fifteenth century, in a reading that is close to the one that served as the basis for the Mass (Ex. 24):

EXAMPLE 24

The chant is quoted entirely only in the Gloria and Credo. In these movements, the melody appears in the tenor, sometimes in long note values. In general, however, it is the initial formula of the introit that, thematically, remains in the forefront. This formula occurs in the whole of the Mass 61 times, and in several places produces a striking effect. This is especially the case in the Sanctus, where a high tessitura makes it reminiscent of the sound of a trumpet, and in the final Agnus dei, where it is sung in all voices, in a vertiginous series of transpositions. The contrast between these two sections – the one lofty, the other restrained – is a fine witness to Josquin's talent in lending musical expression to sacred texts. In Chapter 6, the distribution of the motifs over the various sections of the Mass is specified in more detail, and it is also explained how the resulting series of numbers is related to their medieval mystical signification.

MISSA PANGE LINGUA (NJE 4.3)

The Mass survives, entirely or in part, in 22 sources: four printed books and eighteen manuscripts. Furthermore, four sources contain arrangements for lute of sections of the Mass. The scoring is for four voices with the following ranges: c¹–e² (superius), c–a¹ (altus), c–f¹ (tenor), G–c¹ (bassus). Length: 737 measures.

This Mass, the only one of Josquin's not published by Petrucci, is included in no less than five manuscripts of the Vatican library, all copied between 1513 and 1523. The transmission in general suggests that it is one of the composer's later works, written when he was living in Condé. Two of the manuscripts of which the production was supervised by Petrus Alamire (in Mechlin and Brussels) open with this famous Mass. The Mass also was copied into the 'Occo Codex', which is entirely devoted to music for the Holy Sacrament. The latter manuscript was produced in

1520–1521, also in Alamire's workshop, at the request of the Amsterdam merchant banker Pompejus Occo, chapel warden of the 'Heilige Stede' (called 'Jerusalem'), where a miracle involving a wonderworking host, which had taken place in 1345, was commemorated every year.

The *Missa Pange lingua* was written for the feast of Corpus Christi, observed in the Roman Catholic Church on the Thursday after Trinity Sunday. It is the only Mass setting of the period that takes the hymn of the same name, written by Thomas Aquinas, as a starting point (Ex. 25):

EXAMPLE 25

The third-mode melody consists of six short phrases which provide the seeds for the unfolding of new melodies. The first nine measures of Kyrie I are based on the first phrase (Ex. 26). The second phrase is used in the next section, phrases three and four in the Christe, and phrases five and six in Kyrie II. While only a few phrases of the hymn are heard in the Gloria, Credo and Sanctus, the entire melody reappears in the final Agnus dei. Since both the text of this section and of the hymn bear witness to the Lamb of God who sacrificed himself to expiate the sins of the world, Josquin's decision to quote the entire melody in the highest voice in this section is significant. It is heard first in long note values, then in a more or less free elaboration. Towards the end, the last six notes are transformed into a peaceful motif that turns the closing passage of the Mass into an insistent prayer.

EXAMPLE 26

Josquin's Mass may be seen as an early high point in the development towards a greater homogeneity of the voice parts in a polyphonic complex, and its fully balanced imitation technique paves the way for the Palestrina style. This homogeneity is revealed by the occurrence of the chant motifs in all four voices. Nonetheless, in the Gloria and Credo, sections in which the voices imitate one another alternate with short, homophonic passages, where the text is more easily understood and emphasized. A fine example may be found in the Credo, in the passage "Et incarnatus est ... et homo factus est" (And was incarnate by the Holy Spirit of the Virgin Mary, and was made man.)

Masses based on secular monophonic songs

MISSA L'AMI BAUDICHON (NJE 5.1)

The Mass survives, entirely or in part, in 16 sources: five printed books and eleven manuscripts. The scoring is for four voices with the following ranges: b–g² (superius), e–a¹flat (altus), g–g¹ (tenor), A–e¹ (bassus). Length: 717 measures.

The composition was probably written in France around 1475. Several style elements, such as the use of a head-motif in all Mass movements, the frequent occurrence of duos, and the major-third tonality, point to the influence of Dufay.[3] Josquin based this work on the song 'L'ami Baudechon ma dame', which is so simple that its choice as a starting point for a Mass setting may be surprising, the more so because it contains a rhyme word incongruously obscene in the context of the Holy Liturgy. The scribe of manuscript 781 of the chapterhouse library in Verona, the only source to record the song's text, understandably omitted it (Fig. 24). Judging by its presence in one of the Vatican choirbooks, the composition nevertheless also belonged to the repertory of the Sistine Chapel.

Although in Josquin's time the song was often mentioned in poems and texts about dance and theatre, the reconstruction of the original form of the melody can only be made on the basis of his Mass (Ex. 27). The ternary metre and the repeats of the short phrases mark it as a dance tune. It appears almost exclusively in the tenor, a part that can conveniently be played on a shawm. The melody is consistently repeated in the four-voice passages. In the longer Mass movements it is heard in long note values. These values are not notated but must be deduced from mensuration signs and written directions in Latin, such as "Crescit in duplo" (Increases to double values). In the Credo, the tune is set in inversion, changing the descending melody to an ascending one. This procedure is indicated by a quotation from Luke 14:11: "... every one that exalteth himself, shall be humbled; and he that humbleth himself, shall be exalted." In the passages "Et incarnatus est ..." and "Crucifixus etiam ..." the tenor is said to be "a dumb man not opening his mouth" (Ps. 37:14), which means

---

3   Concerning the Mass's authorship, see the observations made by Rob Wegman, 'Who was Josquin', in *JosqComp*, 31–35, and Fallows, 29–35. In the Critical Commentary to his recent edition of the Mass, NJE 5.1, 26–35, Martin Just discusses the principal stylistic features, and concludes that there is no compelling ground to doubt the attribution in Petrucci's *Missarum Josquin Liber secundus* of 1505.

that this voice part is silent. A child of his time, Josquin undoubtedly took pleasure in inventing riddles and puzzles while elaborating the material at his disposal.[4]

FIGURE 24: Superius and tenor voices of the Kyrie of *Missa L'ami Baudichon*. Verona, Biblioteca Capitolare, Ms. 761, f. 62'.

EXAMPLE 27

---

4   Verona 761 preserves what was probably the original notation of the *cantus firmus*; see Jaap van Benthem, "Kommst in die ersten Kreise!". Josquins *Missa L'ami Baudichon* – ihre Originalgestalt und ihre Überlieferung in Petruccis *Missarum Josquin Liber secundus*', in *Basler Jahrbuch für historische Musikpraxis* 25 (2001), 71–83, and the figure at 74.

MISSA UNE MOUSSE DE BISCAYE (NJE 5.2)

The Mass survives, entirely or in part, in 6 sources: four printed books and two manuscripts. The scoring is for four voices with the following ranges: bflat–e²flat (superius), c–a¹ (altus), c–f¹ (tenor), F–bflat (bassus). Length: 669 measures.

The composition possibly dates from the years 1473–1475, and might therefore be considered to be Josquin's first Mass setting. The formation of melodies and voice combinations are reminiscent of Ockeghem, and certain deficiencies in the composition technique point to a young, not yet mature composer.[5] The text of the Agnus dei is sung to the music of the Kyrie, a cyclic form unique among Josquin's Mass settings. (Gloria, Credo, and Sanctus are thus framed by the same music.) The centre of the composition is the Credo, with 269 measures by far the longest movement. It presents a very sophisticated mensural notation of the *cantus prius factus*.

The ballad 'Une mousse de Biscaye', on which the Mass is based, was also used by Josquin for a chanson (see NJE 28.35). It consists of eight phrases and begins as follows (Ex. 28):

EXAMPLE 28

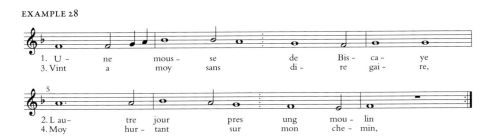

The head-motif of the two higher voices of the chanson is similar to that in the Christe (and Agnus II) of the Mass. Except for the Sanctus, where the melody is quoted in a somewhat condensed form, the eight phrases are incorporated in all movements. The most remarkable aspect of the presentation of the melody is the occasional transformation of a binary metre into a ternary one. This always happens in the first section of each

5   Josquin's authorship of the Mass has been considered "highly problematic" by Jaap van Benthem, 'Was "Une mousse de Biscaye" Really Appreciated by L'ami Baudichon?', in *Muziek en Wetenschap* 1 (1991), 175–194, but his suggestion that the Mass might have been composed by Gaspar van Weerbeke (p. 188-189) is rejected by Eric F. Fiedler on stylistic grounds ('A New Mass by Gaspar van Weerbeke? Thoughts on Comparative Analysis', in *Studien zur Musikgeschichte. Ein Festschrift für Ludwig Finscher*, ed. Annegrit Laubenthal (Kassel 1995), 72–87). Van Benthem's reservations are shared by Anne-Emmanuelle Ceulemans, 'A Stylistic Investigation of *Missa Une mousse de Biscaye*, in the Light of its Attribution to Josquin des Prez', in *TVNM* 48 (1998), 30–50. See also Fallows, 268–269. However, in a lengthy discussion of the Mass, Martin Just argues that the stylistic features of the Mass point to Ockeghem's Masses as a model, and, accepting the attribution in Petrucci's *Missarum Josquin Liber secundus* of 1505, grants it a place in Josquin's oeuvre "as perhaps his earliest Mass"; see the Critical Commentary to his recent edition of the Mass, NJE 5.2, 79–89, at 89.

movement, except for in the Credo. In contrast to *Missa L'ami Baudichon* (see above), the chanson melody is not only quoted in the tenor but also in the other voices, and the short phrases are then expanded and elaborated. In the Credo the chanson melody enters in m. 46 in the tenor, and appears in fourfold augmentation as well as in inversion. This is indicated in the earliest source, Berlin 40021, with a warning (in Latin): "Singer, if you wish to perform this well, do it inversely." The ascending melody thus turns to a descending one. However, undoubtedly to help the musically still inexperienced singers, the scribe also notated the melody in the intended form: "Singers that are not yet grown up should perform it as it stands here." In m. 128, the song resumes its normal form, now in double note values. Also unlike the *L'ami Baudichon* Mass, the polyphony in the Credo is interrupted several times by passages in homophony. Where this is the case, the composer obviously wanted to emphasize the meaning of the text. A fine example may be found at the words "Et iterum venturus est judicare vivos et mortuos." (And He shall come again with glory to judge both the living and the dead.)

MISSA L'HOMME ARMÉ SEXTI TONI (NJE 6.2; Mi 5)
MISSA L'HOMME ARMÉ SUPER VOCES MUSICALES (NJE 6.3; Mi 1)

NJE 6.2 survives, entirely or in part, in 21 sources: eight printed books and thirteen manuscripts. Furthermore, one source contains an arrangement for lute of the "Et resurrexit" from the Credo. The scoring is for four voices, but in the final Agnus dei the superius and altus divide canonically into two parts, a procedure also applied in NJE 9.1. The ranges are as follows: e–c² (superius), Bflat–e'flat (altus and tenor), D–bflat (bassus). Length: 730 measures.

NJE 6.3 survives, entirely or in part, in 37 sources: fifteen printed books and twenty-two manuscripts. Furthermore, three sources contain arrangements for lute or organ of sections of the Mass. The scoring is for four voices with the following ranges: g–d² (superius), c–g¹ (altus), A–a (tenor), F–d¹ (bassus). Length: 765 measures.

Both settings are based on the popular 'L'homme armé' melody. This song, showing an A B A' form, dates from the second half of the fifteenth century, and probably came into existence shortly after the fall of Constantinople, possibly under the auspices of the Order of the Golden Fleece, which consisted entirely of 'armed men'.[6] At that time, Western Europe feared a Turkish invasion and prepared for battle (Ex. 29). It is generally accepted that the *Super voces* cycle with which Petrucci opens his first Book of Josquin Masses from 1502 is older than the *Sexti toni*. Before Josquin chose the song as a starting point for a Mass, many composers had already done so. With his two, structurally entirely different settings, he undoubtedly wished to surpass his predecessors. Unlike the *Super voces* Mass, which is extremely inventive in its archaistic orientation, the *Sexti toni* strikes a more modern tune. This is perhaps why Petrucci placed the works at the opening and at the end of his edition. The *Super voces* Mass can also be seen as an homage to Ockeghem, his "bon père" (see p. 33). The fact that both compositions were copied into manuscripts from the Vatican, together with the *L'homme armé* Masses by eight other composers, could indicate a Roman origin, in the 1490s.

---

6   See William Prizer, 'Music and Ceremonial in the Low Countries: Philip the Fair and the Order of the Golden Fleece', in *Early Music History* 5 (1985), 113–153.

EXAMPLE 29

The older setting derives its name from the notes of the Guidonian hexachord, *sex voces* or *voces musicales*, and is explained by the fact that the 'L'homme armé' melody starts in turn on every note of the *hexachordum naturale*: *c* = ut (Kyrie), *d* = re (Gloria), *e* = mi (Credo), *f* = fa (Sanctus), *g* = sol (Agnus I), *a* = la (Agnus III). The result of this continuous transposition of the tune is that it is performed in a different mode in every Mass movement. However, since the tune is stated in the tenor only and covered by the other voices, the shift in mode is scarcely audible at all. The Mass also contains four proportion canons. In the three sections of the Kyrie, the song is elaborated in canon between the tenor and one of the other voices, with the note values of the *comes* proportionally augmented. The Benedictus consists of three 2 *ex* 1 canons. Finally, the three voices of the Agnus II form a proportion canon to which a symbolic meaning can be attached (see p. 80–82). Other exceptional devices may be found in the second section of the Gloria, and in the Credo in the passage "Et incarnatus est ... cujus regni non erit finis", where in both cases the melody is sung in retrograde motion (Fig. 25). Oddly enough, the following passage, "Et in spiritum sanctum ... ecclesiam", is lacking in all sources of the Mass except for the mid-sixteenth-century manuscript Cappella Sistina 154. A stylistic analysis has shown that it is a later addition.[7] In the final Agnus dei, the tune, having so far been allocated to the tenor, now appears in the superius, preceded by the direction "Clama, ne cesses" (Cry, cease not; Isaias 58:1). This indicates that this voice part of 124 measures should not contain a single rest. As for the performance of this voice, we cannot know for sure what the composer had in mind. Could he have aimed at an instrumental rendering, for example by a shawm, an instrument that allows for circular breathing?[8]

---

7   See Jesse Rodin, 'Finishing Josquin's "Unfinished" Mass: A Case of Stylistic Imitation in the *Cappella Sistina*', in *JM* 22 (2005), 412–453. The absence of this section of the Credo can perhaps be explained by the fact that, in the Roman Catholic Church, the position of the Holy Spirit within the Trinity was debated for centuries. The Eastern Church could never accept that he would have proceeded not only from the Father, but also from the Son. The absence of one or more of the articles relating to the Holy Spirit in numerous other Credo settings of the time seems to indicate that ecclesiastical authorities dealt with the problem locally as they saw fit.

8   See Willem Elders, 'The Performance of *Cantus firmi* in Josquin's Masses Based on Secular Monophonic Song', in *EM* 17 (1989), 330–341, at 333–335.

FIGURE 25: Loose leaf with the resolution to the retrograde section of the *cantus firmus* in the Credo of *Missa L'homme armé super voces musicales.* Jena, Thüringer Universitäts- und Landesbibliothek, Ms. 32.

In the *Sexti toni* Mass, Josquin quotes the melody in the 6th mode, on F. This is unlike most of the earlier settings, among which those by Guillaume Dufay and Antoine Busnois, where the tune is in a minor tonality. In Josquin's setting, the tune is almost always quoted in a more or less embellished version and is not allocated to a single voice. The new approach makes broad use of imitation and sequence. The B section of the melody is highlighted in the "Et resurrexit" in the Credo, where the three motifs are stated four times in the superius (m. 83–104 = 110–131 = 137–158 = 164–185), in each section supported by the lower voices in constantly changing counterpoint (Fig. 26). In the two four-voice sections of the Sanctus the melody is treated canonically, first at the unison, then at the fifth. The imitative duos in the Pleni sunt and Benedictus leave no doubt as to their symbolic nature (see p. 79). Similarly to the *Super voces* Mass, the melody is stated both in normal form and in retrograde, but here, in the final Agnus dei, the two forms are heard simultaneously: the tenor sings the B section first recte and then in retrograde; the bassus first in retrograde and then recte. At the same time, the superius and altus are the leading voices in two freely-composed double canons at the unison, both *ad minimam*. Above the long sustained notes in the low voices, motif imitations in swift succession, mutually related and in seemingly endless motion, evoke an image of heavenly music (see also p. 79). Notwithstanding this amazing example of technical skill, the music in the apotheosis of the Mass fully conveys the spirit of the prayer.

FIGURE 26: Superius voice (top left) of the Credo of *Missa L'homme armé sexti toni* with the fourfold statement of the middle part of the *cantus firmus*. Vatican City, Biblioteca Apostolica Vaticana, Ms. C VIII 234 ('Chigi Codex'), f. 197ᵛ-198.

Masses based on secular polyphonic songs

MISSA D'UNG AULTRE AMER (NJE 7.3)

The Mass survives, entirely or in part, in 12 sources: six printed books and six manuscripts. The scoring is for four voices with the following ranges: g–f² (superius), Bflat–g¹ (altus), c–f¹ (tenor), F–c¹ (bassus). With only 364 measures, it is Josquin's shortest Mass setting, and atypical in several respects.

The composition most likely dates from the 1480s, when Josquin was employed by the Sforza family in Milan.[9] The syllabic character of the polyphonic *lauda* left its mark on the setting of the Gloria and Credo, and the design of the Sanctus matches that of the so-called *motetti missales* in the Ambrosian rite. In this liturgical practice, the Benedictus and Osanna II were replaced by a motet, sung during the benedictions of the bread and the wine.

---

9   In the absence of any work attributed to him, it may seem daring "to see [the singer] Juschinus de Kessalia as the possible composer" of the Mass; cf. Fallows, 329.

The cycle is based on Ockeghem's chanson of the same name. The tenor is quoted in its original form, once in the Kyrie, Gloria, Sanctus and Agnus dei, and twice in the Credo. Furthermore, in the Kyrie and Sanctus the first four measures of the superius are identical to those in the chanson. The choice of this song not only attests to Josquin's esteem for Ockeghem, but can also be explained by its secular words, which are an unconditional declaration of love ("To love another, my heart would be abased ..."). In the text of the Mass, this declaration is addressed to Christ. The words of the elevation motet *Tu solus qui facis mirabilia* (see also p. 156) are a prayer to Christ, who redeemed mankind with his blood. In the Sanctus and Agnus dei, the quotations from the chanson are combined with references in the altus to the relevant chants of the Ordinary cycle XVIII in the *Liber Usualis*. Slightly deviating from the reading in the Solesmes edition, these references may either follow local versions or were adapted to the *cantus prius factus* in the tenor.

MISSA FAYSANT REGRETZ (NJE 8.1)

The Mass survives, entirely or in part, in 13 sources: four printed books and nine manuscripts. Furthermore, five sources contain arrangements for lute of sections of the Mass. The scoring is for four voices with the following ranges: g–e^{2}flat (superius), c–a^1 (altus), d–f^1 (tenor), G–d^1 (bassus). Length: 551 measures.

The similar sequential passages of falling thirds in the outer voices of the Sanctus of the present Mass and the Kyrie II of *Missa Hercules Dux Ferrarie* (see below) could argue for the same period of composition.[10] The *Faysant regretz* Mass uses as its head-motif the first four notes in the superius of the B section of Walter Frye's three-part rondeau *Tout a par moy*, which dates from the 1450s and became very popular in France and Italy. The notes *fa–re–mi–re* are sung to the words "Faysant regretz", which explains the title of the Mass. However, Josquin used other pre-existing melodies as well, in particular in the superius of the Kyrie, Gloria and Credo, where the corresponding Gregorian chants no. XI and Credo I in the *Liber Usualis* are quoted. The way Josquin incorporates the four notes in his Mass is breathtaking. From the very first up to the last measures, the short motif is heard over two hundred times and almost without interruption in one or more voices, at different pitches and in different rhythmic shapes. In the Osanna, the tenor and bassus build a canon at the octave that exclusively consists of a repetition of the head-motif (Ex. 30). In the final Agnus dei the top voice quotes the entire superius melody of the *rondeau*; here the "faisant regretz" motif coincides in m. 77-79 with the words "dona nobis [pacem]". At the same time, the tenor sings the *fa–re–mi–re* motif twenty-five times in succession, while the altus sings the *re–re–mi–re* motif, derived from the initial notes of the tenor of the chanson twenty-four times.

Regarding the reception history of the Mass the following is worth noting. One of its sources is the parchment choirbook Jena 3, which was prepared in the

---

10 A dating of the Mass "around 1504 or a bit later" (see Fallows, 289) must be considered improbable, because it almost undoubtedly precedes *Missa La sol fa re mi*. The latter Mass, copied into the manuscript Cappella Sistina 41 in the years 1495-1498, has been described as "technically ... both a return to, and an extension of, the style of *Faisant regretz* ..." and "an enormous advance on the earlier work." (Noble, *NGD2*, vol. 13, 238).

years 1515–1520 by scribes working under the supervision of Alamire (in Brussels or Mechlin) for Frederick III the Wise, Elector of Saxony. This choirbook opens with Josquin's *Faysant regretz* and *Hercules Masses*, with the difference that the tenor of the *Hercules* Mass is underlaid with the motto "Fridericus dux saxsonie". The miniature at the opening of the *Faysant regretz* Mass on folio 1v depicts Mary's visit to her cousin Elizabeth (Luke 1:39–45). Elizabeth was the patron saint of Thuringia, and Frederick's mother had been named after her. It is clear therefore that both Masses are paying homage to the Elector's family. Beginning with the *fa–re–mi–re* motif, the tenor of Kyrie I is underlaid with the words "Elizabeth kyrie eleison". Since the four syllables of Elizabeth's name fit the four notes of the ostinato motif, it is tempting to conjecture that the copying of the Mass into the manuscript for Frederick's chapel is explained by precisely this motif. One could even imagine that the singers, while performing the Mass on her saint's day, may have pronounced the name "Elizabeth" in the head-motif where it appears in longer note values.

EXAMPLE 30

MISSA FORTUNA DESPERATA (NJE 8.2)

The Mass survives, entirely or in part, in 16 sources: nine printed books and seven manuscripts. Furthermore, two sources contain arrangements for lute and organ of sections of the Mass. The scoring is for four voices with the following ranges: f–f² (superius), Bflat–b¹flat (altus), c–a¹ (tenor), F–d¹ (bassus). Length: 811 measures.

This setting has a counterpart in Obrecht's Mass of the same name: The bassus in the Osanna of the latter composition is identical to the same part in Agnus III of Josquin's setting. Since this melody was not borrowed from the model, either Obrecht took it from Josquin, or Josquin from Obrecht. The sources of both works do not permit a more precise dating, and opinions differ on the question of which Mass was composed first.[11] A dating for Josquin's of around 1490 seems most likely. The text "Fortuna desperata" is dedicated to the ill-fated goddess of Greek-Roman mythology. No other theme in the late Middle Ages and Renaissance has aroused so much interest from the part of writers, artists, and composers. As all three voices of the model are quoted in the Mass, Josquin's setting

---

11   For a recent survey, see Fallows, 161–169.

can be considered an early example of parody technique (see p. 42). The essential feature of this technique is that all Mass movements begin with the first measures of the model, here the three-part song *Fortuna desperata*, which is ascribed to Antoine Busnois in a manuscript in Segovia. In this song, the superius in particular stands out melodically (Ex. 31). Structurally though, the role of the middle voice is more important. This part is entirely quoted in the tenor of the Kyrie, then in the tenor of the Gloria where it appears three times in reduced note values, and finally in the bassus of the second (= last) Agnus dei. The top voice of the song is heard four times in the superius of the Credo, in the course of which different mensuration signs are the key to a continuous reduction of the note values (m. 1–117 = 118–177 = 178–225 = 226–256). This same voice part further acts as the lowest voice in Agnus I. In this section, the notes 1–19 appear in a fourfold augmentation and in inversion. In other words, it is as if Josquin reverses the wheel of Fortune. The sources elucidate this complicated procedure in various ways, in some manuscripts with a reference to Genesis 9:7 ("But increase you and multiply, and go upon the earth, and fill it"; Fig. 27), in the Petrucci print with the direction "In gradus undenos descendant multiplicantes / Consimilique modo crescant antipodes uno", which means that, though the melody is given at the same pitch as in the exemplar, it must be sung eleven tones lower, with augmented note values and in inversion. Glarean refers to Petrucci's performing direction as the "riddle of the sphinx". Finally, the song's lowest voice is used as a starting point for the Sanctus. The melody is quoted in the altus in the original note values and reappears in the Osanna, now in a twofold reduction. Josquin used similar procedures in the following Mass.

EXAMPLE 31

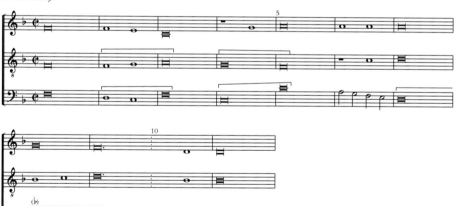

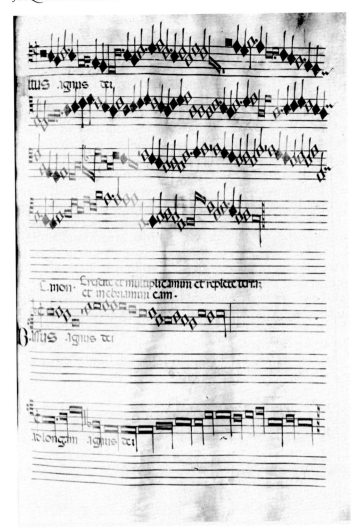

FIGURE 27: The *Fortuna desperata* melody in Agnus dei I of the eponymous Mass, in which the *cantus firmus* is sung in augmented note values and in inversion. Modena, Biblioteca Estense e Universitaria, Ms. M.1.2, f. 126.

MISSA MALHEUR ME BAT (NJE 9.1)

The Mass survives, entirely or in part, in 27 sources: ten printed books and seventeen manuscripts. The scoring is for four voices, but in the final Agnus dei the altus and bassus divide canonically into two parts, a procedure equally applied by Josquin in NJE 6.2. Voice ranges: g–e² (superius), c–a¹ (altus and tenor), E–d¹ (bassus). Length: 863 measures.

Like the song *Fortuna desperata* (see above), the chanson *Malheur me bat* was used by other composers as a model, among them Alexander Agricola and Jacob Obrecht. Set for three voices, the chanson is attributed both to Johannes Martini and Johannes Ockeghem, as well as to a certain Malcort. Judging by the number of sources of these Masses, the setting by Josquin enjoyed the greatest popularity. Recent scholarship has dated it to around 1500. With his ingenious, inventive elaboration of the model, Josquin undoubtedly wished to surpass his colleagues. He employs all voices of the exemplar – in the Sanctus, for example, the first eleven measures are identical to the opening of the chanson. Therefore this work can also be considered as a precursor of the parody Mass, though different procedures are employed. The top voice of the chanson acts as the superius in the Credo. In order to match the much longer liturgical text, the melody is cut into eleven segments that are quoted in succession and, except for segment 11, each sung twice: 1a 1b 2a 2b …10a 10b 11. Together they provide the melodic material for measures 1–154. From m. 155 until the end of the Credo, the entire melody is restated. The same voice of the chanson is used again in the final Agnus dei, where it is likewise stated in the superius, now divided into eight segments. The lowest voice (= tenor) of *Malheur me bat* turns up in the same voice part of the Kyrie, Gloria, Agnus I and Agnus III. In the Gloria, this melody is handled more or less in the same way as the superius in the Credo, with the difference that it is divided into thirteen segments, which are all repeated once. In Agnus I, all notes shorter than a semibreve are omitted, and the others doubled in length. In Agnus III, the melody of the tenor is divided into eight segments, as in the superius. The frame of this six-voice Mass movement thus consists of two voice parts from the chanson, which are combined with two newly-composed double canons at the unison, performed by the altus and bassus. Structurally, this last Mass movement presents the same plan as Agnus III in *Missa L'homme arme sexti toni* (see above). Here too, the continuous motivic repeats follow each other in quick succession. The altus of the chanson appears in each of the four sections of the Sanctus in the same voice, twice entirely in Sanctus and Pleni sunt, then divided into twelve segments in the Osanna in an alternating binary and ternary mensuration. The Benedictus consists of three short duos (Benedictus; qui venit; in nomine domini), and in each of these sections the first eleven measures are quoted, first beginning on the pitch of e_1, then of d_1, and finally of a. Agnus II is a freely-composed canonic duet.

MISSA N'AURAY JE JAMAIS [= 'Di dadi'] (NJE 9.3)

The complete Mass is transmitted in Petrucci's third Book of Masses from 1514 and in two reprints. Agnus II is found independently in a manuscript in Regensburg. The scoring is for four voices with the following ranges: g–c^2 (superius), c–g^1 (altus), c–f^1 (tenor), F–d^1 (bassus). Length: 798 measures.

Just like the *Faysant regretz* Mass (see above), *Missa N'auray je jamais* is based on a work by an English composer: in this case, Robert Morton's four-part chanson of the same name. Judging by the sixteen sources in which it is preserved, it was rather famous. The Mass probably dates from the late 1470s, and was called 'Di dadi' by Petrucci, a title that refers to the dice that are printed at the beginning of the first four Mass movements to indicate the factor by which the note values of the tenor from the chanson must be multiplied: in the Kyrie by two, in the Gloria by four, in the Credo by six, and in the first section of the Sanctus by five (Fig. 28). In order to spare the singers the tricky multiplications, Petrucci also printed the augmented note values. Such consistently rigorous augmentations do not necessarily betray Josquin as archaistic, but put him rather in the role of 'homo ludens' (to adopt Johan Huizinga's term), Man the Player, addressing himself to a private circle of insiders. Up to and including the first section of the Sanctus, the composer only borrows the first phrase of the chanson in the four-voice sections, placing it in the tenor.[12] The chanson melody is subsequently presented entirely in the Osanna and first Agnus dei, likewise in the tenor. The last occurrence of the complete melody is in the final Agnus dei, where it is quoted a fourth lower in the bassus. In both Agnus I and Agnus III, the mensuration sign indicates that the note values must be doubled.[13]

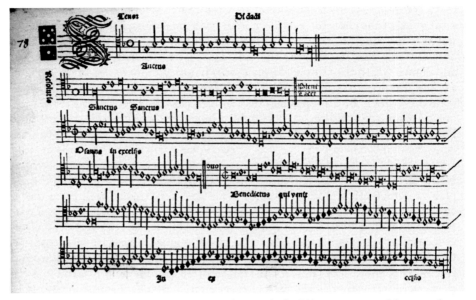

FIGURE 28: The dice in *Missa N'auray je jamais*, indicating the fivefold augmentation of the note values in the tenor voice of the Sanctus. Petrucci, *Missarum Josquin Liber tertius* (Venice 1514).

---

12   In his study 'Symbol and Ritual in Josquin's *Missa Di dadi*', *JAMS* 42 (1989), 1–22, Michael Long offers an interesting interpretation of the use of dice as an exercise in medieval Christian symbolism. Connecting the opening phrase of the chanson with the Elevation of the Host after the first section of the Sanctus, the French text "N'auray je jamais mieulx que j'ay?" (Shall I never have better than I have?) should, according to Long, be understood as the Christian's plea for redemption.

13   As in the case of the other early Mass settings by Josquin, some musicologists have questioned his authorship of *Missa Di dadi*, among them Barton Hudson, the editor of the Mass in *NJE*, vol. 9, Critical Commentary, 70–71, and, recently, Fallows, 323. However, refuting Hudson's arguments, the Editorial Board of the *NJE* decided to publish the Mass as an authentic work.

Mass based on a sacred popyphonic song

MISSA MATER PATRIS (NJE 10.1)

The Mass survives, entirely or in part, in 8 sources: five printed books and three manuscripts. The scoring is for four voices with the following ranges: c–c² (altus primus), c–a¹ (altus secundus), d–f¹ (tenor), F–f¹ (bassus primus). In Agnus III, the bassus divides into two parts, F–g¹ (bassus secundus). Length: 691 measures.

The composition is based on Antoine Brumel's three-voice motet of the same name. Brumel replaced Obrecht as chapelmaster at the Este court in Ferrara in 1505, and died in 1512 at the age of about fifty. The sombre tone of the Mass, as well as the striking passages such as "Et exspecto resurrectionem mortuorum" (And I look for the resurrection of the dead) in the Credo and "dona nobis pacem" (grant us peace) in the Agnus dei, suggest that Josquin may have written this setting as a memorial to his colleague.[14]

The exceptional character of the *Mater patris* Mass was pointed out as early as 1868 by Ambros (see p. 41). For example, the peculiar, sombre four-voice chord successions in the Kyrie, Credo, and Osanna are in the old-fashioned *fauxbourdon* style, with an extra voice a third above. Until recently, these passages, in particular, had caused a number of musicologists to cast doubt on the authenticity of the Mass, but sufficient arguments can be advanced in favour of Petrucci's attribution. The three two-part canons in Pleni sunt, Benedictus and Agnus II, all freely composed, show a remarkable resemblance to the other thirteen canonic duets in Josquin's Masses. And certain melodic and sequential motifs also prove part of the composer's idiom.[15] Perhaps the most amazing section of the Mass is the Osanna, where the "exaudi" motif from the motet is repeated incessantly for forty measures at every modal pitch, showing great musical daring. The tenor of this section ends with the fifth of the final chord falling to the third (*sol–mi–mi*), which can be considered the composer's fingerprint. As in most of Josquin's Masses, the final Agnus dei is the apotheosis. It consists of Brumel's whole motet, framed by two new voices.

Masses based on solmisation themes

MISSA HERCULES DUX FERRARIE (NJE 11.1)

The Mass survives, entirely or in part, in 35 sources: sixteen printed books and nineteen manuscripts. Furthermore, three sources contain arrangements for lute of sections of the Mass The scoring is for four voices, but in the final Agnus dei the altus and bassus divide into two parts. The ranges are as follows: g–e² (superius), c–d² (altus), c–f¹ (tenor), F–d¹ (bassus). Length: 571 measures.

---

14   M. Jennifer Bloxam, 'Masses Based on Polyphonic Songs and Canonic Masses', in *JosqComp*, 151–209, suggests it might have been composed around 1500 (see 192–195). It is however hard to see why Josquin would have chosen such a sombre mood for his Mass – Brumel's model does not provide any reason to do so – if it was not intended as a 'Requiem'.

15   See the Critical Commentary to *NJE* vol. 10, 20–32.

Josquin scholarship offers rather divergent dates of composition for this Mass, between1480 and 1504 (see also p. 19). The motivic character of the voices surrounding the *cantus firmus* in the tenor allows for both an early and a late dating. This melody is a *soggetto ostinato* devised by the conversion of the vowels of "Hercules Dux Ferrarie", using the solmisation syllables of the Guidonian hexachord (Fig. 29). The resulting melody is *re–ut–re–ut–re–fa–mi–re* (Ex. 32):

EXAMPLE 32

[Her - cu - les   Dux   Fer - ra - ri - e]

Josquin was apparently the first composer to have used this procedure. In 1558, Gioseffo Zarlino would coin a term for it, *soggetto cavato*, which means that the theme is 'excavated'. Except for four presentations, the theme occurs always in the tenor, and is in the course of the Mass stated, clearly audibly, 47 times. In the following table the starting notes are given (with italics denoting retrograde):

	Kyrie – Christe – Kyrie	Et in terra – Qui tollis	Patrem – Et incarnatus – Et in spiritum
S	d'		
A			
T	d a	d' d a d'	d a d' d a d' d a d' *d'* *a* d d a d'
B			

	Sanctus – Hosanna –	Benedictus – [Hosanna]	Agnus I – Agnus III
S			d' a'
A	d'		
T	d d a d' d a d' d a d'	d a d' d a d' *d'* a *d*	d a d'
B			

As in several other of Josquin's works based on a *soggetto ostinato*, the 'irregularities' in the presentation of the 'Hercules' motif in Kyrie I, Sanctus and Agnus III suggest that the composer incorporated the number 47 on purpose (see p. 19). Since it appears, in particular in the Gloria and Credo, that it is not always possible to arrive at a proper combination of the syllables of the text phrases and the eight notes of the 'Hercules' motif, it cannot be excluded that it may have been the composer's intention to have these notes sung to the solmisation syllables, just as in his motets *Illibata dei virgo* and *Ut Phebi radiis* (see p. 84 and p. 75). In any case, singing "Hercules Dux Ferrarie" as proposed in the *NJE* becomes problematic when the theme is stated in retrograde. In m. 16–23 and 33–41 of the Credo, two passages in strict imitation symbolize Christ as "the only-begotten Son of God" and "being of one substance with the Father". The Pleni sunt is a two-voice canon at the fifth. The three-voice canonic Agnus II is notated as a single voice part, and none of the sources explains how the canon must be performed. Only in 1960, twenty-three years after the publication of the Mass in the first Josquin edition, was the correct resolution discovered.[16] Again we see that Josquin seems to have taken pleasure in putting singers to the test.[17]

FIGURE 29: Superius and tenor voices of the Gloria of *Missa Hercules Dux Ferrarie* with the *cantus firmus* constructed from the solmisation syllables. Milan, Archivio della Veneranda Fabbrica del Duomo, Librone 3, f. 141'.

MISSA LA SOL FA RE MI (NJE 11.2)

The Mass survives, entirely or in part, in 20 sources: five printed books and fifteen manuscripts. Furthermore, four sources contain arrangements for lute or organ of sections of the Mass. The scoring is for four voices with the following ranges: g–f² (superius), e–a¹ (altus), d–f¹ (tenor), F–d¹ (bassus). Length: 617 measures.

The second Mass based on a *soggetto ostinato* has an entirely different character. According to an anecdote found in Glarean's *Dodecachordon*, Josquin asked a favour of an influential person (not known to the author), who replied, in bad French, "Laise faire moy" (Leave it to me). The phrase sounds like the solmisation syllables *la–sol–fa–re–mi*. It has been speculated that the little miniature of a turbaned prince at the

---

16   See Edward Stam, 'Eine "Fuga trium vocum" von Josquin Desprez', in *Mf* 13 (1960), 28–33.

17   In the 2009 reprint of *NJE* vol. 11, in several places in the Mass, *b*'s have been altered to *b*-flats.

beginning of the altus in the oldest source of the Mass, Cappella Sistina 41, could be the person who addressed these famous words to the composer (Fig. 30). In the 1490s there indeed was a prominent Turk in the Vatican, Prince Jem, a half-brother of the Ottoman Emperor Bayazid II. But the resemblance of this miniature to known portraits of Jem is too vague to corroborate this suggestion. Another possibility is that Josquin derived his theme from the refrain "Lassa far a mi" of a contemporary *barzelletta*, the most popular form in the *frottola* prints. This poem, in the style of Serafino dall'Aquila (see p. 33), would certainly have been known at the court of Ascanio Sforza, Josquin's employer in the 1480s. The Vatican manuscript mentioned can be dated to the 1490s, and the Mass too was probably written in that decade.

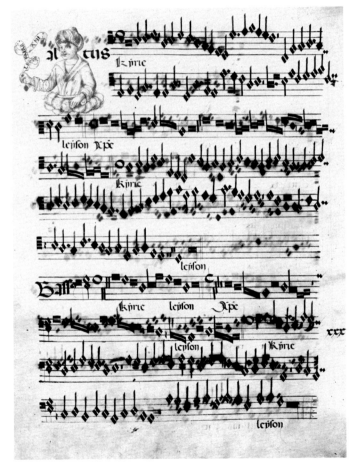

FIGURE 30: The miniature with Prince Jem (?) in the Kyrie of *Missa La sol fa re mi*. Vatican City, Biblioteca Apostolica Vaticana, Ms. Cappella Sistina 41, f. 39.

The five-note phrase is predominant from the beginning to the end of the composition. In the Gloria, Credo, Agnus I, and largely in the Sanctus, the tenor uses this theme without adding other melodic material, at the pitch of either *a* or *e*. It is heard more sparsely in the other voices, except for the superius and bassus in the Gloria and Credo. The opening of the Agnus dei shows how, in spite of the continuous repetitions, monotony is avoided by means of rhythmic variations (see altus m. 1–4, tenor m. 1–3, 3–6 and 6–8, superius m. 3–5, 5–7 and 7–9) (Ex. 33). The altus of the two-voice Agnus II, with sixteen statements in succession, offers another example of the subtle rhythmic variations the five notes can undergo. In total, the theme occurs as many as 226 times – 250 if we include the repeat of Agnus I (see below). Compared with *Missa Faysant regretz*, which, as we saw above, is built on a four-note motif, one cannot escape the impression that, in the present Mass, Josquin proceeded with still greater inventiveness and technical skill. This might suggest that *La sol fa re mi* is the later work. As in the *Ad fugam* Mass (see below), the text of the final Agnus dei is sung to the music of Agnus I, the words "miserere nobis" being replaced by "dona nobis pacem". Finally, in the Gloria and Credo, references are found to Gloria XV and Credo I in the *Liber Usualis*.[18]

EXAMPLE 33

Canonic Masses

The earliest printed source of the two canonic Masses is Petrucci's *Missarum Josquin liber tertius* of 1514, where they are called *Ad fugam* and *Sine nomine*. In the fifteenth century, the term 'fuga' meant a composition written according to a strict imitative technique: The first voice part to enter is repeated literally later by one or more of the other voices. From the seventeenth century onwards this technique was

---

18 At S 104₄-105₂ in the Gloria, the reading of the six secondary sources listed in the Critical Commentary, p. 108, is to be preferred.

called 'canonic'. In other words, we could translate the title of the first Mass as 'In the manner of a canon'. However, we remain in the dark as regards the second Mass. When this work was published by Andrea Antico in Rome, in 1516, it was called *Ad fugam*, a name that we also find in two later manuscripts, Cividale 59 and Toledo 9. Josquin is unlikely to have used the same name twice, or indeed to have circulated his work without a title (*sine nomine*). Both works are freely composed, and were a novelty at the time. Apart from Ockeghem's *Missa prolationum* and some canonic Masses based on pre-existing melodies, only one other canonic Mass is known from Josquin's time, copied without a title into Cappella Sistina 35 and attributed to Josquin's Vatican colleague Marbrianus de Orto.

MISSA AD FUGAM (NJE 12.1)

The Mass survives, entirely or in part, in 9 sources: six printed books and three manuscripts. Furthermore, two sources contain arrangements for lute of sections of the Mass. The scoring is for four voices with the following ranges: c^1-e^2 (superius), $d-b^1$flat (altus), $f-a^1$ (tenor), $A-e^1$ (bassus). Length: 657 measures.

Ad fugam is among Josquin's earliest settings of the ordinary, and probably dates from the late 1470s.[19] Except for the Benedictus, in all sections two of the four voices are canonic. Contrary to most canons in his later oeuvre, the process is rather consistent: The *dux* of the canon, the notated part, appears throughout in the superius, the *comes* enters one or three measures later in the tenor, a fifth lower. Totalling eight measures only, the music of Kyrie I is also used to open the next four movements, and thus serves as an extended head-motif. (A similar procedure may be found in Dufay's *Missa Ecce ancilla domini*.) Imitation occurs sporadically between altus and bassus. Remarkable passages in the Mass are the opening of the second section of the Gloria (m. 50–70), with motifs of an ascending fourth and a descending third, and measures 24–35 of the Sanctus, where the word "sabaoth" is stated five times in succession by the two canon voices in an ascending sequence. The composer seems to have chosen an exact canon form, though the additional flat in the *comes* occasionally causes modal inconsistency with the other voices.

MISSA SINE NOMINE (NJE 12.2)

The Mass survives, entirely or in part, in 12 sources: six printed books and six manuscripts. Furthermore, two sources contain arrangements for lute or organ of sections of the Mass. The scoring is for four voices with the following ranges: $g-e^2$ (superius), $c-a^1$ (altus), $c-g^1$ (tenor), $G-d^1$ (bassus). Length: 617 measures.

It is generally accepted that the *Sine nomine* cycle belongs to Josquin's last Mass settings. This is, among other things, evident from its greater sweetness of sound and the more expressive setting of the text. As in the *Ad fugam* Mass, two of the four voices

---

19 In his unpublished paper *Masses and Evidence: Petrucci's Josquin*, read at Duke University, NC, 1999, Joshua Rifkin raised serious questions about Josquin's authorship. These doubts are however convincingly dismissed by Peter Urquhart in Section 7 of the Critical Commentary in his edition of the Mass, *NJE*, vol. 12. Fallows, 268, exaggerates in saying that the authenticity of this Mass is "widely doubted".

are canonic, but this time each voice is by turns subject to a canonic treatment, and the setting has more varied scoring and rhythmic motion. Furthermore, the imitation technique is frequently applied to the non-canonic parts. In this composition, Josquin's command of counterpoint is sovereign to such an extent that the listener is hardly aware of its canonic structure. This is particularly true for the first movement, because the time interval between the canon voices is larger than normal: in Kyrie I seven measures, in the Christe twelve measures, and in Kyrie II again seven measures. The temporal interval is between one and three measures in the following movements. The pitch interval between the canon voices also changes: it is either a fourth (Kyrie, Credo, Pleni sunt), a fifth (Gloria, Sanctus, Osanna, Agnus I), a second (Agnus II), or an octave (Agnus III). The first of the three short duets of the Benedictus is a proportion canon, with the *comes* starting together with the *dux*, but a fifth lower and at half speed. The *comes* is then reused in the two following duets (Qui venit and In nomine domini) as the basis for new counterpoint.

Single Mass movements

Of the nine single Mass movements in the *NJE*, eight were published in 1505 in Venice, in Petrucci's collection *Fragmenta missarum*. NJE 13.4 is only transmitted in Cambrai 18. In addition to these sources, five manuscripts are known for NJE 13.6, four for 13.1, and one for 13.2–13.3 and 13.7. Since, in the sixteenth century, the interest in such single Mass movements was fading, these works were never reissued, in contrast to Josquin's Masses. Except for *Credo De tous biens playne*, which was copied into Cappella Sistina 41 in the 1490s, Petrucci's edition appears to be the earliest source for these works. They may all well have been written before 1490.

a) Mass movements based on Gregorian chants

GLORIA DE BEATA VIRGINE (NJE 13.7)

The scoring is for four voices with the following ranges: c^1-f^2 (superius), $e-a^1$ (altus and tenor), Bflat–e^1 (bassus). Length: 208 measures.

This work is based on the same chant as Josquin's later *Missa De beata virgine* (see p. 100) It also contains the same tropes. Except for m. 7–10 and 131–138 in which the chant melody is presented in the top voice, it appears throughout in the tenor with occasional imitations in the superius. The musical design as a whole is less ambitious than in the later setting. While the highest pitch of the superius in NJE 13.7 is reached only twice, in NJE 3.3 the highest pitch occurs eight times, always at an appropriate moment in the text. The setting in block chords of the last three tropes (m. 139–145, 152–157 and 167–173) is in strong contrast with the polyphonic treatment of these passages in NJE 3.3 (m. 188–195, 197–203 and 211–217). It has been suggested that the latter Gloria was a reworking of the present one.[20]

---

20   See Walter Wiora, 'The Structure of Wide-Spanned Melodic Lines in Earlier and Later Works of Josquin', in *ProcNY*, 309–316, at 309–310.

CREDOS NJE 13.4, 13.5 and 13.6

The three following settings of the Credo are based on plainsong Credo I which, in the fifteenth and sixteenth centuries, was known as *Credo dominicalis* (for Sundays). This Credo chant consists of a series of short melodic formulas. The chant's opening motif, beginning with the half step *mi–fa–mi*, is frequently repeated both in the chant itself and in the polyphony (Ex. 34):

EXAMPLE 34

A comparison of the chant melodies used in these three settings reveals a number of melodic variants, which could be explained either by differences in local 'dialects', or by the fact that Josquin almost always allowed himself some liberties in the elaboration of plainchant models. In the sources, these settings are designated as "Patrem de villaige" or "Patrem vilayge", a term that was also used for a number of Credo settings by other fifteenth-century composers and is yet to be clarified. The first in this group has been labelled "Quarti toni" in the *NJE* because it is in the 4th mode.

CREDO [Quarti toni] (NJE 13.4)

The scoring is for four voices with the following ranges: f–d² (superius), a–f¹ (altus), d–c¹ (tenor), G–e¹ (bassus). Length: 239 measures.

The chant melody in this Credo is treated as a canon in the altus and tenor, first up to the section "Et incarnatus est ...", and then from "Et resurrexit tertia die" until the end. The interval between the canonic voices is a fifth, and is the cause of a number of cross-relations and diminished fifths. It may therefore seem that, as in other early works (for example the *Missa Ad fugam*), melodic integrity took preference over harmonic aspects. As if to give the work balance, Josquin set the central section, "Et incarnatus est ...", homophonically.

CREDO VILAYGE I (NJE 13.5)

The scoring is for four voices with the following ranges: g–c² (superius), c–g¹ (altus), d–f¹ (tenor), F–bflat (bassus). Length: 392 measures.

This is Josquin's most extensive setting of the text of the Credo, conceived perhaps for a solemn occasion. The chant melody is often literally quoted in long note values, and sometimes treated in canon. On the other hand, there are also phrases that are freely elaborated, either in full or in part. Remarkable are the long-held chords at the words "Et homo factus est" (And was made man) in m. 175–181, as is the ternary rhythmic motion in the superius, m. 307–328, at the words "Qui cum patre et filio simul adoratur ..."(Who together with the Father and the Son is adored ...). Here, the idea of the Trinity is symbolized in the mensuration sign 3. Several duets provide variety in the polyphonic texture. The final section, "Confiteor unum baptisma ..." (I confess one baptism ...), is set in a ternary mensuration.

CREDO VILAYGE II (NJE 13.6)

The scoring is for four voices with the following ranges: d¹–g² (superius), f–a¹ (altus), g–g¹ (tenor), Bflat–d¹ (bassus). Length: 148 measures.

This Credo is in marked contrast with the previous one. The setting of the text is more syllabic, and the written pitch is much higher. Rather often, notes are repeated in two or more voices. Particularly striking are m. 80–84 at the words "Et iterum venturus est ..." (And He shall come again ...), where Josquin seems to evoke the trumpets of the Last Judgement (Ex. 35). This passage is followed by three voices in *fauxbourdon*, an archaistic sound meant to underline the words "cujus regni non erit finis (whose kingdom shall have no end). The final section of this Credo is set in a ternary mensuration.

EXAMPLE 35

b) Mass movements based on secular melodies

CREDO CHASCUN ME CRIE (NJE 13.1)

The scoring is for four voices with the following ranges: c¹–g² (superius), d–b¹flat (altus), f–a¹ (tenor), c–e¹ (bassus). Length: 205 measures.

Though this Credo is a rather peculiar composition, Josquin's authorship is recognized because three independent sources mention him as the composer. The title by which the piece has become known in the literature is problematic. While Petrucci, in 1505, gave it the name *Ciaschun me crie*, two years later it was titled *Patrem des rouges nes* in Cappella Sistina 23. No chanson text is known to begin with the words "Rouges nes". On the other hand, a chanson on the text "Chascun me crie" is known from a Petrucci print from 1504. Even though the relationship between the present Credo and this chanson is only evident in a few short melodic fragments, the latter title has been adopted in the *NJE*. However, it cannot be excluded that the title *Chascun me crie* does not stem from the composer but was invented by Petrucci because of vague reminiscences of the chanson.

Resembling a musical mosaic, the setting is composed of a large number of short phrases that usually are imitated in all voices, occasionally at the unison or the octave. Remarkable too are the brief passages in *fauxbourdon* in m. 101–103, 114–119 and 142–146. Compared to other works in Josquin's oeuvre, the music is uncommonly cheerful. It is reminiscent of Haydn's remark that, "Wenn ich an Gott denke, ist mein Herz so voll Freude, dass mir die Noten wie von der Spule laufen." (Whenever I think of God, my heart is so full of joy that the notes flow from me as from a spool of thread.)

CREDO DE TOUS BIENS PLAYNE (NJE 13.2)

The scoring is for four voices with the following ranges: b–d² (superius), c–g¹ (altus), G–e¹ (tenor), E–d¹ (bassus). Length: 206 measures.

Although this Credo also borrows fragments of the plainsong Credo I, it derives its name from what is considered the most famous chanson of the fifteenth century, Hayne van Ghizeghem's *De tous biens plaine*. This three-part *rondeau* is transmitted in almost thirty sources. The combination of the chant melody with the tenor of the chanson is bold because they are in two different modes, which sometimes cause a clash between the voice parts. A striking example can be found in m. 76, where the chant melody in the altus is in conflict with the tenor of the chanson at the point where *b*natural sounds against *b*flat (Ex. 36). Did Josquin intend this pungent dissonance to depict Christ's crucifixion? In three of the four sections (m. 1–60, 61–121 and 145–206), the entire tenor of the chanson is quoted literally in the tenor. The third section, m. 122–144, devoted to the Holy Spirit, is freely composed as a canon at the unison for two bass voices. Lacking in the Credo of Josquin's *Missa L'homme armé super voces musicales* (see above), it cannot be excluded that this section was added by Josquin at a later date.

EXAMPLE 36

CREDO LA BELLE SE SIET (NJE *13.3)

The scoring is for four voices with the following ranges: e–c² (superius), f–d¹ (altus), A–d¹ (tenor), G–bflat (bassus). Length: 196 measures.

The two sources for this Credo show conflicting attributions: in Petrucci to Josquin, in Cappella Sistina 41 to "Ro. de Fevin". There are substantial differences between the two versions. The editor of Robert de Févin's collected works calls it "either a rather good example of Robert's writing or a less clever example of Josquin's." It is included in the *NJE* as a dubious work. The Credo is based on a popular song that existed in several versions and has also been taken as a starting point for a Mass setting by other composers, among whom Johannes Ghiselin and Marbrianus de Orto. Polyphonic settings of the French song text are known by both Dufay and Josquin (NJE 27.20). However, no pre-existing song melody corresponds with the *cantus prius factus* in Josquin's Credo. A hypothetical reconstruction of the original tune of the ballade, as it appears in the tenor of NJE *13.3, shows an A B A' form (m. 1–89, m. 90–156, and m. 157–196 respectively).[21] The greater length of the first two sections incited the composer to use motivic repeats and long note values.

SANCTUS D'UNG AULTRE AMER / TU LUMEN (NJE 13.10)

The scoring is for four voices with the following ranges: bflat–d² (superius), f–a¹ (altus), f–f¹ (tenor), G–bflat (bassus). Length: 113 measures.

Like the *Credo De tous biens playne* (see above), this Sanctus is based on musical material from both the secular and the chant repertoire. The tenor quotes a version of the plainsong Sanctus XVIII, and is throughout contrapuntally related to the lowest voice part. The highest voice of the Sanctus is derived from the superius of Ockeghem's chanson *D'ung aultre amer*. (In his Mass of the same name, Josquin uses the chanson's tenor voice.) Ockeghem's superius is stated twice, first in the sections Sanctus and Osanna I, then in the Benedictus and Osanna II. Its duple metre becomes triple metre after the first section. In Petrucci's *Fragmenta missarum*, the only source of the piece, the Sanctus is followed by a homophonic setting in breves of the second strophe of the hymn *Jesu redemptor omnium*, in the Ambrosian rite to be sung during the Elevation of the Host.

c) Another setting of the Sanctus

SANCTUS DE PASSIONE (NJE 13.9)

The scoring is for four voices with the following ranges: a–c² (superius), d–g¹ (altus), c–f¹ (tenor), F–a (bassus). Length: 70 measures.

This Mass movement, written for the Passiontide liturgy, is not based on any pre-existing musical material. Though unpretentious, its dark mood may indicate that Josquin wished to draw attention to Christ's suffering and death. Like *Sanctus D'ung aultre amer*, it contains an Elevation motet on a text from a hymn by St. Bonaventure: "Honor et benedictio" praises the Son of God, because he redeemed mankind from hell by his death on the cross. The sections Pleni sunt celi and Benedictus are set as duets – the first for superius / altus, the second for tenor / bassus – and are musically identical.

---

21   See Richard Sherr, 'Mass Sections', in *JosqComp*, 211–238, at 224.

In over 300 sources that could possibly contain works by Josquin, 171 motets have been attributed to him. Sixty-two have been accepted in the *NJE* as authentic, nineteen as doubtful. The remaining ninety are considered to have been wrongly ascribed to him. Except for the cycle *O admirabile commercium* (NJE 21.7), which consists of five individual motets, all other multipartite motets are counted as one composition. Six motets are preserved incompletely. The motets cover the composer's entire period of creative activity. Precise datings are known for only a few of them. As is the case with Josquin's Mass settings, his motets give evidence of a wide range of style components. In the *NJE*, the motets are arranged according to the type of text:

– Motets on texts from the Old Testament
– Motets on texts from the New Testament
– Motets on non-biblical texts in honour of Jesus Christ
– Motets on non-biblical texts in honour of the Virgin Mary
– Motets on other non-biblical texts

Motets on texts from the Old Testament

a) Genesis, Samuel, Job, Ecclesiasticus, The Song of Songs
Of the six motets in this category, only two count as genuine, *Ecce tu pulchra es* and *Planxit autem David*. On the basis of their sources, the first can be dated before 1500, the second before 1504.

ABSALON FILI MI (NJE *14.1)
The motet survives in 3 sources: two printed books and one manuscript. Furthermore, one source contains an arrangement for lute. The scoring is for four voices with the following ranges: eflat–a'flat (superius), A flat–c' (altus), F–bflat (tenor), B flat–eflat (bassus). Length: 85 measures.

The text is a compilation of fragments drawn from the second book of Samuel, Genesis and Job. The late attribution of this freely-composed work to Josquin, found in a German print from 1540, throws some doubts on its reliability. The motet is part of a group of laments in the Renaisance based on texts from the Old Testament. These also include Josquin's *Planxit autem David* (see below) and *When David heard that Absalon was slain* by Thomas Weelkes. Some scholars have tried to link *Absalon fili mi* to an unfortunate event in a noble family of the time. The following names have been suggested: Juan Borgia (*d.* 1497), son of Alexander VI; Arthur (*d.* 1502), son of Henry VII of England; Philip the Fair (*d.* 1506), son of the Emperor Maximilian I.[1] The deep sorrow of the father is expressed in the extremely low register of the voices. The words "sed descendam in infernum plorans" (but I will go down [to my son] into hell lamenting) are symbolized in the then-exceptional modulation through the circle of fifths, down to *D*flat.[2]

DESCENDI IN ORTUM MEUM (NJE *14.3)

The motet survives in three manuscripts, which were all produced by scribes under the supervision of Petrus Alamire in Brussels and Mechlin. The scoring is for four voices with the following ranges: c¹–f² (superius), c–g¹ (altus), e–f¹ (tenor), F–c¹ (bassus). Length: 93 measures.

The text is drawn from The Song of Songs 6:10 and 6:12 (Septuagint 6:11 and 7:1). The Gregorian antiphon of the same name, which was sung at feasts of the Holy Virgin, is the starting point for the music. Each of the four voices opens in imitation with the chant's first four notes. In the course of the setting, other motifs are elaborated in the same way. The repeat of the words "revertere, revertere" (return, return, [O Sulamitess]) in the antiphon surely inspired the composer to deal with them at great length (m. 55-77), before closing the motet with an "alleluia".

ECCE TU PULCHRA ES (NJE 14.6)

The motet survives in 11 sources: three printed books and eight manuscripts. Furthermore, one source contains an arrangement for lute. The scoring is for four voices with the following ranges: d¹–f² (superius), a–d² (altus), a–b¹ (tenor), d–f¹ (bassus). Length: 96 measures.

This text is based on excerpts from The Song of Songs as well: 1:12-16 (Septuagint 1:15-17); 2:1-2 and 4: 5. These verses contain a dialogue between the groom and the bride. Judging by the number of sources in which the motet is preserved, it enjoyed some popularity. Apart from Italy, it was also known in Spain and Germany. The music is freely composed, and on several occasions brief text passages are emphasized. For example, the line "Ecce tu pulcher es, dilecte mi" (Behold thou art fair, my beloved) is set to block chords. Other passages, such as "Ego flos campi" (I am the flower of the field), appear in an imitative setting, sung successively by bassus,

---

1   See *NJE* vol. 14, Introduction to the music, p. XIV.
2   Questioning the reliability of the earliest source for the motet, London 8 G.VII, Peter Urquhart suggests an originally clef-less notation, a notation that would not necessitate any modulation; see 'Another Impolitic Observation on *Absalon, fili mi*', in *JM* 21 (2004), 343–380.

tenor, superius and altus. The dialogue between the groom and the bride cannot be recognized in the scoring, but cadences mark the alternation between the lyrical expressions of tenderness.

PLANXIT AUTEM DAVID (NJE 14.9)

The motet survives in 7 sources: three printed books and four manuscripts. Furthermore, one source contains an arrangement for lute. The scoring is for four voices with the following ranges: g–d² (superius), c–g¹ (altus), Bflat–f¹ (tenor), F–c¹ (bassus). Length: 331 measures.

The text of this great, bipartite motet is based on II Samuel 1:17-27, where King David laments the death of Saul and Jonathan, father and son, both slain in the battle against the Philistines in the mountains of Gilboa (Fig. 31).[3] The text is divided into short phrases and the music is sometimes contemplative, at other times plaintive in character. The polyphonic texture changes constantly: beautifully shaped melodies alternate with passages in homophony, the latter preceded by a general rest. The lines "Incliti Israel ..." (The illustrious of Israel are slain upon thy mountains) and "filie incircumcisorum" (the daughters of the uncircumcised) are set to the sombre sound of *fauxbourdon*. In the three lines that begin with the words "Quomodo ceciderunt?" (How are the valiant fallen?) in m. 55, 244 and 311, Josquin quotes the Gregorian recitation tone of the Lamentations of Jeremiah, which are sung in the Good Friday liturgy. Undoubtedly he was incited to do so by their identical opening word, "Quomodo [sedet sola]" (How doth the city sit solitary!) (Ex. 37). Heinrich Glarean (see p. 37–38) concludes his comments on the motet as follows:

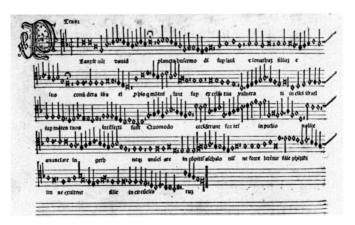

FIGURE 31: The first part of the tenor voice of *Planxit autem David*. Petrucci, *Motetti C* (Venice 1504), no. 33.

---

3   The attribution of this work in the index of the Florentine Ms. II.I.232 to Ninot (le Petit) has been judged to be incorrect for stylistic reasons. Although Fallows, 435, states that the motet is "increasingly considered to be more likely by Ninot than by Josquin", so far only Ludwig Finscher has formulated arguments against Josquin's authorship, judging the motet's musical rhetoric too madrigalistic; see 'Four-Voice Motets', in *JosqComp*, 249–279, at 270. Richard Sherr, however, has convincingly argued in favour of its authenticity; see the Critical Commentary to *NJE* vol. 14, 94–96.

EXAMPLE 37

Nor is there anything in this song that is not worthy of its composer. He has everywhere expressed most wonderfully the mood of lamenting, as immediately after the beginning of the tenor, at the word 'Jonathan'.[4]

QUI EDUNT ME (NJE *14.11)

The motet survives in 4 sources: two printed books and two manuscripts. The scoring is for two voices with the following ranges: d–e¹ (tenor), G–a (bassus). Length: 31 measures.

This short, imitative duo may originally have belonged to a larger composition, which either is lost or has yet to be identified. *Qui edunt me* could have been the second part of a tripartite motet or have formed part of a Mass setting. In the latter case, the music of the duet could have served for the Pleni sunt in the Sanctus, as this section is set for two voices in many Masses, with the words "gloria tua" sung in imitation to melismas. The text, possibly a *contrafactum*, is drawn from Ecclesiasticus 24:29-31 (Septuagint 24:21-22), and is appropriate for celebrating the Eucharist.

RESPONDE MIHI (NJE *14.12)

The motet survives in 2 sources: one printed book and one manuscript. The scoring is for four voices with the following ranges: c¹–e² (superius), f–a¹ (altus), c–e¹ (tenor), A–c¹ (bassus). Length: 165 measures.

This bipartite motet carries a unique attribution to Josquin in a German print from 1545, which cannot be considered as a very reliable source. The text, which

---

4   After Miller, vol. 2, 270.

is drawn from Job 13:22-28, begins with the last two words of verse 22: "Responde mihi" (Do thou answer me). This passage, in which Job asks God about his guilt, forms part of the Office of the Dead. The theme of the text is penitence and mourning, a mood that is most appropriately expressed through music in the 3rd mode. Frequent tone repetitions are reminiscent of a plainsong recitation tone. Measures 1-15, sung by tenor and bassus, and entirely repeated by superius and altus, draw attention to Job's question: "How many are my iniquities and sins? Make me know my crimes and offences." The same procedure is applied at the opening of the second part, this time with the superius and altus repeated by tenor and bassus. Though this typically Josquinian alternation of paired imitations speaks in favour of Josquin's authorship, the piece could also be the work of a very talented follower.

b) The psalms
More than in any other group of motets, authenticity problems are found in the psalm repertory. Of the 52 compositions in this group that have been transmitted with an ascription to Josquin, only eleven are considered genuine by the editors of the *NJE*. Besides these works, the *NJE* contains seven dubious psalm settings. In other words, at the very most 35 per cent of these 52 compositions are thought to be from Josquin's hand. The explanation of this singular situation is to be sought in Germany. In contrast to the Roman Catholic countries in Europe, there was an urgent need for polyphonic settings of psalm texts in the Lutheran territories. The religious communities were no longer content with the relatively small number of psalm motets from Italy and France that had been commercialized in editions of German publishers. Therefore, as a consequence of Luther's great admiration for Josquin (see Chapter 2), the latter tried to expand their repertory with new compositions written in the style of Josquin. It should come as no surprise that some composers (or editors) of the younger generation used Josquin's name as a commercial means to sell their works. However, this situation explains at the same time why the task appointed to the editors of the four *NJE* volumes with psalm motets was by no means an easy one.

The so-called penitential psalms occupy an important place among Josquin's motets. Although these psalms are not a distinct category in the Bible, in the Roman Catholic tradition this term is, since St. Augustine, used for the following psalms from the Vulgate: 6, 31 (32), 37 (38), 50 (51), 101 (102), 129 (130) and 142 (143). In these texts, the theme of which is guilt and distress, the sinner asks for remission. Of the seven psalms – seven is the number of penance – five were set by Josquin. (The most famous example of a complete cycle is that by Orlando di Lasso. His *Psalmi Davidis poenitentiales*, commissioned by Duke Albrecht V of Bavaria, are preserved in two presentation manuscripts. Because of the large miniatures and ornamental borders by the court painter Hans Mielich, these manuscripts are among the greatest treasures of the Bayerische Staatsbibliothek in Munich.)

Only one of Josquin's psalm motets can be dated more precisely. This is the psalm *Miserere mei, deus*, which the Ferrarese court poet Teofilo Folengo, in one of his poems, says was written at the request of Ercole d'Este: "... illud compositum *Miserere*, Duca rogitante Ferrara" (see p. 35). The work must have been composed in the years 1503-1504, when Josquin was in Ercole's service. *Misericordias domini* and *Domine, ne in furore* (NJE 16.6) are among the earliest settings in the repertory of Josquin's psalm motets; the text of the first motet could point to Josquin's possible service at the French court under Louis XI (see p. 22). *Domine, non secundum peccata* dates from the period when the composer was a member of the Papal Chapel. The remaining settings were probably written after 1504, when Josquin was back in Northern France. Two of them, *In exitu Israel de Egypto* and *Memor esto verbi tui*, have been connected with the court of Louis XII.

ALLELUIA. LAUDATE DOMINUM (NJE *15.1)

The motet is only preserved in the partbooks Berlin 7.[5] The original scoring is for four voices: b–e^2 (superius), g–g^1 (tenor), G–c^1 (bassus). Length: 95 measures.

Each of the two verses of the short psalm 116 (117) is treated as an independent section, with an "alleluia" appended to each verse. The tenor consists of long note values and contains elements from the 8th psalm tone. Although the lacking altus hinders a full critical examination of the musical quality of the motet, the consistent repetition of text phrases, an uncommon feature in Josquin's psalm motets, as well as the general musical style suggest that it is a work by a composer of the generation after Josquin.

DE PROFUNDIS CLAMAVI (NJE *15.11)
DE PROFUNDIS CLAMAVI (NJE *15.12)
DE PROFUNDIS CLAMAVI (NJE 15.13)

Of the entire psalm 129 (130), three settings survive with attributions to Josquin. While NJE *15.11 and *15.12 are bipartite and close with the formula "Gloria patri et filio ... seculorum. Amen", NJE 15.13 ends with the prayer that is sung during the absolution at the end of the funeral service: "Requiem eternam ... Kyrie eleison ... Pater noster."

NJE *15.11 – The motet survives, entirely or in part, in 12 sources: five printed books and seven manuscripts. The scoring is for four voices with the following ranges: a–c^2 (superius), d–f^1 (altus), A–d^1 (tenor), D–g (bassus). Length: 167 measures.

The seven attributions to Josquin are in conflict with the one to [Nicolas] Champion, a composer who was a member of the chapel of Philip the Fair, then of Charles V. The motet appears under Champion's name in Vienna 15941, an 'Alamire' manuscript produced in the third decade of the sixteenth century in Brussels or Mechlin. Notated in low clefs, the music is written in the 4th mode and opens imitatively with a motif that in m. 13 descends to *D* in the bassus (Ex. 38). Glarean (see p. 37–38]), who names Josquin as the composer, rightly notes that this low register perfectly expresses the contents of the text: "Out of the depths I have cried to thee, O Lord ..." However, the musical treatment of the text is less effective in the second part of the motet, and the imitation technique is not as coherent as is usually the case with Josquin.

---

5   This manuscript survives without the altus voice part.

EXAMPLE 38

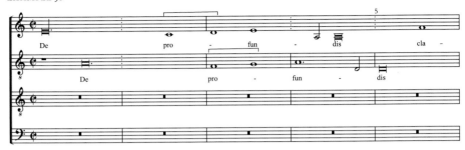

NJE *15.12 – The motet survives in 5 sources: one printed book and four manuscripts. The scoring is for four voices with the following ranges: c¹–g² (superius), e–a¹ (altus and tenor), c–d¹ (bassus). Length: 174 measures.

There are only two German sources that attribute this work to Josquin. As far as their ascriptions are concerned, these sources are mostly unreliable. In the remaining sources, the motet is anonymous. Although NJE *15.12 is of good musical quality and contains passages that could be expected from Josquin, there is also, as in the previous motet, the question of inconsistent imitations, as for example in m. 31–41. At this point, the superius and altus melodically deviate from the tenor and bassus. In m. 60–72, the paired imitations show their usual pattern, but at the opening of the second part the repeat of verse 6 in the tenor and bassus does not match the music in the higher voices. Finally, when comparing the high register of the voices with that in the surely authentic setting NJE 15.13, it appears that the composer of NJE *15.12 conceived the text rather as a Pauline song than as a penitential psalm in which the remission of sins is asked for.[6]

NJE 15.13 – The motet survives in 5 sources: one printed book and four manuscripts. The scoring is for five voices with the following ranges: a–c² (superius), e–g¹ (altus), c–f¹ (tenor), A–c¹ (bassus primus), E–bflat (bassus secundus). Length: 117 measures.

Attributed to Josquin in all of its sources, this motet is undoubtedly a late work; the earliest source is dated 1521, the year of the composer's death. As in Josquin's other five-voice motets, the polyphony is determined by a particular structural principle, in this case a three-voice canon in the superius, altus and first bassus (Fig. 32). Apart from some short melodic formulas, the text is set syllabically, and the frequent note repetitions, reminiscent of a plainsong recitation tone, identify NJE 15.13 as a liturgical composition. The motet's gloomy mood would perfectly fit the memorial service for which it must have been written (see p. 79).

---

6   Luther associated the psalm with St. Paul, who considered the text to express hope of the remission of sins through faith.

FIGURE 32: The superius voice of the five-voice *De profundis clamavi*, copied ca. 1550 by Jodocus Schalreuter in Wittenberg. Utrecht, library of Peter Hecht.

DOMINE, DOMINUS NOSTER (NJE *16.4)

The motet survives in 4 sources: one printed book and three manuscripts. The scoring is for five voices with the following ranges: a–d^2 (superius), c–a^1 (altus), c–f^1 (tenor primus), g–e^1 (tenor secundus), G–b (bassus). Length: 159 measures.

Although this setting of the complete psalm 8 is ascribed to Josquin in only two sources from about 1550 – for this reason the motet has been published in the *NJE* as a doubtful work – various elements strongly argue in favour of his authorship.[7] First, the ingenious *cantus firmus* in the second tenor has symbolic meaning, as explained in Chapter 6. Second, the composition displays elements that are characteristic of Josquin's style. Among these are the use of paired imitations (as in m. 101–110) and the continuous alternation of imitative sections with chord progressions in homophony. In addition, the emphasis laid on important moments in the

---

7 Pointing to some contrapuntal infelicities, John Milsom judges the motet to be a misattribution or forgery; see 'Motets for Five or More Voices', in *JosqComp*, 281–320, at 311. However, since the extant sources contain a rather high number of errors, it cannot be excluded that the uneven quality of the motet is due to its late transmission. The psalm motet *Misericordias domini* (see p. 143) provides another example where several emendations had to be made in order to arrive at a plausible reading; see the Critical Commentary to *NJE*, vol. 18, 81.

text is a stylistic feature of Josquin's later oeuvre. Examples may be found in m. 9–17 at the words "Quam admirabile est nomen tuum" (How admirable is thy name) and in the last line, "in universa terra" (in all the earth).

DOMINE, EXAUDI ORATIONEM MEAM (NJE 16.5)

The motet survives, entirely or in part, in 7 sources: two printed books and five manuscripts. The scoring is for four voices with the following ranges: a–d² (superius), d–g¹ (altus), c–e¹ (tenor), G–c¹ (bassus). Length: 341 measures.

In this setting, the text of psalm 142 (143) deviates somewhat from the Vulgate, particularly in verse 1, where the second half is replaced with psalm 53 (54). The disproportional distribution of the verses over the three parts of the motet, with 99, 158 and 88 measures respectively, indicates that Josquin was guided above all by the verbal contents. While part I comprises the beginning of a prayer to God, in part II the psalmist recalls the past and concludes with the desire to "teach me to do thy will"; part III develops this reflection: "Thy good spirit shall lead me into the right land ..." With the minor second at the word "exaudi", the opening sets a grave tone for the entire motet and brings to mind Josquin's psalm motet *Miserere mei, deus* (see below), which is also set in the Phrygian mode (Ex. 39). The syllabic declamation of the text is interrupted only occasionally by melodic figuration, for example at the word "vivens" (living) in m. 42–48. Other remarkable moments may be found at the end of part I, where the verse "in me turbatum est cor meum" (my heart within me is troubled) is emphasized, and in m. 167–182 of part II, in which all voices descend stepwise through an octave: "... et similis ero descendentibus in lacum" (lest I be like unto them that go down into the pit).

EXAMPLE 39

Do - mi - ne ex - au - di o -

DOMINE, NE IN FURORE (NJE 16.6)

The motet survives, entirely or in part, in 13 sources: five printed books and eight manuscripts. The scoring is for four voices with the following ranges: c–f¹ (superius), c–e¹ (altus and tenor), F–a (bassus). Length: 207 measures.

Of the long penitential psalm 37 (38), Josquin set only the following verses: 2–4, and 7 (part I); and 11, 22 and 23 (part II). Written for low voices, the motet is in the same mode as NJE 16.5 and 18.3. On the basis of the treatment of the text, the work can be grouped with Josquin's earliest psalm motets: little account is taken of word accents and the many melodic figures make it difficult to understand the words. Imitation plays a prominent part in the polyphonic texture, and the melodic phrases usually correspond with the grammatical units. The low register of the voices – *f*¹ is the highest note of the superius – results in a certain harmonic compactness. The circular melodic formula in m. 98–114 at the words "miser factus sum" (I am become miserable) and "et curvatus sum" (and am bowed down) is also heard in the opening of *Domine, exaudi orationem meam* (see above), a motet probably composed after 1504 (Ex. 40).

EXAMPLE 40

DOMINE, NE IN FURORE (NJE 16.7)

The motet survives, entirely or in part, in 7 sources: two printed books and five manuscripts. The scoring is for four voices with the following ranges: c¹–d² (superius), d–a¹ (altus), d–f¹ (tenor), G–c¹ (bassus). Length: 167 measures.

Verse 1 of psalm 6, the first of the penitential psalms, is identical to verse 1 of NJE 16.6 commented on above. The whole text comprises ten verses. These are divided over two parts. Compared with NJE 16.6, the polyphonic texture is more transparent and more varied. The composer also gives great thought to the declamation of the text. Clauses that are important to him are set in block chords. This is, for example, the case with "Miserere mei, domine" in m. 24–27 and "Salvum me fac propter misericordiam tuam" (O save me for thy mercy's sake). At the end of part I, the words "lacrimis meis stratum meum rigabo" (I will water my couch with my tears) are set to wailing 6/3 chords in the lower voices (Ex. 41). In part II, the music reaches a climax in verse 9 at the words "Quoniam exaudivit dominus vocem fletus mei" (the Lord hath received my prayer).

EXAMPLE 41

DOMINE, NE PROJICIAS ME (NJE *16.9)

The motet survives in 4 sources: two printed books and two manuscripts. The scoring is for four voices with the following ranges: c¹–d² (superius), d–f¹ (altus), c–e¹ (tenor), E–a (bassus). Length: 215 measures.

The setting of this bipartite motet appears under Josquin's name only in two German prints. Since the later of these two prints is a reprint of the earlier, we are thus left with just one independent ascription. In contrast to normal practice, the text is a compilation of verses from no less than nine different psalms and I Esdras 9:6. Together, these lines constitute a prayer to God of an old and sick person. Although the motet is written in accordance with the 'rules of the art' and with observance of a proper declamation of the text, Josquin's authorship is doubtful for its late, unique attribution. The fact that some distinct musical motifs resemble those in other, authentic motets – for example, the passage at the words "suscipe me" (uphold me) in m. 133–139 reminds the listener of the beginning of the third part of his famous *Miserere mei, deus* – has been used both as an argument in support of and against Josquin's authorship.

DOMINE, NON SECUNDUM PECCATA (NJE 16.10)

The motet survives, entirely or in part, in 10 sources: three printed books and seven manuscripts. The scoring is for four voices with the following ranges: c¹–e²flat (superius), c–b¹flat (altus), f–f¹ (tenor), F–c¹ (bassus). Length: 239 measures.

The text, a supplication to God about the miseries of human life, consists of verse 10 from psalm 102 (103) and verses 8–9 from psalm 78 (79). The composition forms part of a group of twelve settings of the same text, all found in manuscripts of the Sistine Chapel. The text is actually that of the tract of the Mass for Ash Wednesday. NJE 16.10 occupies a special place among Josquin's psalm motets for three reasons. Firstly, its structure matches the instructions in a *Ceremoniale* from 1505, drawn up by the papal master of ceremonies: the instance that the pope rises from his throne (m. 88), thereupon kneels down (m. 123), and, after the prayer for God's help, returns to his throne (m. 210).[8] Secondly, this is the only psalm motet which shows an alternating scoring in the duets. Thirdly, this work is not freely composed but based on the plainsong tract. This is easily perceived at the opening, when the superius sings the words "Domine" to the melody of the tract (Ex. 42). Similarly, in the course of the motet, which shows great stylistic variety, references are made to the chant melody, particularly in the superius and tenor.

EXAMPLE 42

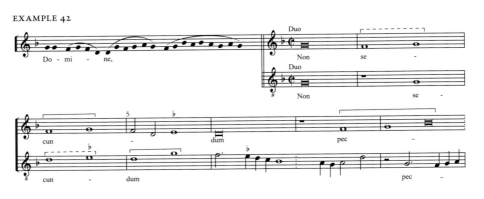

---

8   See Sherr, '*Illibata dei virgo nutrix* and Josquin's Roman Style', Appendix 458.

DOMINUS REGNAVIT (NJE *17.1)

The motet survives, entirely or in part, in 4 sources: two printed books and two manuscripts. The scoring is for four voices with the following ranges: c¹–c² (superius), f–g¹ (altus), c–e¹flat (tenor), F–g (bassus). Length: 176 measures.

The text of this bipartite motet consists of the entire psalm 92 (93), followed by the closing formula "Gloria patri et filio ... seculorum. Amen." Although this composition was long considered to examplify the style of Josquin's late psalm motets, in the recent analysis of the music in the critical commentary to the edition doubts are raised about his authorship, and these doubts are strengthened by the fact that the transmission is limited to late German sources. In particular, the octave leaps in m. 59–61, 65–67, 72–74, 86–87, 90–91, 94–95 and 97–98 look suspicious, even though they illustrate the text sung in the passages verses 4–6, in which the words "elevaverunt" (have lifted up), "elationes" (the surges), and "in altis" (on high) ask to be 'painted'. Though this rhetorical figure is not uncommon in Josquin, it is rather stereotyped here. Lack of variety is also more generally evident in this work, both in the formation of melodic motifs and in the harmonic progressions.

IN EXITU ISRAEL DE EGYPTO (NJE 17.4)

The motet survives, entirely or in part, in 8 sources: two printed books and six manuscripts. Furthermore, five sources contain arrangements for lute or guitar. The scoring is for four voices with the following ranges: c¹–d² (superius), c–g¹ (altus and tenor), G–b (bassus). Length: 401 measures.

This extended, tripartite motet is based on the entire psalm 113 (114) and concludes with the formula "Gloria patri et filio ... seculorum. Amen". It is Josquin's only psalm setting in which a Gregorian psalm tone is used: in this case, the so-called *tonus peregrinus* ('wandering' tone), which is connected with the text describing the exodus of Israel from Egypt. The "Amen" is followed by the antiphon *Nos qui vivimus*. The text of this antiphon is inspired by the last verse of the psalm to which it was connected in Josquin's time. The polyphonic texture is very transparent: except for part III, four-voice writing is limited to short passages. The musical progress of the composition shows great variety in the setting of the 27 individual verses. We shall elucidate some of the rhetorical aspects of the music.

A first example may be found in verse 3, "... Jordanis conversus est retrorsum" (Jordan was turned back). After the conclusion of this verse, the word "retrorsum" is repeated in the tenor only, thus strengthening the effect of retreating. In m. 42–43, the bassus and altus enter with leaps of an octave and a fifth respectively at the word "montes" (mountains). A contrast between low and high is created in m. 62f.: this verse mentions again the (low) retreating Jordan in altus, tenor, and bassus, followed by the springing mountains, the octave and fifth intervals of which are now heard in the tenor and superius. In m. 93–97, archaistic 6/3 chords give voice to God's severity: "a facie dei Jacob" (at the presence of the God of Jacob). Where the psalmist, in verse 12 of part II, criticizes the idolatry of the pagans, Josquin draws attention to the poorness of the silver and golden idols in repeating a six-note motif over ten measures, alternately in the bassus/tenor and altus/superius voice pairs. In the last part he changes the binary mensuration to a ternary one in verse 21, at the words "Benedixit domui Israel" (He has blessed the house of Israel), allowing the four voices to express their joy unanimously. Finally, the descent into hell of the sinners in verse 26 is depicted by repeating a falling motif in all voices (Ex. 43).

EXAMPLE 43

INIQUOS ODIO HABUI (NJE *17.6)

The motet survives only in Bologna R142, copied between 1530 and 1550, and of which only the tenor partbook is preserved. The original scoring is for four voices. Length: 81 measures.

The text in the tenor of this incomplete work is taken from the verses 113–116 of psalm 118 (119). The obstinate character of the musical motifs is reminiscent of the tenor voice of NJE *16.4 (see above). However, Bologna R142 contains no less than five chansons by Josquin with Latin texts, and it can therefore not be excluded that the psalm verses are not the original text of this short composition. Since *Iniquos odio habui* cannot be evaluated stylistically, it is included in the *NJE* as doubtful.

MEMOR ESTO VERBI TUI (NJE 17.14)

The motet survives, entirely or in part, in 15 sources: four printed books and eleven manuscripts. Furthermore, one source contains an arrangement for lute. The scoring is for four voices with the following ranges: a–f^2 (superius), a–c^2 (altus), c–g^1 (tenor), A–d^1 (bassus). Length: 327 measures.

This bipartite motet is based on the verses 49–64 from psalm 118 (119), followed by the shortened closing formula "Gloria patri et filio et spiritui sancto". Just like NJE 17.4, *Memor esto* was probably composed during Josquin's service with Louis XII. The text is both a song of praise and a supplication to God, beginning with the words: "Be thou mindful of thy word to thy servant". An anecdote in Glarean's *Dodecachordon* (see p. 37–38]), which has since become renowned, relates the motet to the king himself, as a gentle reminder of a so far unfulfilled promise to grant a prebend. However, since further historical evidence is lacking, the truth of this account remains unclear. Among the more notable aspects of the motet is a transparent texture. This is partly formed by paired voices that not only alternate with one another, but are also treated in imitation. For example, the first verse is sung by the tenor and bassus (m. 1–11), then repeated an octave higher by the superius and altus. In this case, the imitation in the paired voices is at the unison, causing a stretto-like effect. At the end of the composition it becomes obvious that the opening of the motet must have been of special importance for Josquin, because from m. 311 onwards the music of the first verse is repeated, but now in reduced note values and with voices entering in a different order (Ex. 44). Some verses, such as no. 8 at the end of the first part, are set syllabically and sung to a recitation tone. Nevertheless, the conclusion of the motet indicates that any liturgical function is unlikely. The repeat in m. 66–68 of "non declinavi" (I declined not), where all voices are heard simultaneously in homophony, shows that Josquin wanted to focus attention on these words. Should this be seen as a second hint to King Louis in the context of his promise to the composer?

EXAMPLE 44

MIRABILIA TESTIMONIA TUA (NJE *18.2)

The motet survives only in a manuscript in a private library in Utrecht, copied in Wittenberg ca. 1550, and of which only the superius partbook is preserved. The original scoring is for four or five voices. Length: 314 measures.

The text in the superius of this incomplete work is taken from verses 129–134 of psalm 118 (119). Although certain stylistic features are reminiscent of Josquin, such as the declamation of the text and the return of the opening at the end of the motet, the absence of lower voices makes further analysis of the music impossible. The composition is therefore included in the *NJE* as doubtful.

MISERERE MEI, DEUS (NJE 18.3)

The motet survives, entirely or in part, in 19 sources: nine printed books and ten manuscripts. Furthermore, two sources contain arrangements for lute. The scoring is for five voices with the following ranges: c'–d² (superius), d–g' (altus), e–f' (tenor primus), c–g' (tenor secundus), G–c' (bassus). Length: 422 measures.

The tripartite setting of the entire psalm 50 (51) is Josquin's most celebrated psalm motet. According to Glarean (1547), it was "in everyone's hands". The text is a supplication of man to God for remission of his sins, so that he can praise him with a pure heart. Just as in his setting of psalm 113 (see above), Josquin uses rhetorical means to express the contents of the text. That he fully succeeded in this can be gathered from the comments of the German publisher Hans Ott, who edited the work in 1537 (see p. 39). The eloquence of the music is most obvious in the repeat, after each verse, of the words "Miserere mei, deus". This happens 21 times in total. (The reason for choosing this number is explained in Chapter 6.) Five-voice scoring is unusual in Josquin's psalm settings – only NJE 15.13 and *16.4 are for five voices as well – and in this motet is the result of the composer's decision to reserve one voice to repeatedly deliver the prayer "Miserere mei, deus". This voice, the first tenor, recites the syllables of the refrain at the same pitch, except for an inflexion at the first syllable of "deus" (Fig. 33). However, the refrain's obstinate character is counterbalanced by the continually changing musical setting of the other voices. The psychological impact of the prayer depends of the way it is set. For example, in m. 365–369 of part III, where two voices gradually descend an entire octave (Ex. 45), the refrain is very insistent. An even more impressive passage is found in m. 321–331 at the verse "utique holocaustis non delectaberis" (with burnt offerings thou wilt not be delighted). The words "non delectaberis" are stated eleven times. In medieval numerology the number 11, considered to be a transgression of the perfect number 10, was also understood as a transgression of divine law. So we may perhaps assume that the composer, by way of this repetition, wanted to make clear God's rejection of burnt offerings.

FIGURE 33: The ostinato voice of the first part of *Miserere mei, deus*. Grapheus, *Novum et insigne opus musicum* (Nuremberg 1537), no. 13.

EXAMPLE 45

MISERICORDIAS DOMINI (NJE 18.4)

The motet survives, entirely or in part, in 7 sources: four printed books and three manuscripts. The scoring is for four voices with the following ranges: c^1-e^2 (superius), $c-g^1$ (altus), $c-e^1$ (tenor), $E-a$ (bassus). Length: 280 measures.

The text of this tripartite motet, which has been related to Louis XI in Chapter I, is a compilation of nine verses from the psalms 30 (31), 32 (33), 85 (86), 88 (89), 122 (123) and 144 (145). Furthermore, some words from the Lamentations of Jeremiah 3:22 are interpolated; the origin of two other verses is unknown. While lines 2–4 in part I begin with the word "misericordia", lines 5–10 in part II describes the power of God's mercifulness; the text of part III consists of three psalm verses that are also used as the conclusion of the *Te deum*. In the eighteenth century, the motet was mentioned as an example of the "solemnity and science" of Josquin's style by Charles Burney (see p. 40). The musical setting forms a great contrast with that of Josquin's psalm settings after 1500 and contains parallel fifths and octaves, which are rarely found in the later works. On the other hand, the nice sequence at the words "omnibus invocantibus eum" (to all who call upon him) in m. 149–158, with the outer voices moving in parallel tenths, is very characteristic of the composer (Ex. 46).

EXAMPLE 46

EXAMPLE 46 (continued)

QUI HABITAT IN ADJUTORIO ALTISSIMI (NJE 18.7)

The motet survives, entirely or in part, in 17 sources: three printed books and fourteen manuscripts. Furthermore, seven sources contain arrangements for lute. The
scoring is for four voices with the following ranges: g–c² (superius), c–f¹ (altus and
tenor), G–bflat (bassus). Length: 282 measures.

This bipartite motet is based on the entire psalm 90 (91) and repeats at the end,
as does *Memor esto verbi tui* (see above), the first words of verse 1, in more or less
the same musical setting as at the opening. The psalm, which in the monastic
tradition is still sung daily in the Office before bedtime, has been called a song of
confidence in God, "eminent above others". That Josquin must have been aware
of this can be gathered from m. 40–47, where he repeats the words "sperabo in
eum" (in him I will trust) in all voices. Although the musical texture is not as
transparent as in *Memor esto*, here the technique of voice pairing is used as well.
See, for example, m. 92–105 where, at the words "ab incursu et demonio meridi-
ano" in verse 6, there is a reference to the coming "of invasion, or of the noonday
devil". Archaistic 6/3 chords (m. 102–105) are used to evoke the imminent dan-
ger. In m. 4–5, the word "altissimi" (of the most High) is painted in the superius
with a leap of an octave; another rhetorical figure is found in m. 233–236, where
the composer uses ascending melodic lines at the words "clamavit ad me" (he has
cried to me) (Ex. 47). NJE 18.7 can be counted among Josquin's most widely-
disseminated works.[9] In the 1540s, Ludwig Daser based one of his Masses on it;
in 1565, Valentin Bakfark published an arrangement for lute in Kraków; and in
1616, some hundred years after *Qui habitat* was composed, the *diaria* of the Sistine Chapel still indicate that the work was sung at the offertory in the Mass on
the first Sunday of Lent.

---

9   See Leeman L. Perkins, 'Josquin's *Qui habitat* and the Psalm Motets', in *JM* 26 (2010), 512–564.

EXAMPLE 47

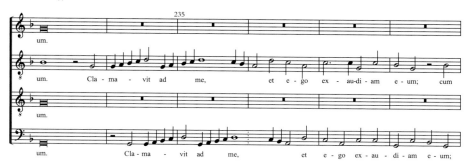

QUI HABITAT IN ADJUTORIO ALTISSIMI (NJE *18.8)

The motet survives, entirely or in part, in 4 sources: two printed books and two manuscripts. The scoring is for twenty-four voices in canon, with the following ranges: c¹–f²
(superius), e–a¹ (altus), c–f¹ (tenor), F–c¹ (bassus). Length: 154 measures.

The first eight verses of psalm 90 (91) served as a starting point for an entirely different setting of the text than that of NJE 18.7. The present work is a gigantic canon for four parts, each consisting of six voices, a procedure absolutely unique in the musical repertory of the sixteenth century.[10] As is explained in Chapter 6, it looks as though the composer conceived the canon in order to musically portray particular passages from the Book of Revelation. The technical complexity did not stop him from stressing the important moments in the text. For example, in order to evoke the idea of the thousands of impious that "shall fall at thy [= God's] side", the word "cadent" (they shall fall) is carried in a downward motion throughout all voices. As in NJE 18.7, the word "altissimi" in verse 1 is set to a leap of an octave in the superius. The conclusion shows clearly the sense of verse 8, "et retributionem peccatorum videbis" (and [thou] shalt see the reward of the wicked). The limited tradition of the motet, exclusively found in German sources, is undoubtedly due to its extravagant scoring, which makes it *de facto* less appropriate for performance (see also pp. 90–91).

USQUEQUO, DOMINE, OBLIVISCERIS ME (NJE 18.12)

The motet survives in 4 sources: two printed books and two manuscripts. The scoring is for four voices with the following ranges: c¹–d² (superius), d–a¹ (altus), c–f¹
(tenor), F–bflat (bassus). Length: 193 measures.

This bipartite motet, based on the entire psalm 12 (13), repeats the first half of verse 1 at the end. However, in contrast to *Memor esto* and the four-voice *Qui habitat*, in which the text of the opening also returns at the end, this time the musical setting is identical for a duration of no less than nineteen measures. Considering the exclusively posthumous, German transmission, which gives only one independent ascription to Josquin, this procedure could be used as an argument against his au-

---

10 For an argument in favour of Josquin's authorship, see p. [62].

thorship.[11] In spite of that, the setting of the text, which is a prayer to God for protection against the enemy of mankind, contains structural and affective elements that are characteristic of Josquin. For example, we regularly come across passages in which the pairing of voices is employed to create a contrast with three- or four-voice writing, and the setting of the conspicuous words "Respice, et exaudi me, domine" (Consider, and hear me, O Lord, my God) lends a strong climax to the prayer by means of ascending motif repetitions (Ex. 48). A plain reference to the recitation tones of psalms in Gregorian chant may be found in m. 166–171. At this point, tone repetition occurs in all voices at the words "et psallam nomini domini" (yes, I will sing to the name of the Lord).

EXAMPLE 48

11   Having received very little attention in the more recent scholarly literature, the motet is nevertheless considered genuine by Leeman L. Perkins, whose analysis reveals, alongside the motet's conformity to the general stylistic traits of Josquin's psalm motets, "iterative procedures very much like those associated ... with Josquin's unique compositional voice"; see 'Josquin's *Qui habitat* and the Psalm Motets', 552.

Motets on texts from the New Testament

This category comprises nine authentic and two doubtful compositions. Seven are based on texts drawn from the gospel of Luke, two on texts from Matthew, one on a text from John, and one on texts from Matthew and Luke. Of the motets *Factum est autem* and *Liber generationis* that are based on the genealogy of Christ, only the second setting was widely disseminated. Although all the sources date from after 1500, these motets were almost certainly composed before the end of the fifteenth century. Since the plainsong recitation formulas that have been used as *cantus prius factus* are related to those from the royal abbey of St. Martin's in Tours, these motets have been associated with Josquin's service at the French court.[12] The *Magnificat tertii toni* is found in one of the earliest musical sources of Josquin's works, Berlin 40021, which dates from the late fifteenth century. The work cannot as yet be linked with a specific period of the composer's life. *Homo quidam fecit cenam magnam, Missus est Gabriel angelus*, and the *Magnificat quarti toni* probably originated in the 1490s. The gospel motets *In illo tempore assumpsit Jesus* and *In principio erat verbum* exhibit stylistic features of the late Josquin, and certainly date from after 1500. As for the six-voice double motet *Pater noster – Ave Maria*, it has been argued that Josquin wrote it while in Ferrara.[13] Stylistically, however, it seems more likely that it is one of his later works, if not his very last. Except for this double motet, the order in which the works are commented on is synchronic with the life story of the Virgin Mary and Jesus Christ, as reported in the three gospels.

MISSUS EST GABRIEL ANGELUS (NJE 20.7)

The motet survives, entirely or in part, in 13 sources: one printed book and twelve manuscripts. The scoring is for four voices with the following ranges: f–d² (superius), c–g¹ (altus), Bflat–f¹ (tenor), F–bflat (bassus). Length: 85 measures.

The text combines the antiphons *Missus est Gabriel* and *Ave Maria* for the feast of the Annunciation to the Virgin Mary (March 25), with texts drawn from Luke 1:26-28, and where it is said that she will become the mother of God. The question of the extent to which Josquin made use of the melodies of these antiphons cannot easily be answered. While it is evident that, from m. 40 onwards, Josquin is quoting the familiar antiphon *Ave Maria* (see p. 68), no chant melody corresponds with the one cited in the opening of the motet. On the other hand, the Magnificat antiphon of Annunciation, which opens with the words "Gabriel angelus", begins with the same leap of a fifth as the motet. Therefore it may seem plausible that Josquin allowed himself some liberty in quoting the plainsong melodies. Stylistically, the motet is characterized by imitation and duet-writing; the long melismas in the graceful melodies make the music highly melodious.

---

12 See Jeremy Noble, 'The Genealogies of Christ and their Musical Settings', in *Essays in Music and Culture in Honor of Herbert Kellman*, ed. Barbara Haggh (Paris 2001), 197–208.

13 Daniel E. Freeman, 'On the Origins of the *Pater noster – Ave Maria* of Josquin Des Prez', in *Musica Disciplina* 45 (1991), 169–219.

MAGNIFICAT TERTII TONI (NJE 20.1)
MAGNIFICAT TERTII TONI (Verses 1–8) (NJE *20.2)
MAGNIFICAT QUARTI TONI (NJE 20.3)
MAGNIFICAT QUARTI TONI (Verse 6) (NJE *20.4)

Four entire or partial settings of Mary's canticle "Magnificat anima mea domini" (Luke 1:46-54) have survived. In the two complete and authentic settings, NJE 20.1 and 20.3, the even-numbered verses are polyphonic, alternating with the odd verses in plainsong.

NJE 20.1

The motet survives only in Berlin 40021. The scoring is for four voices with the following ranges: $a–d^2$ (superius), $c–a^1$ (altus), $c–f^1$ (tenor), $F–c^1$ (bassus). Length: 188 measures.

The 3rd Gregorian psalm tone appears in verses 2, 6 and 12 in long note values in one of the voices, and is paraphrased in verses 4 and 10, in the form of motifs, in two or more voices. In verse 8, all voices begin with the first notes of the recitation tone, but are otherwise freely composed. When in this verse, God is said to have sent away the rich "empty", Josquin seems to give prominence to this idea by having the word "inanes" (empty) sung to ever lengthier melismas (Ex. 49).

EXAMPLE 49

NJE 20.3

The motet survives in five manuscripts. Furthermore, one source contains an arrangement for organ. The scoring is for four voices with the following ranges: $g–d^2$ (superius), $c–g^1$ (altus), $c–f^1$ (tenor), $E–b$ (bassus). Length: 297 measures.

In one of its sources this Magnificat is anonymous. The remaining manuscripts attribute it to four different composers (see p. 57). NJE 20.3 differs from NJE 20.1 in the setting of the first verse, since, after the plainsong incipit "Magnificat", the rest of this verse is set for all voices. Cappella Sistina 44 transmits a version in which all verses appear in polyphony. The scribe used the music of five even-numbered verses twice, in order to provide the odd verses with polyphony as well (7 = 2, 9 = 4, 11 = 6, 5 = 10, and 3 = 12).[14] The 4th Gregorian psalm tone is almost always heard in one or more voices in long note values. The lowest voice part in verse 10 consists of the four-note motif *sol–fa–sol–ut*, notated four times in decreasing note values; this is identical to the motif at the opening of the familiar antiphon *Salve regina*. In the last verse, the psalm tone is treated as a canon at the upper fourth in tenor and bassus (Ex. 50).

EXAMPLE 50

NJE *20.2

The motet survives only in Segovia s.s. The scoring is for four voices with the following ranges: a–e² (superius), c–a¹ (altus and tenor), A–e¹ (bassus). Length: 152 measures.

There can be no doubt that, in its unique source, this *Magnificat* is transmitted only in part. Verses 2 and 6 are for four voices, verse 4 is a duet, and verse 8, the last one in the manuscript, is for three voices. In other words, in the original version the verses 10 and 12 were most probably written again in four parts. Although the opening is reminiscent of the 3rd psalm tone, in the course of the composition this recitation formula is much less prominent than in NJE 20.1.

NJE *20.4

Of this setting, only verse 6, "Fecit potentiam", is known. It is found in a Spanish collection for lute from 1554, and has been reconstructed in the *NJE* as an instrumental duo of 75 measures.

At the opening, the 4th psalm tone can be recognized. It has been suggested that this single verse could be a surviving fragment of a full composition.

IN PRINCIPIO ERAT VERBUM (NJE 19.8)

The motet survives, entirely or in part, in 10 sources: two printed books and eight manuscripts. Furthermore, two sources contain arrangements for organ and lute. The scoring is for four voices with the following ranges: f¹–f² (superius), f–c² (altus and tenor), Bflat–d¹ (bassus). Length: 252 measures.

The text of this tripartite motet is taken from John 1:1–14 and is recited at Christmas in the daytime Mass as well as at the very end of the daily Eucharistic service,

---

14   See Motetten no. 78 in the old Josquin edition.

after the dismissal (Fig. 34). In the first verse, the son of God is called "the Word" that brings life and light to mankind (v. 4), by which it will be redeemed (v. 14). The disproportionate distribution of the fourteen verses over the three parts does full justice to the verbal contents of the gospel: part I (v. 1–5 in m. 1–77) concerns the Word before the incarnation of Jesus Christ; part II (v. 6–13 in m. 78–208) relates that John the Baptist was sent by God to bear witness to the light; and part III (v. 14 in m. 209–252) describes the glory of the Word that was made flesh. It seems that, in composing this motet, Josquin aimed to reveal the mystical character of the gospel text as much as possible. The musical discourse is simplified: the text is predominantly treated syllabically and the melodic formulas are repetitive. Variety is achieved in the alternation of passages in two- to four-voice imitative polyphony with those where the four parts sing the same words simultaneously. In part II, the binary mensuration is momentarily interrupted three times by triplets in all voices, always in order to emphasize the textual contents. In v. 6, where the evangelist introduces John the Baptist, the entry of the superius is given prominence by a high register (Ex. 51). The first words of the final part, "Et verbum caro factum est", are spread over eight measures in sustained chords. Highlighting Christ's incarnation, they create the most solemn moment in the motet.[15]

FIGURE 34: The opening of the superius voice of *In principio erat verbum* in the first volume of Berg & Neuber's *Evangelia dominicorum et festorum dierum* (Nuremberg 1554), no. 2.

---

15 Considering that the motet is attributed to Josquin in nine out of ten sources, several of them independent, it is surprising that Finscher, in *JosqComp*, 264, fn. 33, judged this important motet to be doubtful, though recognized it as authentic three years later in *MGG2*, vol. 9, col. 1220. Fallows, in his Josquin monograph, seems to ignore the motet entirely.

EXAMPLE 51

LIBER GENERATIONIS JESU CHRISTI (NJE 19.13)

The motet survives, entirely or in part, in 14 sources: five printed books and nine manuscripts. The scoring is for four voices with the following ranges: c¹–d² (superius), a–g¹ (altus), A–f¹ (tenor), E–a (bassus). Length: 391 measures.

The text of this comprehensive genealogy, recorded in Matthew 1:1–16, follows the three eras of the Old Covenant. This threefold division is maintained in the motet: part I consists of v. 1–6; part II of v. 7–11; and part III of v. 12–16. In the monastic tradition, the genealogy is sung during Christmas Matins. Josquin based his motet on a recitation formula that, in his time, was used in the diocese of Tours. Consisting of five notes, this formula begins as follows (Ex. 52):

EXAMPLE 52

The melody is mostly found in the tenor but is sometimes quoted in the other voices as well, particularly at the beginning of the first and last parts. The musical progress is regularly punctuated by cadences, allowing the listener 'to resume the thread' of the monotonous enumeration of names, as for example at "Abraham autem genuit Isaac" and "Esram autem genuit Aram". In the closing measures, Josquin draws attention to the birth of Christ by setting his name in all voices to the falling motif *sol–mi–mi*. In contrast to the four-voice outer movements, the polyphonic texture of the three-voice central section is more transparent and concludes with a passage in ternary mensuration. Notwithstanding the seemingly endless inventory of the 39 generations, the musical setting of the text remains highly varied. Glarean, who included the entire motet in his *Dodecachordon* (see p. 37–38), made the following comment:

> The song possesses great majesty and it is wonderful that from such unfruitful material, namely a bare nomenclature of names, he [= Josquin] has been able to create just as many delights as if it had been some ornate narrative.[16]

FACTUM EST AUTEM (NJE 19.3)

The motet survives, entirely or in part, in 2 sources: one printed book and one manuscript. The scoring is for four voices with the following ranges: a–c² (superius), c–f¹ (altus), A–e¹ (tenor), F–b (bassus). Length: 395 measures.

The genealogy of Jesus in Luke 3:24–38 differs in structure from that in Matthew (see above). Not only are the names enumerated in reverse order, but Luke also follows the lineage that runs from David via Nathan, and not the royal lineage. Furthermore, the genealogy, which goes back to Adam and includes a greater number of generations, is preceded by Christ's baptism in the Jordan (Luke 3:21–23). Like *Liber generationis*, this motet too is tripartite: part I consists of v. 21–23; part II of v. 24–31, leading us to Jesse; part III of v. 32–38, and concludes with Jesus' journey to the desert. In the monastic tradition, the genealogy is sung during Epiphany Matins. Josquin based his motet on a recitation formula that, in his time, was used in the diocese of Tours; its range goes from *g–a¹*. The melody is most easily recognized in the tenor voice of the first part. The four-voice scoring is regularly reduced to three or two voices. In both the second and third parts, sections in ternary mensuration enliven the rhythmic progress. Each of the three parts opens with the same motif, treated in imitation, and in this way contributes to creating global coherence. The following example shows the opening of the last part (Ex. 53):

EXAMPLE 53

HOMO QUIDAM FECIT CENAM (NJE 19.4)

The motet survives, entirely or in part, in 3 sources: one printed book and two manuscripts. The scoring is for five voices with the following ranges: a–g² (superius), f–g¹ (altus), g–a¹ (tenor primus), d–a¹ (tenor secundus), Bes–f¹ (bassus). Length: 129 measures.

The text of this bipartite motet is the same as that of the responsory, sung in the First Vespers of the Feast of Corpus Christi. It combines the parable of the wedding guests (Luke 14:16–17) and Proverbs 9:5. The melody of the responsory is treated canonically in the two tenor voices: in part I at the lower fourth, and in part II at the unison. The superius in particular, with a range of almost two octaves, produces a lively counterpoint against the quietly moving tenor voices. The text of the verse is as follows: "venite, comedite panem meum et bibite vinum, quod miscui vobis" (Come, eat my bread, and drink the wine which I have mingled for you). In m. 111–118, the bassus sings the words "et bibite" five times to the same motif (Ex. 54). Could the repeated statements of these words be understood as Josquin's incentive to drink the wine which, in the celebration of the Eucharist, has been changed into the blood of Christ?

EXAMPLE 54

IN ILLO TEMPORE ASSUMPSIT JESUS (NJE 19.5)

The motet survives, entirely or in part, in three manuscripts. The scoring is for five voices with the following ranges: c¹–f² (superius), e–a¹ (altus), e–f¹ (tenor), A–c¹ (bassus). Length: 121 measures.

This motet, based on Matthew 20:17–19, concerns the third prophecy of the Passion, and represents Josquin's last composition on the life of Jesus Christ as chronologically reported in the gospels.[17] In the liturgy, the text is that of the gospel in the Votive Mass on Good Friday in honour of the Holy Cross. It is only in the tenor, m. 6–15 and 55–60, that Josquin uses the plainsong recitation tone. In m. 61–76, all four voices sing in a threefold sequence the words "et filius hominum tradetur" (and the Son of man shall be betrayed). This musical passage is subsequently repeated at the words "principibus sacerdotum et scribis" (to the chief priests and the scribes). Made up of the motif *sol–mi–mi*, the ascending sequence produces a strong climax in the middle of the motet (Ex. 55). The passage which, in m. 97–105, refers to the mockery, the scourge, and the crucifixion is equally emphasized by means of a threefold chordal setting.

---

17   NJE 21.5, the subject of which is the passion of Christ, is commented on below.

EXAMPLE 55

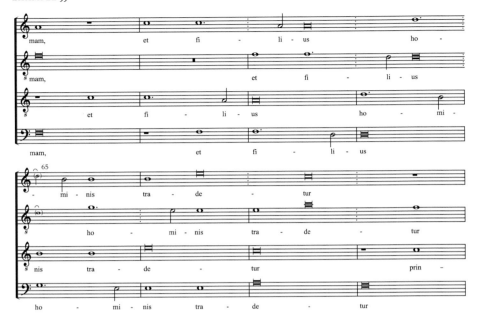

PATER NOSTER – AVE MARIA (NJE 20.9)

The motet survives, entirely or in part, in 25 sources: three printed books and twenty-two manuscripts. The scoring is for six voices with the following ranges: c^1–d^2 (superius), c–g^1 (altus primus and altus secundus), e–f^1 (tenor primus), d–d^1 (tenor secundus), G–b (bassus). Length: 198 measures.

The many sources of this double motet bear witness to its wide dissemination. In addition to the printed editions published in France and Germany, it was copied into manuscripts in Italy, Spain, the Czech Republic, Germany and Denmark (Fig. 35). The text consists of the familiar prayer to God the Father (Matthew 6:9–13) in the first part, and the "Ave Maria" (Luke 1:28 and 42) in the second part. It seems unlikely that the motet, which is thought to be the earliest polyphonic setting of these combined prayers, would have had a liturgical function in Josquin's time. In the second part, Luke's v. 42 ("et benedictus fructus ventris tui") is followed by a prayer to the Virgin Mary based on a non-biblical text very popular in the sixteenth century. The prayer ends with the words "pray for us sinners, that we may see you with the elect."

Although the tenor voices, at some points in the *Pater noster*, are reminiscent of the liturgical recitation tone used with the same text, Josquin, perhaps for harmonic reasons, seems to have remodelled the formula. In these voices, the newly written melody is treated as a two-voice canon at the fifth. Canon technique is also applied in the second part, where the tenor voices begin with a brief quotation from the antiphon *Ave Maria*. This time the two voices are in unison. In Chapter 5 it was pointed out that Josquin used this antiphon in five of his motets. However, in NJE 20.9, he transformed the melody after the first phrase into his own song in honour of Mary. This motet is certainly one of his most important and a fine example of his late motet style, where great attention is given to the audibility of the text. One only has to listen to the fourfold repeat of the last phrase of the *Ave Maria* to realize that we are dealing with a perfect example of a prayer set to music. Josquin himself seems to have been of this opinion. In his will was stipulated that this motet should be sung yearly on the anniversary of his death (see p. 20).

FIGURE 35: The opening of the six-voice *Pater noster - Ave Maria*. Toledo, Catedral, Obra y Fabrica, Ms. Reservado 23, f. 98'-99.

Motets on non-biblical texts in honour of Jesus Christ

All fourteen motets in this category are considered authentic. In Josquin's time, nine of them had their place in the liturgy. These are *Ave verum corpus*, *Tu solus qui facis mirabilia*, *Victime paschali laudes*, the five motets of the cycle *O admirabile commercium*, and *Qui velatus facie fuisti*. The texts of *O bone et dulcissime Jesu* and *O domine Jesu Christe* are found in medieval books of hours. *Huc me sydereo* is based on a fifteenth-century humanistic poem. For the prayer texts *Magnus es tu domine* and *O bone et dulcis domine Jesu*, no other sources are known.

Regarding chronology, it is assumed that *Ave verum* and the two *O bone ... Jesu*-motets date back to Josquin's early years in France, and that *Huc me* and the cycle *O admirabile commercium* were composed after he had returned to France, in 1504. The remaining motets most likely originated in Italy.

AVE VERUM CORPUS (NJE 21.2)

The motet survives, entirely or in part, in 7 sources: five printed books and two manuscripts. The scoring is for three voices with the following ranges: c¹–f² (superius primus), a–d² (superius secundus), c–g¹ (altus). Length: 115 measures.

Dating from the thirteenth century and written in Northern Italy, this Eucharistic text takes Christ sacrificed on the Cross as its subject. It originated from a trope for the Sanctus of the plainsong Mass no. VIII (*De angelis*), which was sung after the Benedictus. Petrucci's *Motetti de passione* from 1503 is the earliest source. The Gregorian chant is paraphrased and is most easily recognizable in the second superius. The layout of the five sections, turned into letters, is *a a' b b' c*. Sections *a* and *b* are for the two superius parts and are repeated with an additional third voice. Section *c* is for three voices. By using a high register, Josquin seemingly wanted to imitate the singing of angels.

TU SOLUS QUI FACIS MIRABILIA (NJE 22.5)

The motet survives, entirely or in part, in 12 sources: six printed books and six manuscripts. The scoring is for four voices with the following ranges: d¹–d² (superius), f–b¹flat (altus), f–f¹ (tenor), F–bflat (bassus). Length: 110 measures.

The motet is bipartite. Part I is also found in sources together with Josquin's *Missa D'ung aultre amer* (see p. 110). In the Ambrosian liturgy in Milan, this part substituted the Benedictus and second Osanna, and was sung during the Consecration. Whether NJE 22.5 had the same function remains unclear. The opening of the text recalls v. 4 of psalm 135 (136): "Qui facit mirabilia magna solus" (Who alone doth great wonders). In the second part of the prayer, the poet says that Jesus Christ is his one and only love. Josquin underscores this idea by quoting the first four measures of the highest voice of Ockeghem's chanson *D'ung aultre amer* (To love another) twice in succession (Ex. 56). The music mainly consists of sustained chords, characterizing its devotional style. These chords alternate with short, imitatively treated paired voices in m. 38–45 and 53-60. The frequent use of fermatas contributes to the motet's character of quiet introspection.

EXAMPLE 56

VICTIME PASCHALI LAUDES (NJE 22.6)

The motet survives, entirely or in part, in 4 sources: two printed books and two manuscripts. Furthermore, one source contains an arrangement for organ. The scoring is for four voices with the following ranges: g–d² (superius), c–a¹ (altus), Bflat–g¹ (tenor), F–c¹ (bassus). Length: 119 measures.

In terms of structure, this bipartite motet is a good example of what has been called 'combinative techniques'.[18] In this case, the compositional process is marked by the connecting of texts and melodies from the sacred and secular repertories. Verse 1 of the familiar sequence *Victime paschali laudes*, which dates from the eleventh century and is about the Risen Christ, appears in the tenor in long note values. The three short phrases of verses 2a and 2b are set to the same melody, and quoted as follows: 2a in the altus, bassus, and tenor successively; 2b entirely in the tenor. Likewise, in the second part the chant is presented alternately in the three lower voices. The superius material is borrowed from two French chansons. In part I, Josquin uses the entire top voice of Ockeghem's *D'ung aultre amer* (Ex. 57; see also the previous motet); in part II the top voice of Hayne van Ghizeghem's *De tous biens plaine* appears (Ex. 87 at p. 220). The answer to the question of why Josquin decided to combine these two *cantus prius facti* with the text of the sequence is to be sought in their great popularity rather than their textual content. He incorporated both songs in some of his other compositions as well (see p. 110 and 219). In the sources of *Victime paschali laudes*, only the textual incipits of the chansons are given.

EXAMPLE 57

---

18 See Maria Rika Maniates, *Combinative Techniques in Franco-Flemish Polyphony: a Study of Mannerism in Music from 1450 to 1530* (Ph. D. diss., Columbia University, 1965).

O ADMIRABILE COMMERCIUM (NJE 21.7a)
QUANDO NATUS EST (NJE 21.7b)
RUBUM QUEM VIDERAT MOYSES (NJE 21.7c)
GERMINAVIT RADIX JESSE (NJE 21.7d)
ECCE MARIA GENUIT (NJE 21.7e)

The cycle survives, entirely or in part, in 7 sources: two printed books and five manuscripts. Furthermore, one source contains an arrangement for organ of all five motets. The scoring is for four voices with the following ranges: (a) c^1–d^2 (superius), d–g^1 (altus), f–f^1 (tenor), Bflat–bflat (bassus). Length: 103 measures. (b) c^1–d^2 (superius), f–g^1 (altus), g–g^1 (tenor), c–bflat (bassus). Length: 91 measures. (c) g^1–d^2 (superius), g–g^1 (altus), f–d^1 (tenor), A–g (bassus). Length: 63 measures. (d) e^1–f^2 (superius), f–a^1 (altus and tenor), Bflat–bflat (bassus). Length: 66 measures. (e) d^1–f^2 (superius), e–g^1 (altus), e–f^1 (tenor), G–bflat (bassus). Length: 73 measures.

These five motets are based on the texts and melodies of the eponymous antiphons sung at the Feast of the Circumcision of our Lord (January 1).[19] The antiphons' great popularity is demonstrated, among other things, by their numerous polyphonic settings. For example, in the repertory of polyphonic motets before 1550, no less than eighteen other settings of *O admirabile commercium* can be found. Josquin's motets form a unique cycle in his oeuvre because of their cyclic function in the liturgy. The first two motets are about Jesus Christ, the third and fourth are devoted to the Virgin Mary, and the fifth to both. In medieval chant sources, the antiphons are found in the Saturday Office of Our Lady.

Although the chant melodies are occasionally quoted in all four voices, they are paraphrased primarily in the tenor. The five-note exclamation "O" in the first antiphon is extended to a melody of fourteen notes (Ex. 58). The change in m. 19, at the word "commercium", from a minor to a major sonority can be understood as symbolic (see p. 77). In the second motet, the elaboration of the motif at the word "descendisti" in m. 57–65 is nearly identical with that in m. 19–25 of the Gloria of Josquin's *Missa Hercules Dux Ferrarie*. In the final measures of the third motet, polyphonic writing is abandoned in favour of a syllabic, clearly audible setting of the words "intercede pro nobis" (intercede for us). In the fourth motet, the allusion to the Tree of Jesse – "orta est stella ex Jacob" (a star is risen out of Jacob) – is musically emphasized in m. 18–36. The change to a ternary mensuration in m. 41–46 of the last motet, as well as the constantly repeated "alleluia" in m. 57–73, bring the cycle to a joyful conclusion.

---

19   Richard Sherr examines in some detail the question of how these motets, in their performance context, could be understood liturgically; see 'Conflicting Levels of Meaning and Understanding in Josquin's *O admirabile commercium* Motet Cycle', in *Hearing the Motet. Essays on the Motet of the Middle Ages and Renaissance*, ed. Dolores Pesce (New York 1997), 193–212. But see also Paul A. Merkley and Lora L.M. Merkley, *Music and Patronage in the Sforza Court* (Turnhout 1999), 483–484.

EXAMPLE 58

QUI VELATUS FACIE FUISTI (NJE 22.3)

The motet survives, entirely or in part, in 8 sources: four printed books and four manuscripts. The scoring is for four voices with the following ranges: a–c² (superius), d–g¹ (altus), c–f¹ (tenor), E–c¹ (bassus). Length: 502 measures.

This work consists of six short motets based on poems attributed to St. Bonaventure (*d.* 1274) that were written for the Office of Passiontide, and describe Christ's suffering and death. Petrucci's edition *Motetti de passione* from 1503 is the only source of the composition. The last part, *Christum ducem*, was re-issued by Petrucci in 1514 as an independent piece, and is, at 130 measures, much longer than the preceding motets. It is assumed that the cycle is not transmitted in its original order. Moreover, the last lines of the fifth poem – "and lead us to the heavenly joy of eternal peace" – would form a more logical conclusion than those of the sixth poem, in which it is asked to be "granted with blessed joys". The section "Honor et decus" in m. 207–234 of part IV is identical with m. 33–60 of Josquin's *Sanctus de passione* NJE 13.9 (see p. 127). The verses, most of them rhyming, are grouped together in short sections ending with long sustained block chords. Where Bonaventure quotes the first line of a Gregorian hymn – this happens eight times in total – Josquin set these lines to their plainsong melodies. The absence of a coordinating formal principle is compensated by the use of the same musical material in the course of the cycle. To a certain extent, this procedure evokes the character of a litany. By treating the voices alternately in polyphony and homophony, Josquin succeeds in creating marked contrasts, both harmonically and rhythmically. In places, short passages in a ternary mensuration enliven the rhythmic progress. The falling triads in the altus and bassus at the beginning of part III, reminiscent of the opening of his *Stabat mater*, lend great dramatic tension to the words "In flagellis potum fellis" (Amidst scourges thou drankest).

O BONE ET DULCISSIME JESU (NJE 21.9)

The motet survives, entirely or in part, in 6 sources: one printed book and five manuscripts. The scoring is for four voices with the following ranges: d¹–d² (superius), f–a¹ (altus), d–g¹ (tenor), A–c¹ (bassus). Length: 203 measures.

This freely-composed, bipartite motet is based on a prayer text found, in various versions, in fifteenth-century books of hours. They all begin with the words "O bone Jesu" and are addressed to Christ, who is praised for his loving kindness and asked for remission of sins. It is assumed that these prayers have their origin in a meditation of Anselm of Canterbury (*d.* 1109). Anselm's meditation also inspired the Franciscan theologian Bernardino of Siena (*d.* 1444) to write a prayer. It has been suggested that Josquin wrote the motet during his service at the court of Duke René of Anjou (see p. 22), who held Bernardino in great esteem.[20] Among the stylistic features characteristic of the young Josquin are the alternating paired voice parts, the imitatively treated sequence in m. 26–33 at the words "per tuam misericordiam" (by your mercifulness), the alternation of sections in binary and ternary mensuration, and, in the four-voice homorhythmic section in m. 161–169, the delayed, syncopated entry of the tenor.[21]

O DOMINE JESU CHRISTE (NJE 22.1)

The unique source of this motet is Petrucci's *Motetti de passione* from 1503. The scoring is for four voices with the following ranges: g–b¹ (superius), c–f¹ (altus and tenor), F–a (bassus). Length: 338 measures.

The prayers set in this motet are traditionally attributed to Gregory the Great, and were written to be recited before the effigy of the Man of Sorrows in order to obtain indulgences. Each of the five parts opens with the invocation "O domine, Jesu Christe" in sustained block chords, always in a new harmonic setting. The music is almost purely homophonic. Yet by means of brief melismatic melodic figures, Josquin succeeds in achieving a certain degree of variety without sacrificing the prayer's austere character. In the first two parts, the text describes Christ's sufferings on the cross, and in the third part his entombment. Part IV is a devotional plea for remission of sins. In part V, the praying person begs Christ to have mercy upon their soul, when the time comes for it to leave their body. The low register of the voices contributes to the mystical character of the music, and the threefold sequence at the end of part III gives prominence to the words "Deprecor te / ut tua mors / sit vita mea" (I beseech thee / that thy death / may be my life).

HUC ME SYDEREO (NJE 21.5)

The motet survives, entirely or in part, in 17 sources: six printed books and eleven

---

20 See Patrick Macey, 'Josquin, Good King René, and *O bone et dulcissime Jesu*', in *Hearing the Motet ...*, 213–242.

21 Cf., e.g., *Ave Maria* NJE 23.6, m. 94.

manuscripts. The scoring is for six voices with the following ranges: g–d² (superius), bflat–g¹ (altus), f–e¹ (tenor), G–g¹ (sextus), G–d¹ (bassus primus), D–d¹ (bassus secundus). Length: 192 measures.

This bipartite motet is one of Josquin's most dramatic compositions. Two versions are transmitted, for five and for six voices respectively.[22] The question of which of the two versions should be considered as the original has been the subject of several studies. While it is impossible to determine with certainty whether the sextus is an addition to the original texture or was conceived at the same time as the other five voices, most scholars agree that it stems from the hand of Josquin himself.[23] However, the question of the sixth voice cannot entirely be settled without considering that *Huc me sydereo* has a six-voice companion piece, *Ave nobilissima creatura*. Each of these motets is based on an antiphon, the texts of which are different but their melodic settings identical (see p. 178).[24] And since texts form an integral part of Josquin's motets, the conjunction of *Ave nobilissima creatura* and *Huc me sydereo*, because of their complementary contents and the circumstantial evidence of their *cantus prius facti*, can no longer be ignored.

Huc me sydereo is a humanistic, elegiac text by Maffeo Vegio (1407–1458), written in hexameters. It was published posthumously in Turin in 1521. In verses 1–4 and 9–12, Christ speaks from the cross; verses 5–8 are those of a 'commentator'. Throughout the poem, the word "amor" – a metonym for God – functions as a leitmotif. In m. 19–35, Christ's descent from the starry Olympus is depicted in long melodic descending lines (Ex. 59). Another example of word-painting may be found at the end of the first part, where the repeated rhythmic motif at the words "verbera tanta pati" (to bear heavy scourges) stresses the blows of the lash. The antiphon *Plangent eum*, sung at Lauds on Holy Saturday, serves as *cantus firmus*. Entering in m. 49 in long notes, it is repeated twice in part II, in ever smaller values. The text of the antiphon – They shall mourn him like an only-begotten son, for the innocent Lord has been slain – constitutes a symbolic background to Vegio's poem.

---

22 Omitting not only the sextus but also the *cantus firmus* voice, Brussels 9126 transmits the motet in a four-voice version.

23 Some musicologists have suggested that the sixth voice was written by someone else. On pages 282–285 of his Josquin monograph, Fallows gives an excellent summary of the various opinions, voiced since 1977 by Jeremy Noble, John Caldwell, Bonnie Blackburn, Jaap van Benthem, Joshua Rifkin and Stephanie Schlagel.

24 See Willem Elders, 'Zusammenhänge zwischen den Motetten *Ave nobilissima creatura* und *Huc me sydereo* von Josquin des Prez', in *TVNM* 22 (1971–72), 67–73. The conclusions drawn in this study are shared by both Noble (*NGD2*, 233) and Blackburn (Critical Commentary to NJE vol. 21, 58).

EXAMPLE 59

MAGNUS ES TU DOMINE (NJE 21.6)

The motet survives, entirely or in part, in 7 sources: three printed books and four manuscripts. The scoring is for four voices with the following ranges: a–d² (superius), d–f¹ (altus), c–d¹ (tenor), G–e¹ (bassus). Length: 110 measures.

The opening of this bipartite motet, based on a prayer to Christ, quotes verse 6 from Jeremiah 10: "Thou art great, and great is thy name in might." The prayer's last phrase is inspired by verse 4 of psalm 12 (13): "[Enlighten my eyes] that I never sleep in death." The numerous textual variants in the sources of the motet can perhaps be explained by the fact that the prayer is not known from other, non-musical sources, and obviously did not belong to the standard repertory of sacred texts. As is the case in Josquin's motets *Tu solus qui facis mirabilia* (see p. 156) and *Illibata dei virgo* (see p. 179), stylistically the two parts contrast with one another: while the structure of the first part is polyphonic, the second verges on a homophonic texture, where the short lines of the poem are treated as independent phrases, separated by rests. In m. 76–87, at the words "et nunc, redemptor domine …" (and now, Redeemer Lord …), the binary mensuration is changed to a ternary one, in order to highlight the begging for Christ's personal intervention.

O BONE ET DULCIS DOMINE JESU (NJE 21.8)

The motet survives, entirely or in part, in 5 sources: one printed book and four manu-scripts. Furthermore, one source contains an arrangement for lute. The scoring is for four voices with the following ranges: c¹–f² (superius), c–g¹ (altus), a–f¹ (tenor), A–b (bassus). Length: 97 measures.

The two upper voices of this motet are based on an unidentified prayer to Christ, affirming belief in the dogmas of the Church and imploring his compassion. At the same time, the tenor sings a plainsong version of the *Pater noster* from the Ordinary of the Mass, and the bassus the antiphons *Ave Maria* and *Benedicta tu in mulieribus* (see also p. 68). Since Christ taught his disciples the Lord's Prayer (Matthew 6:9–13), and since the Virgin Mary, as Mother of God, acts as a mediator between man and the Lord, the juxtaposition of these chants attests to Josquin's full comprehension of the motet's main text. Striking moments in the music are, among others, the opening, in which the words "O good and sweet Lord Jesus" are emphasized in the soft harmony of thirds and sixths, and the closing measures, where the unexpected melodic climax in the superius at "fidelis" draws attention to the meaning of the motet's final words: "[servus] tuus sum fidelis" (I am your faithful servant).

Motets on non-biblical texts in honour of the Virgin Mary

The 37 motets in honour of the Virgin Mary constitute about half the total number of motets published in the *NJE*.[25] Nine of them, mostly deriving their texts from the Bible, have been commented upon earlier in this chapter. Of the settings of non-biblical texts, eighteen are based on liturgical or paraliturgical texts – eight sequences, seven antiphons, two hymns, and one chant from the Proper of the Mass. Four texts stem from medieval books of hours, and four from contemporary poetry. One motet, NJE *23.12, has a text found in yet another sixteenth-century setting; the text of NJE 25.14 consists of seven prayers, some of them containing quotations from antiphons. Josquin often found his inspiration in Gregorian chant. This is clearly shown by the large number of motets in which one or more plainsong melodies are quoted (see also Chapter 5).

Twenty-four of the motets discussed below are considered authentic, four as dubious. Following the three periods of Josquin's compositional activity proposed in Chapter 4, the motets can be dated as follows:
(a) From 1475 to 1489 – the two *Alma redemptoris mater* settings, the two *Ave Marias*, the sequences *Gaude virgo* and *Mittit ad virginem, Recordare, virgo mater*, the four-voice *Salve regina, Ut Phebi radiis*, and *Vultum tuum deprecabuntur*
(b) From 1489 to 1504 – the two *Ave maris stella* settings, *Illibata dei virgo*, the five-voice *Inviolata, Obsecro te, domina*, the five-voice *Salve regina, Stabat mater, Virgo prudentissima*, and *Virgo salutiferi*
(c) From 1504 to 1521 – the sequences *Ave mundi spes Maria* and *Benedicta es, Ave nobilissima creatura, Ave virgo sanctissima*, the twelve-voice *Inviolata, O virgo prudentissima, O virgo virginum, Preter rerum seriem* and *Regina celi, letare*

Antiphons
All these motets are based on the texts and melodies of the eponymous antiphons, although in NJE 23.4 and NJE 25.12 these are not used in their entirety.

ALMA REDEMPTORIS MATER (NJE 23.1)
ALMA REDEMPTORIS MATER / AVE REGINA (NJE 23.2)
NJE 23.1 survives, entirely or in part, in 5 sources: three printed books and two manuscripts. The scoring is for four voices with the following ranges: c–g¹ (superius), d–g¹ (altus), e–g¹ (tenor), A–d¹ (bassus). Length: 116 measures.

---

25   This includes the second part of the *Pater noster – Ave Maria*, which in the sources is often found as an independent motet, and the motets NJE 21.7c and 21.7d from the *O admirabile commercium* cycle.

NJE 23.2 survives, entirely or in part, in 7 sources: one printed book and six manuscripts. The scoring is for four voices with the following ranges: b–g² (superius), f–a¹ (altus), g–g¹ (tenor), A–d¹ (bassus). Length: 155 measures.

Both motets are bipartite and set texts from the four so-called 'great' Marian antiphons. The double motet, in which two antiphons are brought together, is almost certainly older than the other setting, which treats the antiphon *Alma redemptoris mater* as a two-voice canon at the unison (see below). The superius of NJE 23.2 opens with the first notes of the antiphon in a form that is identical to that of the altus voice in Ockeghem's *Alma redemptoris mater*. Whether or not this is meant as a tribute must remain an open question. The transparent writing of the parts and the lengthy duos are archaistic and show the influence of Dufay. The beautiful melody of *Alma redemptoris mater* is given to the outer voices, that of *Ave regina celorum* to the altus and tenor (Ex. 60). The two antiphons are divided over the motet in such a way that, at the beginning of the second part, a subtle union is created between the words "Tu que genuisti" (You gave birth to) and "Gaude gloriosa" (Rejoice glorious [virgin]). Moreover, in m. 68–77, the word "gloriosa" is strongly emphasized by a fivefold repeat in a stepwise descending sequence.

Josquin demonstrates his great talent for elaboration also in NJE 23.1. The finely balanced melody is quoted from m. 5 and 7 onwards in the altus and tenor voices, and it is remarkable that, notwithstanding the canonic construction, it is easily recognizable. While the plainsong melisma at the word "alma" in NJE 23.2 occupies four measures, in this setting it extends over no less than nine (Ex. 61). Superius and bassus open in the same way. The words "Nature marvelled" (because Mary gave birth to her own, sacred creator) are emphasized in the superius (Ex. 62).

EXAMPLE 60

EXAMPLE 61

EXAMPLE 62

AVE MARIA (NJE 23.4)

The motet survives, entirely or in part, in 2 sources: one printed book and one manuscript. Furthermore, one source contains an arrangement for lute. The scoring is for four voices with the following ranges: f^1-g^2 (superius), $d-a^1$ (altus), $f-g^1$ (tenor), Bflat–d^1 (bassus). Length: 67 measures.

Since only the tenor partbook of the manuscript Bologna R142 is preserved, Petrucci's *Motetti C* of 1504 is the unique complete source of the motet. The text is a compilation of the angel Gabriel's salutation to Mary (Luke 1:28), Elizabeth's benediction (Luke 1:42), and the seventh responsory from Christmas Matins. Melodic quotations from the antiphon are limited to the first thirteen measures (see p. 68). The imitative style is coupled with the formation of elegant melodies. M. 42–57 contain an interruption in ternary mensuration. The words "Et benedicta sint beata ubera tua" (And blessed be your happy breasts) are here sung to circular melodic motifs, called *circulatio* in musical rhetoric. It has been suggested that this figure is meant as an allusion to the roundness of the Virgin's breasts.[26] In spite of the simple technical means, Josquin has succeeded in conferring eloquence to the music.

O VIRGO VIRGINUM (NJE 24.10)

The motet survives, entirely or in part, in 5 sources: one printed book and four manuscripts. The scoring is for six voices with the following ranges: d^1-d^2 (superius), $f-g^1$ (altus primus), $e-f^1$ (altus secundus), $c-e^1$ (tenor), A–bflat (bassus primus), F–bflat (bassus secundus). Length: 187 measures.

In the first part of the motet, the Virgin Mary is asked a question which is answered in the second part. The antiphon *O virgo virginum*, one of the most popular among the so-called 'O-antiphons', was intended for the fourth Sunday of Advent, and was notably in use with the Dominicans. A version of the melody found in a manuscript from St. Martin's Abbey in Tours is almost identical to the *cantus firmus* in the motet. The antiphon is quoted by Josquin in long note values, clearly audible in the superius, with some of the phrases sung an octave lower in the tenor, either in anticipation of the entry of the top voice or in imitation. The dense texture of the six-voice writing regularly alternates with passages for three or four voices. The questioning phrases appropriately conclude with the motif *mi–re–ut–sol* (su-

---

26 See Warren Kirkendale, '*Circulatio*-Tradition, "Maria lactans", and Josquin as Musical Orator', in *AcM* 56 (1984), 69–92, at 84–86.

perius, m. 99–100) or *fa–mi–re–la* (altus, m. 135-136). In m. 114–119, the words "filie Jesusalem" (daughters of Jerusalem) are set to a long series of chords in *fauxbourdon*. The sombre mood of the motet is reminiscent of the late motet *Preter rerum seriem* (see below).

REGINA CELI, LETARE (NJE *25.2)

The motet survives, entirely or in part, in 2 manuscripts. The scoring is for four voices with the following ranges: c'–d² (superius), f–a' (altus and tenor), Bflat–c' (bassus). Length: 164 measures.

This bipartite motet, the third of the four so-called 'great' Marian antiphons, is intended for Eastertide. Each of the four phrases ends with an "alleluia", which greatly contributes to the joyful character of the music. The plainsong melody is imitatively treated in all four voices, with the result that the motet is thoroughly permeated throughout with the chant. Helmuth Osthoff rightly calls attention to the almost song-like appealing beauty of the formation of melodies and sonority.[27] The most remarkable element in the motet is the conclusion. From m. 125 onwards, the "alleluia", as an exclamation of joy because of Christ's resurrection, is repeated continuously (Ex. 63). In this passage, the principal melodic motif is derived from a melisma that, in the version of the antiphon in a printed book from the early sixteenth century at Cambrai, totals no less than thirty-five notes on the second syllable. If the only attribution of the motet to Josquin in Bologna Q20 can be trusted, this *Regina celi* probably stems from the last period of the composer's activity. Stylistically, the motet points to a later generation of composers.[28]

EXAMPLE 63

---

27 *Josquin Desprez*, vol. 2 (Tutzing 1965), 43.

28 Severe comments on the motet have been made by Jeremy Noble; see 'Another *Regina celi* Attributed to Josquin', in *From Ciconia to Sweelinck ...*, 145–152. On p. 21 of the Critical Commentary, *NJE* vol. 25, Noble's reservations regarding the authenticity question are summarised in six points, and discussed at length in the subsequent pages. Since no conclusive arguments against the only attribution can be formulated, the motet has been published as a doubtful work. Two other settings of the antiphon ascribed to Josquin have been judged to be spurious.

SALVE REGINA 4V (NJE 25.4)
SALVE REGINA 5V (NJE 25.5)

NJE 25.4 survives in 3 manuscripts. The scoring is for four voices with the following ranges: d¹–g² (superius), a–d² (altus), e–g¹ (tenor), B–d¹ (bassus). Length: 125 measures.

NJE 25.5 survives, entirely or in part, in 14 sources: three printed books and eleven manuscripts. The scoring is for five voices with the following ranges: d¹–g² (superius), c–a¹ (altus primus), g–g¹ (tenor), f–a¹ (altus secundus), Bflat–d¹ (bassus). Length: 177 measures.

The antiphon *Salve regina* is the oldest and most famous of the four so-called 'great' Marian antiphons. The text has been attributed to several authors, among whom Hermann of Reichenau (*d.* 1054) and St. Bernard of Clairvaux (*d.* 1153). Josquin's settings may have been performed in so-called *Salve* services, after the evening office of Compline, which became popular in the late Middle Ages, particularly in Flanders. The 1482 charter of the Marian Brotherhood in Antwerp stipulates, among other things, that in these daily services four singers and twelve choirboys should be used, and the service be preceded by the ringing of the church bells.[29] In m. 1–4, 15–18, 98–99, 104–105 and 110–111 of the four-voice canonic setting (see p. 70), Josquin set the exclamation "O" in all voices, in quick succession, to an interval of a second. It is most likely that he repeated this motif to imitate the ringing of bells (Ex. 10 above).

In the setting for five voices, the phrases of the antiphon are divided over three parts. The elaboration of the plainsong melody is examined in Chapter 5 (p. 70), while the symbolic meaning of the ostinato motif in the tenor voice is explained in Chapter 6 (p. 85–86).

VIRGO PRUDENTISSIMA (NJE 25.12)

The motet survives, entirely or in part, in 7 sources: three printed books and four manuscripts. The scoring is for four voices with the following ranges: f–d² (superius), d–g¹ (altus), d–f¹ (tenor), F–bflat (bassus). Length: 73 measures.

The text of the antiphon is inspired by three verses from The Song of Songs (1:4, 6:3, and 6:9). Intended for the Feast of the Assumption of the Virgin Mary (August 15), the antiphon is sung before the Magnificat in First Vespers. Josquin paraphrases the plainsong melody in one or more voices up to and including the words "tota formosa" in m. 48–55. At this point, the tenor sustains the note *d* over four measures, above which the superius and altus repeat the word "formosa" (comely), in imitation and close succession, obviously in order to highlight the beauty of the daughter of Sion. The sevenfold, symbolic repeat of the words "ut sol" is illustrated in Chapter 6, Ex. 17.

Sequences

Except for the *Stabat mater*, all motets in this category employ the melody of the eponymous Gregorian sequence. These chants set poems where the verses form rhyming pairs. Each of the double versicles is sung to the same melody.

---

29   See *NJE* 25, music volume, n. 21.

AVE MUNDI SPES MARIA (NJE 23.10)

The motet survives in one manuscript only. The scoring is for four voices with the following ranges: [d¹–e¹] (superius), e–a¹ (altus), c–a¹ (tenor), G–c¹ (bassus). Length: 301 measures.

The motet lacks the highest voice because its only source, Vienna 15941, has lost one of the four original partbooks. Since Josquin based the polyphony on the entire sequence melody and used the technique of paired voices throughout, the missing superius can, for the most part, be easily reconstructed out of the musical material in the three other voices.[30] The text, attributed to Adam of St. Victor (*d.* 1146) and consisting of eight paired plus two appended versicles, is a song of praise to the Virgin Mary, who is asked to intervene with her son. The polyphonic texture is transparent, and the constantly alternating duets are wholly permeated by the sequence melody. At the end of the first two parts, the binary mensuration changes to ternary, thus emphasizing the nourishing of the child and the opening of the heavenly gates. The exclamation "O" at the opening of the third and last part is set to the motif *sol–mi–mi*, sung by all voices in a descending sequence (Ex. 64).

EXAMPLE 64

---

30   See the Critical Commentary to *NJE* vol. 23, 126. Though accepted as authentic by Noble (*NGD2*, vol. 13, 243) and Finscher (*MGG2*, vol. 9, col. 1219), the motet is largely ignored in scholarly literature as well as in Fallows' Josquin monograph.

BENEDICTA ES, CELORUM REGINA (NJE 23.13)

The motet survives, entirely or in part, in 35 sources: eleven printed books and twenty-four manuscripts. Furthermore, twenty-eight sources contain arrangements for lute or organ of one or more parts. The scoring is for six voices with the following ranges: d^1-d^2 (superius), $c-a^1$ (altus), $c-g^1$ (tenor secundus), $d-e^1$ (tenor primus), $G-b$ (bassus secundus), $G-a$ (bassus primus). Length: 176 measures.

The large number of sources of the vocal version of the motet and numerous instrumental arrangements are proof of the great popularity of *Benedicta es* in the sixteenth century (Fig. 36). It is therefore not surprising that seven composers, among whom Palestrina, based a parody Mass on the motet (see p. 43), and that it was also taken as a starting point for a "Magnificat" by Orlando di Lasso. The south-Netherlandish composer Jean Guyot even added six new voices to the six original ones! Dating from the thirteenth century, the sequence consists of three paired versicles. Each single versicle comprises three or four phrases, the last two of which are set to the same melody in all six versicles. Unlike other composers from the sixteenth century who are known to have set the same text to music, Josquin divides the rhyming text disproportionately over the three parts of his motet: part I contains the versicles 1a–b and 2a–b; part II versicle 3a; part III versicle 3b. It would appear that he was guided by the textual contents rather than the form of the sequence. While versicles 1 and 2 are a glorification of the Virgin, versicle 3a describes how the word was made flesh, and versicle 3b is a prayer to Mary to intervene with her son. In part I, the chant's first phrase is elaborated in canonic imitation by the superius and tenor primus, while the second phrase is quoted more freely by these same voices. Part II, scored for two voices, richly paraphrases the third phrase. In part III, which is again for six voices, this same melodic phrase appears imitatively, in a ternary rhythm, in all voices.

FIGURE 36: The opening of the six-voice *Benedicta es, celorum regina,* copied in 1559 by Anthonius de Blauwe for St. Peter's Church in Leiden. Leiden, Gemeentearchief, Ms. 1439, f. 159ʳ-160.

INVIOLATA, INTEGRA ET CASTA ES 5V (NJE 24.4)
INVIOLATA, INTEGRA ET CASTA ES 12V (NJE *24.5)

NJE 24.4 survives, entirely or in part, in 23 sources: eight printed books and fifteen manuscripts. Furthermore, five sources contain arrangements for lute of one or more parts. The scoring is for five voices with the following ranges: a–d² (superius), a–g¹ (tenor secundus), c–g¹ (altus), d–c¹ (tenor primus), F–c¹ (bassus). Length: 144 measures.

NJE *24.5 survives, entirely or in part, in 2 manuscripts. The scoring is for twelve voices with the following ranges: g¹–g² (discantus primus and secundus), a¹–e² (cantus primus), a¹–d² (cantus secundus), g–a¹ (altus primus and secundus), c–g¹ (altus tertius), c¹–f¹ (tenor primus), c–e¹ (tenor secundus), c–c¹ (bassus primus), G–a (bassus secundus), F–g (bassus tertius). Length: 48 measures.

Josquin's five-voice *Inviolata* was widely disseminated in Western Europe. The great popularity of the original Gregorian chant is attested, among other things, by the many settings made by other sixteenth-century composers. Some of these settings are musically indebted to NJE 24.4. While the text of the sequence originated in the twelfth century, the melody is already found in sources from the eleventh century. The text, which is about Mary's 'immaculate conception', consists of four paired versicles, each of two lines. Then follow three exclamations – O benigna, O regina, O Maria – and a final verse. As has been noted in Chapter 5, the elaboration of the sequence melody differs in the two motets (see p. 71). An interesting aspect of these works is the use of symbolism. In the five-voice setting, Josquin uses harmonic means to express the immaculate conception musically (see p. 77–78); in NJE *24.5, the twelve-voice scoring alludes to the Woman of The Book of Revelation (see p. 89–90).[31]

MITTIT AD VIRGINEM (NJE 24.6)

The motet survives, entirely or in part, in 4 sources: two printed books and two manuscripts. The scoring is for four voices with the following ranges: c¹–a² (superius), e–b¹ (altus), g–c² (tenor), B–d¹ (bassus). Length: 222 measures.

The sequence on which the motet is based originated in France, in the early twelfth century. It consists of six paired versicles, all of five lines. In Josquin's setting, the last double versicle has been omitted, and the doxology "Qui nos salvet per omnia seculorum secula. Amen" (Who may save us for all ages to come. Amen) is appended. The sequence, traditionally sung at the Feast of the Annunciation to the Virgin Mary (March 25), is a poetic expression of the story of Gabriel's annunciation, as related in Luke 1:26–38. Quoted in long note values, the plainsong melody alternates between the superius and tenor, but is sometimes found in the

---

31 Since its first publication in the old Josquin edition, few scholars have considered the attribution of the twelve-voice setting to Josquin in Kassel 38 as convincing. While it is evident that its musical style cannot be compared with anything else written by Josquin, the same holds for Brumel's twelve-voice *Missa Et ecce terraemotus* and Gascongne's twelve-voice canon *Ista est speciosa*, both of which have never had their authenticity doubted. All three compositions must have been absolute novelties at the time. For arguments in favour of Josquin's authorship, see the Critical Commentary to *NJE* vol. 24, 82–84.

other voices as well. For example, in m. 163–185, the melody of versicle 4b is transposed to the bassus, to emphasize the angelic message: "Virgin, accept what God is giving you, so that you will fulfil in a chaste way His plan, and honour your vow." In the following lines – "The maiden listened to the messenger and took heed of what he said" – the music gains momentum by a change of mensuration, to quieten again only in the final phrase. In m. 193, the top voice reaches the then rarely used a^2.

PRETER RERUM SERIEM (NJE 24.II)

The motet survives, entirely or in part, in 41 sources: seven printed books and thirty-four manuscripts. Furthermore, eleven sources contain arrangements for lute or organ of the first part or the entire motet. The scoring is for six voices with the following ranges: d^1–d^2 (superius), d–a^1 (altus primus and secundus), d–e^1 (tenor), G–bflat (bassus primus), F–bflat (bassus secundus). Length: 185 measures.

The late, bipartite *Preter rerum seriem* is one of Josquin's most impressive works. A greater contrast than with the early *Mittit ad virginem* (see above) is hardly imaginable. One only has to listen to the opening of the two motets to realise this. For Ambros, *Preter rerum seriem* was one of Josquin's most original creations:

> Highly mysterious, short motifs like strange hieroglyphs are woven together; it is as if one were entering a temple of the Mysteries over which stretches the starry sky, the notes of the cantus firmus in the minor perfect mode, with 'interior signs' [i.e. the long stems of the longs] like powerful columns of an Egyptian temple supporting the mighty structure of the whole.[32]

The Gregorian sequence, employed as *cantus firmus*, dates from the thirteenth century and consists of three paired versicles. But for the last four notes of versicles 3a and 3b, the version in Josquin's motet is identical with the one found in a gradual-sequentiary copied ca. 1529-1531 in 's-Hertogenbosch (Ex. 65). Although the sequence is often associated with feasts of the Virgin Mary, some sources assign it to Christmas Eve. Since the text focuses on the birth of Jesus, it seems likely that Josquin wrote this motet for December 25, and for this reason wanted to evoke the darkness of the night right from the beginning (Ex. 66). The plainsong melody first appears in long note values in the tenor (m. 1–12) and is then repeated by the superius. This results in a high degree of symmetry. In the second part, the long notes are changed to shorter values, and the melody is also heard in other voices than the superius and tenor. From m. 140 onwards, at the words "Dei providentia" (God's providence), the mensuration becomes ternary, providing a joyful mood and creating a fine counterbalance with the opening.

---

32   *Geschichte der Musik* (Leipzig 1862-1882), vol. 3, pp. 224-225: "höchst geheimnissvoll, kurze Motive wie seltsame Hieroglyphen ineinandergewebt; es ist als trete man in einen Mysterientempel, über den sich der hohe Sternenhimmel wölbt, die Noten des Cantus firmus im Modus minor mit 'inneren Zeichen' wie gewaltige ägyptische Tempelsäulen die mächtige Tectonik des Ganzen stützend." I am grateful to Herbert Kellman for the English translation.

EXAMPLE 65

Pre - ter re - rum se - ri - em   Pa - rit de - um ho_ mi - nem   Vir - go ma - ter.
Nec vir tan - git vir - gi - nem   Nec pro - lis o - ri - gi - nem   No - vit pa - ter.

EXAMPLE 66

STABAT MATER (NJE 25.9)

The motet survives, entirely or in part, in 35 sources: nine printed books and twenty-six manuscripts. Furthermore, eighteen sources contain arrangements for lute or organ of the first part or the entire motet. Phalèse published a setting for solo voice and lute. The scoring is for five voices with the following ranges: c^1–f^2 (superius), c–a^1 (altus primus), f–a^1 (tenor), Bflat–f^1 (altus secundus), F–d^1 (bassus). Length: 180 measures.

The poem "Stabat mater" is considered to be of thirteenth-century Franciscan origin, and has been attributed to, among others, Johannes Fidenza, St. Bonaventure, and John Pecham, an English student of Bonaventure in Paris. As a sequence, *Stabat mater* consists of ten double strophes, each of three lines, in trochaic feet, with the rhyming scheme *a a b*. However, Josquin omitted the strophes 6 and 7, and divided the remaining eight strophes evenly over the two parts of his motet. The text in the first part offers a poignant description of the suffering mother of Christ. The strophes in the second part are a prayer to the Holy Virgin for salvation. The poem came into use as a sequence in the late fifteenth century as part of the Church festival of the Seven Sorrows of Mary, and became extremely popular, particularly in Flanders after 1492, when the first Brotherhoods of the Seven Sorrows were founded. The three earliest polyphonic settings of the text, all dating from ca. 1500, are by Josquin, Gaspar van Weerbeke, and John Browne. The earliest known version of the "Stabat mater" poem as a sequence is found in a Dominican gradual, copied at the end of the thirteenth century in the region of Bologna. Later versions have their origin in fifteenth-century South Germany. Since Josquin, except for his *Stabat mater*, always used the original Gregorian chant as *cantus prius factus* in his sequence motets, it seems likely that, when he composed the motet, he did not know any standard plainsong version. Instead, as *cantus firmus* he chose the tenor of a popular French love song (see p. 74). The four other voices either constitute a polyphonic texture around the *cantus firmus*, or, in order to render the text more audible, proceed in homophony. In doing so, Josquin gives prominence to the verbal content, sometimes in contemplative lines, sometimes in more dramatic passages. The latter is the case in strophe 9b: "Threatened by flames and fire, May I be defended by you, O virgin, On the day of judgement." Here, the binary mensuration is momentarily interrupted by a ternary rhythm, with shifted accents in the entire texture (Ex. 67).

EXAMPLE 67

Hymns
Unlike the sequence, in the hymn all strophes are sung to the same melody.

AVE MARIS STELLA (NJE 23.8)
AVE MARIS STELLA (Strophe 4) (NJE 23.9)

Both works survive in one manuscript only, in Bologna and the Vatican, respectively. The scoring of NJE 23.8 is for four voices with the following ranges: d¹–g² (superius), c¹–d² (altus), f–a¹ (tenor), Bflat–d¹ (bassus). Length: 199 measures. NJE 23.9 is also for four voices: c¹–d² (superius), d–g¹ (altus), c–d¹ (tenor), G–b (bassus). Length: 56 measures.

Chapter 5 explained that Josquin used the old first-mode melody of the hymn, sung at Vespers of many feasts of Our Lady, as a starting point for four compositions (see p. 66-68). In both NJE 23.8 and NJE 23.9 he adheres to the hymn's original liturgical function. Nevertheless, the two settings are in marked contrast with one another.

While the plainsong melody in the undoubtedly earlier NJE 23.9 is treated in long note values as a strict canon in the superius and tenor, with the altus and bassus moving in free counterpoint, NJE 23.8 sets the complete text in seven sections, with the melody appearing in all voices, mainly imitatively. The latter motet consists of two parts, the first part comprising strophes 1–4, and the second strophes 5–7. Despite the fact that the motet is, so to speak, through-composed, the openings of the individual strophes remain clearly recognizable thanks to a leap of a fifth in the plainsong melody.

The Proper of the Mass

Apart from the tract *Domine, non secundum peccata* (NJE 16.10), Josquin chose only one other text for a polyphonic setting from the variable chants of the Mass.

RECORDARE VIRGO MATER (NJE 25.1)

The motet only survives in the second book of Antico's *Motetti novi* from 1520. The scoring is for four voices with the following ranges: d¹–e² (superius primus and secundus), c¹–d² (superius tertius), a–c² (altus). Length: 128 measures.

This bipartite motet is based on the offertory of the same name, sung at feasts of the Virgin Mary as part of the *Missa De beata virgine*. The plainsong melody quoted by Josquin corresponds, to a large extent, with the version found in a late fourteenth-century gradual from the Church of Our Lady in Tongeren. In the composer's time, there existed two versions of the chant, one with a long melisma at the syllable 'a' preceding the closing word "nobis", and one where a new text was sung to this melisma. Since this new text is the main constituent of the motet's second part, it may seem that Josquin's *Recordare* is a musical prayer to the Virgin rather than part of the celebration of the Mass. The motet's overall musical character shows some definite archaic traits on the one hand, as well as some innovative features on the other. In contrast to the polyphonic first part, the second part presents a regular alternation of polyphonic and homorhythmic sections. The high tessitura of the four voices suggests that it may have been commissioned by a female religious order.[33]

Books of Hours

The Book of Hours, called in Latin *Horae*, was the most popular prayer book of the laity in the late Middle Ages. The contents of these often sumptuously illuminated manuscripts or printed books consist, among other things, of the little office of the Virgin (i.e. special prayers in her honour), prayers to the saints, and the Hours of the Passion and Cross, as well as sections from the burial service.

---

33   Although Josquin's authorship of this motet is doubted by several scholars, it has been adopted in the *NJE* as authentic for the following reasons: 1) Antico's attributions are generally reliable. 2) The exceptional tessitura is matched by that of Josquin's *La belle se siet* (see p. 196). 3) The appropriate distribution of the text over the two parts points to the composer's awareness of the textual contents, similar to four other motets by Josquin. 4) The restatements of the head-motif are reminiscent of those in Josquin's *Virgo salutiferi*. 5) The daring treatment of *ficta* in m. 1–10 is also encountered in Josquin's *Fortuna d'un gran tempo* (see p. 221). For a more detailed discussion, see the Critical Commentary to *NJE* vol. 25, 4–8.

AVE MARIA (NJE 23.6)

The motet survives, entirely or in part, in 25 sources: two printed books and twenty-three manuscripts. Furthermore, two sources contain arrangements for organ. The scoring is for four voices with the following ranges: c^1–f^2 (superius), f–b^1 (altus), g–a^1 (tenor), G–d^1 (bassus). Length: 152 measures.

The *Ave Maria* NJE 23.6, also known as *Ave Maria ... virgo serena*, is often considered in the literature as a model of Josquin's compositional style and is, for many music lovers, his most familiar work (Fig. 38). The main part of the text consists of five strophes, that refer to the following five joys of Mary: her conception and nativity, the annunciation of the angel Gabriel, her purification and her assumption. These strophes, found in German and French books of hours, are introduced by the lines "Ave Maria, gratia plena, dominus tecum, virgo serena" (Hail, Mary, full of grace, The Lord is with you, gentle Virgin), and conclude with the little prayer "O mater dei, memento mei. Amen" (O Mother of God, remember me. Amen). The opening lines as well as the melody to which they are set are derived from the eponymous sequence; the final words were well-known as an inscription on medieval portraits and gravestones (Ex. 68). Each of the seven sections is treated as an independent unit. The motet's main stylistic features are its points of imitation, paired duets and homorhythmic passages. The exceptionally high quality of the music was already recognized early in the sixteenth century, as can be concluded from Petrucci's first edition of motets of 1502. In this collection, *Motetti A*, it appears at the head. Furthermore, numerous later compositions are musically related to the motet. For example, Verona 218 contains an eight-voice setting of the same text where the second superius is note-for-note identical to the superius of Josquin's motet. And Ludwig Senfl, who greatly admired Josquin, wrote a six-voice *Ave Maria* in which he used the most important musical motifs from Josquin's piece.

FIGURE 38: The opening of the superius and bassus voices of *Ave Maria* (NJE 23.6). Hradec Králové, East Bohemian Museum, Knihovna, Ms. II.A.7 ('Speciálník Codex'), f. 64'.

EXAMPLE 68

GAUDE VIRGO (NJE 24.2)

The motet survives in 3 sources: one printed book and two manuscripts. Furthermore, an excerpt is found in a musical treatise. The scoring is for four voices with the following ranges: d¹–f² (superius), a–d² (altus), d–a¹ (tenor), d–d¹ (bassus). Length: 106 measures.

Gaude virgo is perhaps Josquin's most joyous motet, and also one of his most appealing. From the many joys of Mary mentioned in late medieval literature, the text selects the following five: Gabriel's annunciation, Christ's nativity, resurrection and ascension to heaven, and Mary's assumption. Hence there is some thematic overlap with the previous motet. The text, a rhymed prayer consisting of six strophes arranged in pairs with an appended "alleluia", can be found in versions of different lengths in many medieval books of hours. The version used by Josquin corresponds with that in a manuscript of the Church of Our Lady in Tongeren. Strophes 1–5 begin with the word "Gaude" (Rejoice). The last one concludes with "gaudium". Although a sequence melody is known to which the text was sung in Josquin's time, it was not used by the composer. Instead, his motet is freely composed. Many striking motifs and syncopations are introduced. This is particularly the case in strophe 2b, where the line "Gaude, Christo ascendente" (Rejoice, in Christ ascending) is treated rhetorically with stepwise ascending melodic lines (Ex. 69).

EXAMPLE 69

AVE NOBILISSIMA CREATURA (NJE 23.11)

The motet survives, entirely or in part, in 6 sources: three printed books and three manuscripts. The scoring is for six voices with the following ranges: bflat–d² (superius), d–g¹ (altus primus), c–g¹ (altus secundus), f–e¹ (tenor), F–c¹ (bassus primus), F–g (bassus secundus). Length: 268 measures.

As we have seen earlier in this chapter (see p. 161), this bipartite motet forms a musical diptych with *Huc me sydereo* (NJE 21.5).[34] The text is found in a manuscript now in Darmstadt, dating from ca. 1520, and entitled *Libellus precum* (Little prayer book). Portions of it were incorporated in various books of hours. The text set by Josquin is in the first person throughout; it begins with a greeting to Mary which incorporates the well-known angelic salutation (Luke 1:28), and continues with a series of invocations that enumerate many of the Virgin's prerogatives.

---

34   Doubts about Josquin's authorship have been expressed by John Caldwell, Howard Mayer Brown, Jaap van Benthem and Joshua Rifkin; see the Critical Commentary to *NJE* vol. 23, 141. However, the suggestion made by some scholars that the motet may have been modelled on *Huc me sydereo* should be rejected, because it is difficult to see why an 'imitator' would have chosen the much shorter Passion motet as a model for this joyous and lengthy ode to the Virgin. Moreover, as discussed in the Authorship-section in the Critical Commentary to NJE 23.11, various melodic features are characteristic of Josquin, and m. 215–230 show the same motivic structure as Josquin's motets *Memor esto* (m. 1–15 / 311–319; Ex. 44) and *Virgo prudentissima* (SA m. 51–54). Fallows, who mentions the motet only in passing in his Josquin monograph (p. 284, fn. 34), seems to have overlooked the discussion of the motet in the *NJE*.

The motet ends with the traditional supplication that includes both Mother and Son. The antiphon employed as *cantus firmus* in the tenor was at that time associated with feasts of the Virgin Mary, and derives its text from Luke 1:28 and 1:42: "Benedicta tu in mulieribus, et benedictus fructus ventris tui" (Blessed art thou among women, and blessed is the fruit of thy womb). In other words, the antiphons used in *Ave nobilissima creatura* and *Huc me sydereo* subtly connect Christ's conception and his death on the cross. Their melodies are identical but for two repeated notes, and they are also elaborated similarly. In each motet, they enter, in long note values, in m. 49, and are likewise sung twice in the second part, in proportionally reduced values. The polyphonic texture of *Ave nobilissima creatura* is dense, and conveys the same atmosphere as some other late works by Josquin.

OBSECRO TE, DOMINA (NJE *24.8)

The motet survives in a tablaturebook for vihuela only. The scoring is for five voices with the following ranges: a–f² (superius), d–a¹ (altus), g–g¹ (tenor), d–g¹ (quintus), A–d¹ (bassus). Length: 118 measures.

This composition is included in a 1547 edition of pieces for two vihuelas, collected and arranged by the Spanish lute virtuoso Enriquez de Valderrábano. One of the two vihuela parts contains a fragmentary text which appears to be a free paraphrase of a lengthy prayer, found in numerous fifteenth-century books of hours. The text addresses the Virgin Mary, who is asked for aid in the hour of death. In the vocal reconstruction of the intabulation, the text of the source has been completed.[35] The tenor of the motet is a *cantus firmus* in long note values, and is indicated with numbers marked with red dots in the tablature. How the composer, by means of a twelvefold repeat of a short motif, alludes to the crown of the Woman of The Book of Revelation is described in Chapter 6, p. 89.

Contemporaneous poems
The name of the poet is known only for *O virgo prudentissima* and *Virgo salutiferi*. With *Illibata dei virgo*, it cannot be excluded that Josquin himself wrote the text, at least partially. The sophisticated poem on which *Ut Phebi radiis* is based seems to reveal the hand of a rhetorician.

ILLIBATA DEI VIRGO (NJE 24.3)

The motet survives, entirely or in part, in 2 sources: one printed book and one manuscript. The scoring is for five voices with the following ranges: bflat–e² (superius), d–g¹ (altus primus and secundus), d–d¹ (tenor), F–c¹ (bassus). Length: 192 measures.

Unfortunately, one of the sources for the work, Petrucci's *Motetti a cinque libro primo*, is missing the partbook containing the altus secundus voice. The other source, Cappella Sistina 15, has suffered extensive ink corrosion. Although recently restored, several passages remain hardly legible. However, a careful comparison of the two sources made it possible to publish a trustworthy transcription of this fa-

---

35   See the Critical Commentary to *NJE* vol. 24, 111–114.

mous motet in the *NJE*. This transcription deviates occasionally from the one in the old Josquin edition. The first part of the text contains an acrostic which reveals the name 'Josquin Des Prez':

Illibata dei virgo nutrix,	Spotless Virgin, nurse of God,
Olympi tu regis o genitrix,	O Mother of the Olympian King,
Sola parens verbi puerpera,	who alone brought forth the Word,
Que fuisti Eve reparatrix,	who has made good the sin of Eve
Viri nephas tuta mediatrix,	and are the mediator for man's sin,
Illud clara luce dat scriptura.	as the Scriptures reveal.
Nata nati alma genitura,	Born of your Son to be his mother,
Des ut leta musarum factura	grant that the joyous handiwork of the Muses
Prevaleat ymis, et suave	shall prevail in our songs, and that our throats
Roborando sonos ut guttura	may coax the sounds to come out in a powerful
Efflagitent, laude teque pura	yet tender way, and in pure praises to you
Zelotica arte clament ave.	call out with zealous art: 'ave'.

Whereas the first part of the poem shows such great complexity that it could point to a professional hand, the simplicity of the text in the second part of the motet is reminiscent of the contents of a book of hours. This contrast is mirrored in the music: at first, long melismatic duets in a ternary mensuration, surrounding the sustained notes of the continuously repeated ostinato motif *la–mi–la* in the tenor; subsequently, the shorter, mainly syllabically set lines of the prayer, mostly in a binary mensuration. In this part of the motet, the ostinato motif appears in reduced note values, and the four freely-written voices harmoniously fuse together with the tenor. Dividing this part into shorter sections, Josquin reserves again a ternary mensuration for lines 21 and 22, in which Mary is praised by means of the solmisation syllables *la–mi–la* (= Ma-ri-a): "Salve tu sola, consola amica 'la mi la' canentes in tua laude" (Hail to you, sole beloved, console them who sing 'la mi la' to your praise). Being the apotheosis of the motet, this section is followed by what can be called a tender litany of invocations to the Virgin. (See also p. 84).

O VIRGO PRUDENTISSIMA (NJE 24.9)
The motet survives, entirely or in part, in 7 sources: three printed books and four manuscripts. The scoring is for six voices with the following ranges: d¹–d² (superius), c–g¹ (altus primus), c–f¹ (altus secundus), c¹–g¹ (tenor secundus), f–c¹ (tenor primus), G–bflat (bassus). Length: 190 measures.

This bipartite motet is based on a poem by Angelo Poliziano (*d.* 1494), friend and protégé of Lorenzo de' Medici. Of the original ten strophes, Josquin omitted four, making the poem "an even stronger, more personal, and more dramatic plea to the Virgin ... than Poliziano appears to have intended."[36] As in his *Benedicta es* (see p. 169), Josquin divides the text disproportionally over the parts of his motet. In the

---

36   Howard Mayer Brown, 'Notes Towards a Definition of Personal Style: Conflicting Attributions and the Six-part Motets of Josquin and Mouton', in *ProcU*, 185–207, at 190.

first part, Mary is exalted in a description of her power and in an enumeration of her attributes (strophes 1–4), in the second part she is asked to intervene with the Lord Jesus Christ on behalf of the praying person (strophes 5–6). The motet is based on the antiphon *Beata mater*, sung at feasts of the Virgin. Of this antiphon, numerous versions are known, but none of them corresponds entirely with the *cantus firmus*. In part I, the chant is stated, mainly in breves, in the tenor primus, and repeated in canon after two measures at the fifth above in the tenor secundus. The chant appears once more in part II, in shorter note values and with some changes in the melody. Josquin adopts an unusual procedure in his setting. He not only uses the text of the antiphon in the *cantus firmus*, but in the second part also interpolates Poliziano's text in three different places with the three short phrases of the chant. In spite of the six-voice scoring, the texture is transparent throughout. Paired duets provide colourful contrasts in the opening. The third strophe is sung by the superius and altus secundus; Mary is called here "the star of the sea", and dark whirlwinds are evoked by the change to a ternary mensuration. The second part opens with the word "Audi" (Hear [your humble servants praying to you]), sung in m. 109–116 and 125–131 no less than sixteen times by the freely-composed voices, introducing the final prayer sung by the whole ensemble.

UT PHEBI RADIIS (NJE 25.10)

The motet survives in 2 sources: one printed book and one manuscript. The scoring is for four voices with the following ranges: c^1–d^2 (superius), f–a^1 (altus), f–g^1 (tenor), c–bflat (bassus). Length: 73 measures.

This short motet is, structurally, one of Josquin's most playful works. The origin of the text is unknown, but the virtuoso hexameters seem to be from the hand of a rhetorician rather than that of the composer himself. In each of the two strophes, the verse begins with the name of one or more notes of the Guidonian hexachord. This is done in an additive way, ascending in the first strophe, descending in the second strophe:

Ut Phebi radiis soror obvia sidera luna,
*Ut re*ges Salomon sapientis nomine cunctos,
Ut re mi pontum querentum velleris aurum,
etc.

*La*tius in numerum canit id quoque celica turba,
La sso lege ferens eterna munera mundo:
La sol fa ta mina clara prelustris in umbra,
etc.

Translation
Ut – As the Moon, sister of Phoebus, rules with her rays the stars in her path,
Ut re – As Solomon rules all kings in the name of the wise,
Ut re mi – As the oars of those in quest of the Golden Fleece rule the sea,
etc.

La – Everywhere the heavenly host in verse sings this also,
La sol – Bringing gifts to a tired world according to Law Eternal:
La sol fa – In fact, a radiant gem, shining bright in the dark,
etc.

Since both strophes refer to Gideon's fleece (Judges 6:36–40), some authors have suggested that the motet could have been written for one of the meetings of the Order of the Golden Fleece.[37] Historical evidence, however, is lacking. The first strophe gives a nice example of Homeric similes. These develop into the verse, "So you, O Virgin Mary, rulest over all that is." In the second strophe, the heavenly host sings the praises of the birth of Christ to "an inviolate mother". It therefore cannot be excluded that the fleece refers to the hymen of Mary, who is said to have conceived through the Holy Spirit without sexual intercourse. If this interpretation is correct, the motet may have been destined for Christmas Eve, in which the coming of the Son of God, the "radiant gem, shining bright in the dark", is celebrated, i.e. the beginning of the history of man's salvation. The last verse is a 'memento' addressed to "Christ Jesus, King, God on high."

The Guidonian hexachord not only serves as a guiding principle for the composition of the text, but also as a starting point for the tenor and bassus. The procedure followed by Josquin is described p. 75 in Chapter 6, and the symbolic meaning of the ascending and descending series of solmisation notes explained. Above the breves in the two low voices, the superius and altus sing the poetic main text, frequently imitating each other.

VIRGO SALUTIFERI (NJE 25.13)

The motet survives, entirely or in part, in 10 sources: five printed books and five manuscripts. Furthermore, one source contains an arrangement for organ of the last part. The scoring is for five voices with the following ranges: d^1–e^2 flat (superius), c–a^1 (altus primus), d–e^1 (tenor), c–g^1 (altus secundus), G–c^1 (bassus). Length: 213 measures.

This refined tripartite motet is based on a text by Ercole Strozzi (*d.* 1508), a poet at the court of Ercole d'Este at Ferrara (Fig. 39). The poem, which shows erudite humanistic traits, is a song of praise to the glorious Virgin, who as "mother of the thundering God" and as "benign star of the turbulent sea" brings salvation to mankind. As in the five-voice *Inviolata* (see p. 71), two of the five voices are canonic. In the present motet, the familiar antiphon *Ave Maria* serves as *cantus firmus* in the canonically treated tenor and superius. It appears once in each of the three parts (see p. 68–69). The three freely-composed voices are marked by graceful melodic lines. The entry of the antiphon in m. 43 has a climactic effect. In the middle part, the quotation of the antiphon seems to involve a chromatic turn in the harmony in m. 145, probably meant to symbolize the meaning of the text in the other voices (see p. 77). In the final passage, all voices unite in an overwhelming "alleluia".

---

37 See Prizer, 'Music and Ceremonial in the Low Countries', and Jaap van Benthem, 'A Waif, a Wedding and a Worshipped Child: Josquin's *Ut Phebi radiis* and the Order of the Golden Fleece', in *TVNM* 37 (1987), 64–81.

Texts of unknown origin
The first of the two remaining Marian motets is transmitted with its title only. The text of the second motet is a compilation of six prayers to the Virgin, the origin of which is unknown, with a final prayer addressed to Jesus Christ. Four of these texts contain phrases from antiphons.

FIGURE 39: The opening of the altus and bassus voices of *Virgo salutiferi*. Florence, Biblioteca Medicea-Laurenziana, Ms. 666 ('Medici Codex'), f. 112'.

AVE VIRGO SANCTISSIMA (NJE *23.12)

The motet survives only with the title 'Ave sanctissima virgo' in the *Selectissimae necnon familiarissimae cantiones ...*, printed in 1540 in Augsburg, in which seven other works are ascribed to Josquin in addition to the present piece. The scoring is for five tenor voices with the range c–f¹. Length: 53 measures.

The words "Ave sanctissima virgo" are found as the opening of a prayer in a Flemish book of hours from the end of the fifteenth century. In the order "Ave virgo sanctissima", they form the first line of a song of praise in a medieval psalter with honorary titles of Mary. However, neither of these texts appears to be a good 'candidate' for the present wordless motet. On the other hand, the little rhyming poem *Ave virgo sanctissima*, set by Francisco Guerrero and first published in 1566, can be combined with the music without any difficulty. In this little poem, the Virgin is called "star of the sea", a "precious pearl", and a "fragrant rose". In the Augsburg edition, *Ave virgo sanctissima* forms part of a group of eleven canons for two to eight voices. In the present motet, the five voices imitate one another at the unison, always after two measures. As a consequence of this procedure, the harmonic building material is per force confined to a few chords. In the graceful melody, ascending and descending rows of notes alternate, as do sections in longer and shorter note values. If the poem set to the melody in the *NJE* is indeed the original text, it appears that the composer wanted to highlight the words "gloriosa" and "rosa" with lengthy melismas.

VULTUM TUUM DEPRECABUNTUR (NJE 25.14)

The motet survives, entirely or in part, in 13 sources: two printed books and eleven manuscripts. Furthermore, two sources contain arrangements for organ of part V. The scoring is for four voices with the following ranges: c¹–f² (superius), e–b¹flat (altus), d–g¹ (tenor), A–e¹ (bassus). Length: 570 measures.

The transmission of this multipartite cycle, which consists of seven motets, is more complex than of any other of Josquin's motets. There are doubts as to whether he conceived the cycle as one work at all, since Petrucci's 1505 edition *Motetti libro quarto* is the only source that includes the entire cycle. Almost all manuscripts contain up to four parts of the cycle in various combinations. Six manuscripts contain part V, *Mente tota*, as an independent composition. Moreover, no *cantus prius factus* is used as a guiding element. Only at the opening of the first motet does the superius quote the corresponding phrase from the plainsong introit of the same name. The opening of part II, *Sancta dei genitrix*, is reminiscent of the well-known Litania Lauretana. In *Christe, fili dei*, the altus is derived from the chanson *J'ay pris amours*, which was widely disseminated in Josquin's time. Doubts as to whether these seven works were conceived together are therefore justified. If this were nevertheless the case, *Vultum tuum* would be Josquin's lengthiest motet. The text of the cycle has been made up of six prayers to the Virgin, to which a seventh prayer is appended, addressed to Christ.

The motets show great stylistic variety. The four-voice polyphony regularly gives way to short duets, and in five motets, the binary mensuration changes briefly to a ternary rhythm. In the homorhythmic sections the top voice is very tuneful. In *Mente tota*, Josquin uses a seemingly endless sequence to express the idea that the faithful, after having changed their conduct, may in the end meet with Christ's joy (Ex. 70). Likewise in the last part, where each of the three text phrases begins with the words "Christe, fili dei" (Christ, Son of God), Josquin employs the rhetorical figure of musical repetition, in order to lend the words greater eloquence.

EXAMPLE 70

Motets on other non-biblical texts

This category includes only two motets, both based on texts from the liturgy. *Absolve, quesumus, domine* was almost certainly composed in 1505 or soon after. The hymn *Nardi Maria pistici* dates from Josquin's Roman period.

ABSOLVE, QUESUMUS, DOMINE (NJE 26.1)

The motet survives only in Toledo 21. The scoring is for six voices with the following ranges: c¹–d² (superius), f–a¹ (altus primus), c¹–g¹ (tenor primus), c–f¹ (altus secundus), f–c¹ (tenor secundus), F–f (bassus). Length: 107 measures.

The motet is based on the last prayer in the Requiem Mass. The text is as follows: "Absolve, O Lord, we beseech Thee, the soul of Thy servant N. from every bond of sin ..." In liturgical books, this text uses the letter N (of "nomini") to indicate the Christian name of the deceased. In the same way, the motet, in its only source, does not specify the name of the deceased. However, particular elements in the music suggest that the letter N should be substituted by the name "Jacobi". As explained in Chapter 6, p. 74 and 84–85, the motet contains both a musical reference to one of Jacob Obrecht's works and a numerological reference to his name. In other words, Josquin seems to have dedicated this motet to his colleague. The two tenor voices perform, in long note values, the introit from the plainsong Requiem Mass, treated canonically at the fifth. In the Toledan manuscript, the music is copied in black notes (see p. 76).[38]

NARDI MARIA PISTICI (NJE 26.7)

The motet survives only in Cappella Sistina 15. The scoring is for four voices with the following ranges: f¹–e² (superius), f–a¹ (altus), f–f¹ (tenor), Bflat–d¹ (bassus). Length: 19 measures.

Dedicated to Mary Magdalene, this hymn consists of two strophes respectively beginning with the lines "Nardi Maria pistici" and "Honor, decus, imperium". Josquin is the only composer known to have made a polyphonic setting of the second strophe. This is to be sung after the plainsong version of the first strophe. The four phrases of the text are divided over four equally short sections. The melody of the original hymn is quoted, slightly embellished, in the superius, with a brief anticipation in the tenor in phrases 1, 3 and 4. Whereas strophe I describes the anointing of Christ's feet by Mary Magdalene, strophe II is an homage to the Holy Trinity.

---

38   Josquin's authorship of the motet has been questioned by Martin Just in his review of fascicle 49 of the old Josquin edition; see *Mf* 18 (1965), 110. Admitting that "the general idiom is suggestive of Josquin", John Milsom's judgement is cautious; see 'Motets for Five or More Voices', in *JosqComp*, 281–320, at 301–303. The principal objections – the unique late Spanish source and the motivic density – are rejected however in Willem Elders, 'Josquin in the Sources of Spain. An Evaluation of Two Unique Attributions', in 'Recevez ce mien petit labeur': *Studies in Renaissance Music in Honour of Ignace Bossuyt*, edd. Mark Delaere and Pieter Bergé (Leuven 2008), 61-70, at 65–67.

A hundred and ten secular works have been catalogued with at least one attribution to Josquin. For about a quarter of these, however, the ascriptions are considered incorrect, either because of the unreliability of the relevant source(s), or because of the stylistic aspects of the music. For more than twenty other works, Josquin's authorship is doubtful.

The majority of the secular works in the *NJE* are chansons with a French text. In addition, 28 pieces survive with only a title or with the first few words of a text. As will be seen, twelve of these were written for instruments. Of the remaining sixteen, twelve open with words in French, one with words in Dutch or German, and two have no title or text incipit. Nonetheless, there can be little doubt that the pieces in this last group were originally composed for voices. The absence of text in the sources might be due to the fact that music copyists and printers outside of the Southern Netherlands and France may not always have felt it necessary to offer music with a French text to their clientele. The *NJE* proposes a reconstruction whenever the text can be completed from a secondary source, such as a contemporary anthology of verse or another composition beginning with the same words. The wordless pieces are examined below in two separate groups.

It can be concluded from the great variety of stylistic features, that secular works cover almost the entirety of Josquin's compositional activity, just like his Masses and motets. The works for three and four voices generally date from an earlier period than the five- and six-voice chansons. The latter, nearly all found in editions published in Antwerp by Susato or in Paris by Attaingnant and Le Roy & Ballard, are without exception preserved with a complete text. If, with the three- and four-voice chansons, the term 'voice parts' is used in the description of the scoring, this means that one or more voices appear without text in the *NJE*.

Secular works for three and four voices

Josquin's chansons for three and four voices that survive with text can be divided into two categories: (a) Chansons following the tradition of the medieval courtly song; (b) Chansons connected with orally transmitted popular songs, borrowing from these not only their text but usually their melody as well. Although category (b) comprises twice as many works as category (a), Josquin may have practised the art of the courtly song, with its sometimes elaborate form, for longer than that of the unpretentious popular song. This is suggested by the fact that category (a) includes early settings such as *A la mort* and *Ce povre mendiant* as well as the late *Mille regretz*. This category also contains chansons that show great stylistic differences. In the case of *Adieu mes amours*, the two categories overlap.

Chansons from the courtly song tradition

A LA MORT (NJE 27.1)

The chanson survives only in Florence 2439. The scoring is for three voice parts with the following ranges: a–e² (superius), g–g¹ (tenor), A–d¹ (bassus). Length: 49 measures.

The text of this chanson addresses the Virgin Mary, and is symbolically related to the Gregorian hymn "Ave maris stella". The hymn's first phrase appears as *cantus firmus* in the bassus, where it is stated twice in long note values, first beginning on the pitch of *d*, then of *A* (see p. 66 and Fig. 16). In the transposition to a fourth below, the modality of the plainsong melody undergoes subtle changes. In m. 1-14, the two upper voices are treated in imitation. Thereafter, they continue in free polyphony.

CE POVRE MENDIANT (NJE 27.5)

The chanson survives in 3 manuscripts. The scoring is for three voice parts with the following ranges: b–d² (superius), A–f¹ (tenor), A–a (bassus). Length: 45 measures.

The French text, the transmission of which is slightly corrupt, is about a mendicant friar complaining of his miserable situation. In this respect, the quotation of verse 16 from psalm 87 (88) in the lowest voice part is entirely appropriate: "Pauper sum ego" (I am poor). These words are set to a six-note motif which is identical to the closing formula of the 8th psalm tone. The motif is sung five times in succession, descending stepwise. In the sixth and last presentation it returns to the initial pitch (Ex. 71). The two upper voices are musically independent of each another.

EXAMPLE 71

Pau - per sum e - go,

Pau - per sum e - go,

MILLE REGRETZ (NJE 28.25)

The chanson survives, entirely or in part, in 11 sources: three printed books and eight manuscripts. Furthermore, fourteen sources contain arrangements for lute or keyboard. The scoring is for four voices with the following ranges: c^1–e^2 (superius), a–a^1 (altus), d–e^1 (tenor), A–c^1 (bassus). Length: 40 measures.

This poignant farewell song is one of Josquin's most popular works. Although no literary source of the text is known, in Attaingnant's edition of the chanson it is attributed to Jean Lemaire de Belges (see p. 34). The choice of the 3rd mode (see p. 71) contributes significantly to the doleful mood of the setting, which is particularly evident in the descending melodic lines in m. 19-24 (Ex. 72). The Antwerp music printer Tylman Susato wrote the chanson *Les miens aussi bref* as a "responce" to *Mille regretz*, Cristóbal de Morales quoted the top voice in his Mass of the same name, and Luys de Narváez made an arrangement for lute, entitled "La cancion del Emperador", by which he may have wanted to remind the listener that the chanson was a favourite composition of Charles V.

EXAMPLE 72

PLUS N'ESTES MA MAISTRESSE (NJE *28.27)

The chanson survives only in Attaingnant's *Trente sixiesme livre contenant xxx. chansons* ... from 1549. The scoring is for four voices with the following ranges: b–c^2 (superius), c–f^1 (altus), d–e^1 (tenor), G–a (bassus). Length: 67 measures.

In the only source of the chanson, the text is somewhat corrupt. The opening refrain – You are no longer my mistress; I must serve another – is also used as the conclusion. The composition shows several contrapuntal infelicities, and the style of the chanson further contributes to its doubtful authenticity.

PLUS NULZ REGRETZ (NJE 28.28)

The chanson survives, entirely or in part, in 23 sources: three printed books and twenty manuscripts. Furthermore, seven sources contain arrangements for lute or keyboard. The scoring is for four voices with the following ranges: a–d² (superius), d–g¹ (altus), d–f¹ (tenor), F–c¹ (bassus). Length: 73 measures.

The poem is a *rondeau* by Jean Lemaire de Belges (see p. 34), written for the celebration of the Treaty of Calais between Emperor Maximilian I and King Henry VII of England. First performed on January 1, 1508, *Plus nulz regretz* is Josquin's one and only secular composition that can be dated accurately. Judging by its many sources, it long remained his most famous chanson. It is the only song among the 58 works copied into the chanson album of Margaret of Austria (Brussels 228) that carries an attribution. Josquin's name appears in the banderole of the initial 'P' at the opening of the superius (Fig. 40). The poem introduces Saturn, Phoebus Apollo, War and Venus, thus evoking the end of battle on the one hand, and the flowering of buds and the red rose of love on the other. For the most part, the text is set syllabically and the verses are treated as single thematic groups, first alternating between paired voices, then imitatively. Performed as a *rondeau*, the chanson is over six minutes long.

FIGURE 40: The initial with Josquin's name in *Plus nulz regretz*. Brussels, Bibliothèque Royale, Ms. 228, f. 27ʳ.

QUANT JE VOUS VOYE (NJE 27.32)

The chanson survives in 3 sources: two printed books and one manuscript. The scoring is for three voices with the following ranges: f¹–e² (superius), g–g¹ (tenor), B–f¹ (bassus). Length: 39 measures.

Although the editors of this cheerful chanson rightly state that the text is corrupt in both London 35087 and Antico 1536 – the German print of 1542 was 'reprinted' from Antico – they have refrained from suggesting a hypothetical reconstruction. As can be concluded from the governing rhyming scheme as well as from the textual content, lines 7 and 8 of the original poem are missing. The resulting ambiguities about text placement in m. 9–19 can be eliminated by reconstructing the two missing lines, and inserting them in this section. Hereupon, in m. 19–20, the structure of the chanson suggests that now the complete refrain from m. 1–8 should be sung. (The editors consider m. 19–20 to be an "abbreviated medial refrain".) The most plausible transcription of the text is obtained by emending and combining the two readings: "When I see you, So carried away by joy I am That it seems to me I am a king. Quite free from care, I find myself ..."[1] The text is set syllabically throughout most of the chanson, and the music has the character of a round dance.

QUE VOUS MADAME (NJE 27.33)

The chanson survives, entirely or in part, in 14 sources: two printed books and twelve manuscripts. Furthermore, three sources contain arrangements for lute or keyboard. The scoring is for three voices with the following ranges: c¹–f² (superius), g–a¹ (tenor), c–d¹ (bassus). Length: 62 measures.

The text of this chanson is a *virelai*, a form of French poetry that consists of a refrain (A), followed by two distiches sung to the same music (B), then a new strophe which is set to the music of the refrain, and concludes with the refrain. Here, a man assures a woman of his everlasting loyalty. The lowest voice is a responsory from Compline on the first Sunday of Lent, stated in long note values. The text runs: "In pace in idipsum dormiam et requiescam ..." (I will both lay me down in peace and sleep ...). The responsory tells us who the chanson is addressed to: not the chatelaine from the courtly tradition but the heavenly Woman. In Compline – the liturgical evening prayer service – the Christian asks her for protection against the evils of night.

VIVRAI JE TOUSJOURS (NJE *28.37)

The chanson survives only in Cambrai 125-128. The scoring is for four voices with the following ranges: a–d² (superius), d–g¹ (altus), d–f¹ (tenor), G–a (bassus). Length: 65 measures.

The problems in the transmission of this chanson are more or less the same as with *Plus n'estes ma maistresse* (see above). The authenticity of this chanson is also doubtful. The lover tells his mistress that his desire will only be satisfied if she appreciates his grief.

Chansons from the folk song tradition

ADIEU MES AMOURS (NJE 28.3)

The chanson survives, entirely or in part, in 18 sources: four printed books and fourteen manuscripts. Furthermore, nine sources contain arrangements for lute

---

1   See Marianne Hund and Willem Elders, 'Unravelling Josquin's *Quant je vous voy*'. With a postscript on *El grillo*, in *EM* 41 (2013; forthcoming).

or keyboard. The scoring is for four voice parts with the following ranges: d¹–d²
(superius), f–b'flat (altus), f–d¹ (tenor), Bflat–a (bassus). Length: 60 measures.

As mentioned above, this chanson is on the borderline between the chansons
from the courtly song tradition and those originating in folk song. The text and
melody, alternately sung in the tenor and bassus, are found in the monophonic
chansonnier of Bayeux, where they have the form of a *virelai* (see above, *Que vous
madame*). The text in the superius is a *rondeau*. Both texts begin with the words
"Adieu mes amours". The top voice continues with a long poem where the singer
bids farewell to his sweetheart because his purse is no longer filled by the king, in
the two low voices he takes leave for the same reason until next spring. The beautiful melismatic melody in the superius contains three brief vocalises (Ex. 73).

EXAMPLE 73

A L'OMBRE D'UNG BUISSONNET (NJE 27.2)

The chanson survives in 4 sources: two printed books and two manuscripts. The
scoring is for three voices with the following ranges: g–d² (superius), d–b'flat (ten-
or), G–d¹ (bassus). Length: 77 measures.

Robin finds Bellon (la belle Marion?) in the shade of a thicket, where she is
making a garland. Although he offers her a large chunk of his bread, she does not
respond to his advances. The cheerful melody, of unknown origin, is quoted in
imitation in all voices. Strophes 1, 2 and 5 contain three lines, and are interrupted
by two distiches. The latter are for two voices and set to the same music. The first
is sung by Robin (bassus and tenor), the second by Bellon (tenor and superius), an
octave higher. The final lines of strophes 2 and 5 are musically similar to the last
line of strophe 1.

BAISIEZ MOY (NJE 28.4)

The four-voice version of the chanson survives, entirely or in part, in 11 sources: seven printed books and four manuscripts. Furthermore, two sources contain arrangements for lute. The scoring is for four voice parts with the following ranges: c¹–c² (superius), g–g¹ (altus), f–f¹ (tenor), c–c¹ (bassus). Length: 38 measures.

Already in the fourteenth century, "baiser" meant both "kiss" and "make love". When the boy suggests she might have sex with him, the girl replies that she will not because her mother would not like it. The melody of the folk song, of unknown origin, is quoted in the bassus and, after one measure, is answered canonically, a fourth higher, in the tenor (Fig. 41). Simultaneously, superius and altus perform a 'counter melody', which likewise is treated as a canon at the fourth, and in m. 11–15 and 26–30 derives its material from the song (Ex. 74). The *NJE* provides no text in the upper voices. From most of the sources, however, can be concluded that these voices may have been conceived vocally as well.[2] The opening of Josquin's chanson is quoted literally in the Kyrie of Mathurin Forestier's five-voice *Missa Bayse moy*.[3]

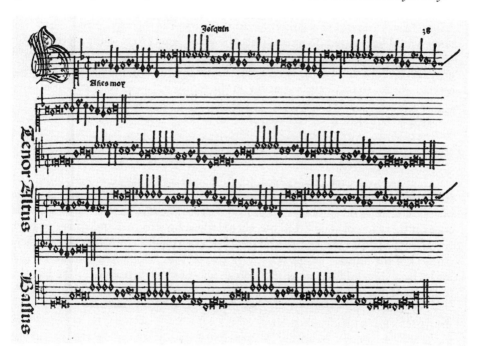

FIGURE 41: The four-voice canonic *Baisiez moy*. Petrucci, *Canti B* (Venice 1503), no. 34.

---

2   The King's Singers (RCA Victor 09026 61814 2) have recorded the chanson in a four-voice version.

3   It seems highly improbable that the six-voice version of *Baisiez moy* is also from Josquin's hand. It is anonymous in the earliest source, Petrucci's *Canti B* of 1502, and its first attribution to Josquin dates only from 1545. The expansion with an additional canonic pair of voices, which produce several contrapuntal infelicities, transforms the light-footed chanson into a clumsy piece of music.

EXAMPLE 74

BELLE POUR L'AMOUR DE VOUS (NJE 28.5)

The chanson survives in 2 manuscripts. The scoring is for four voices with the following ranges: a–c² (superius), d–f¹ (altus), d–d¹ (tenor), A–g (bassus). Length: 38 measures.

Boy: "Sweetheart, I specially came to this town for the love of you." Girl: "Nobody would have cared if you hadn't." The tenor seems to be quoting the original song of unknown origin. Whereas phrases 1–3 are repeated in the bassus at the lower fifth, from m. 29 onwards the four voices continue independently from each other, in order to focus the attention on the repeat of the words "demandoy mye".

DICTEZ MOY BERGERE (NJE *28.10)

The chanson survives, entirely or in part, in 2 manuscripts. The scoring is for four voices with the following ranges: c¹–d² (superius), g–a¹ (altus), c–d¹ (tenor), G–a (bassus). Length: 57 measures.

This chanson is attributed to both Josquin and La Rue. The double canonic structure (4 *ex* 2), both canons at the upper fourth as in *Baisiez moy* (see above), and the bucolic character of the text point to Josquin's authorship. La Rue's oeuvre does not contain this kind of song. "Tell me, shepherdess, how to pass and where to go, I've come from the river. So, please, tell me." The chanson has an A B A' form, where B consists of the phrase "Je suis venu de la riviere" and A' of a repeat of m. 1–14, followed by a threefold repeat of the words "Dictez le moy (bergere)". The charming folk song is quoted in the altus, and followed after one measure in the superius.[4]

EN L'OMBRE D'UNG BUISSONNET (NJE 27.7)

The chanson survives, entirely or in part, in 7 sources: four printed books and three manuscripts. Furthermore, one source contains an arrangement for lute. The scoring is for three voices with the following ranges: c¹–c² (superius), g–g¹ (tenor), Bflat–e¹ (bassus). Length: 43 measures.

---

4   The declamation of the text in the two upper voices can be brought more in line with the character of a folk song by contracting in m. 1–2, 16–17 and 31–32 the two syllables of "Dictez" to "Dite", allowing "moy" to be sung on the second note, and the second, accentuated syllable of "bergere" to be sung on the fourth, highest note.

The narrator finds Robin in the shade of a thicket on a river bank, declaring his love to a shepherdess, who replies: "Robin, what do you mean?" As in NJE 27.2 (see p. 192), imitation plays a part in the polyphony, though to a lesser degree (Ex. 75). The musical material of the first two verses is also used for verses 3 and 4. The dialogue in the following lines is introduced by the words "and said to her", set to repeated notes in the two outer voices.

EXAMPLE 75

EN L'OMBRE D'UNG BUISSONNET (NJE *28.13)

The chanson survives, entirely or in part, in 8 sources: three printed books and five manuscripts. The scoring is for four voices with the following ranges: e¹–c² (superius), b–g¹ (altus), f–d¹ (tenor), G–a (bassus). Length: 41 measures.

This third chanson on the amorous encounters of Robin and Bellon is one of a group of polyphonic settings beginning with the words "A [En] l'ombre" that has been called "a musical and bibliographical jungle."[5] The text of the present setting is a shortened version of that of NJE 27.2 (see p. 192). In NJE *28.13, the song melody is quoted in the altus, and after one measure is answered canonically in the superius at the upper fourth. As in *Baisiez moy* and *Dictez moy bergere*, the lower voices likewise develop a canon at the fourth. The dense four-voice texture lacks the melodic and rhythmic light-footedness of the two three-voice settings. The chanson prompted Antoine Brumel to imitate Josquin's (?) double-canon technique at the interval of the upper fourth throughout his *Missa A l'ombre d'ung buissonet*, but without using much of the melodic material of the original song.

ENTRÉE SUIS (NJE 27.8)

The chanson survives in 2 manuscripts. The scoring is for three voice parts with the following ranges: c¹–e² (superius), f–a¹ (tenor), c–e¹ (bassus). Length: 45 measures.

The two sources show considerable differences in the seven-line text, which has been emended in the *NJE* on the basis of the text of Josquin's four-voice setting of the same song (NJE 28.14, see below). The text of the four-voice setting, however, suggests that the opening of NJE 27.8 should rather be read as "Entré(e) *je* suis". Depending on the choice of reading, either the girl or the boy is upset because she (he) cannot find a new boy- (or girl)friend. A folk song of unknown origin is quoted in the tenor, and there are anticipatory imitations throughout in the

---

5   See the Critical Commentary to *NJE* vol. 28, 177.

superius. The musical material of the first two verse lines returns in lines 3 and 4. The instrumental bassus acts as a lively counterpart.

ENTRÉ JE SUIS (NJE 28.14)

The chanson survives, entirely or in part, in 13 sources: three printed books and ten manuscripts. The scoring is for four voices with the following ranges: d¹–e² (superius), Bflat–g¹ (altus), D–a¹ (tenor), Bflat–d¹ (bassus). Length: 55 measures.

This four-voice setting is based on the same text as the previous chanson, and the tenor voices of both are almost melodically identical. In the present setting, which must have been written somewhat later, all parts are vocal. The melody in the tenor is imitated after two measures by the bassus, a fifth lower. Also in contrast to the earlier setting, the last verse line "Le sarai je ou non?" (Shall I know it or not [whether I will find a lover]?) is spun out over no less than fifteen measures.

GUILLAUME SE VA CHAUFFER (NJE *28.17)

The chanson survives in 6 sources: five printed books and one manuscript. The scoring is for four voice parts with the following ranges: f¹–b¹flat (superius primus and secundus), the tenor sings the note d¹ only, G–d (bassus). Length: 26 measures.

The only attribution to Josquin of this chanson is found in Marin Mersenne's *Harmonie universelle* of 1636. The earliest source in which the chanson survives with its text is the song book of the Swiss clergyman Johannes Heer, dating from the 1510s, who is assumed to have copied the chanson when he was studying in Paris. He gave it the title "Carmen gallicum Ludovici XI regis Francorum". Glarean included the chanson in his *Dodecachordon* of 1547, naming the tenor "regis vox", the voice of the king. As the shortest and most straightforward chanson in the *NJE*, this voice part holds the tone *d¹* for the duration of the whole piece, while the bassus repeats the interval *G–d* twenty-five times and the canonic superius voices sing the text to a simple seven-/eight-note motif, which is repeated continuously. Glarean's treatise is the source of the anecdote that the musically ignorant (?) king would have been given this one note to sing. However, it cannot be excluded that the king himself composed the music, and that Mersenne, over a century later, may have been mistaken about the attribution. The text says that Guillaume is warming himself by the fireplace.

JE RIS (NJE *28.19)

The chanson survives in 3 manuscripts. The scoring is for four voices with the following ranges: a–c² (superius), c–f¹ (altus and tenor), A–c¹ (bassus). Length: 37 measures.

The four-line poem expresses contradictory feelings: "I laugh but a tear is in my eye. I sing without having any joy ..." As such, the text brings to mind the oxymoron in Alain Chartier's poem *Triste plaisir et douleureuse joie*, on which Binchois based his renowned *rondeau*. It seems unlikely that the chanson is related to a folk song. The descending melodic lines in the tenor, often imitated in the other voices, perfectly match the character of the text.

LA BELLE SE SIET (NJE 27.20)

The chanson survives only in Antico's *La couronne et fleur des chansons a troys* from 1536. The scoring is for three voices with the following ranges: G–d¹ (bassus primus), F–d¹ (bassus secundus), F–bflat (bassus tertius). Length: 149 measures.

NJE 27.20 is Josquin's longest chanson. The text goes back to a medieval folk romance relating the moving story of a girl sitting at the foot of a tower, where the
chatelain, her father, has imprisoned her beloved. In view of the dialogue between
the father and the daughter, the scoring for three low male voices is striking. To the
father's question of whether she wants a husband or a lord, the negative answer is
quite unequivocal because of the sustained notes of the top voice in m. 63f. The text
returns to the fore in m. 121f., where the father says that her friend "will be hanged
tomorrow at daybreak" (Ex. 76). By regularly making use of repeated notes, Josquin
reinforces the narrative character of the music. There is an earlier setting of the song
by Dufay. In addition, two Mass settings by Johannes Ghiselin and Marbriano de
Orto, and a Credo (NJE *13.3) attributed to Josquin are modelled on the song.

EXAMPLE 76

MON MARY M'A DIFFAMÉE (NJE 27.27)

The chanson survives, entirely or in part, in 4 sources: one printed book and three
manuscripts. Furthermore, one source contains an arrangement for lute. The scoring is for three voices with the following ranges: d'–f² (superius), g–g' (tenor), d–a'
(bassus). Length: 34 measures.

Consisting of five strophes with a varied rhyme, the text relates the story of a woman beaten by her husband, because she has a lover. The original melody, found in the
fifteenth-century song book Paris 12744, is quoted in the tenor, and imitated in the
other voices. The many note repetitions contribute to the narrative character of the
chanson. The musical setting of the first two lines is also used for lines 3 and 4.

SI J'AY PERDU (NJE 27.34)

The chanson survives in 4 sources: two printed books and two manuscripts. The
scoring is for three voices with the following ranges: c–g' (superius), c–e' (tenor),
G–d' (bassus). Length: 71 measures.

In this chanson a girl complains of having lost her friend, even though he had
promised to be loyal "for the entire month of May". The original melody, found in
the fifteenth-century song book Paris 12744 where it takes the form of a *ballade*,
is quoted in the tenor, and each of the ten phrases is imitated in the superius, a
fourth or a fifth higher. The ten-line poem is set to music according to the following
formal outline: A B A B C C D E D E'. The last line in particular, "et qu'en voullez
vous donc dire de moy?" (And what then will you say about me?), where all voices
participate in a stretto-like motion with short note values, is elaborated with great
virtuosity.

SI J'AY PERDU (NJE 28.32)

The chanson survives in 3 manuscripts. Furthermore, nine sources contain arrangements for lute. The scoring is for four voices with the following ranges: d¹–c² (superius), f–g¹ (altus), d–e¹ (tenor), G–bflat (bassus). Length: 44 measures.

The eight-line poem in this four-voice setting has lines 1–4 and 7–8 in common with the text of the three-voice setting NJE 27.34 (see above). In the *NJE* the text has been expanded by two strophes, taken from the same song book as the *cantus prius factus* of the two preceding chansons (NJE 27.27 and NJE 27.34). Since the last two lines are treated as a refrain, the poem shows the form of a *ballade*. The outline of the melodic material as well as the text in the song book show several differences with the two polyphonic settings. This can be attributed to the oral tradition within which this type of song circulated. Although Helmuth Osthoff suggested that Josquin's authorship of the four-voice *Si j'ai perdu* may have been a mistake of the scribe of the 'Strozzi Chansonnier', which carries the only attribution for the present setting,[6] the piece has been adopted in the *NJE* as authentic. However, there is reason to question this decision. The chanson lacks the lively character of the earlier setting. M. 25-34 are unworthy of a great composer, and, more in general, the music is nowhere stamped with some mark of Josquin.

SI J'EUSSE MARION (NJE *27.35)

The chanson survives only in Antico's *La couronne et fleur des chansons a troys* from 1536. The scoring is for three voices with the following ranges: f–a¹ (superius), f–f¹ (tenor), Bflat–d¹ (bassus). Length: 49 measures.

No folk song is known to survive with the text of *Si j'eusse Marion*. Yet the melody stated in the tenor of the chanson clearly has the character of a chanson rustique. The boy (Robin?) dreams of having Marion entirely for himself, leading her to the woods "to dance a tourdion" – a lively dance in triple metre – before taking her to his home. The eight-line poem is set to the scheme A B A B' C D E F. The outer voices mostly anticipate the melody in the tenor with a richly embellished version of it.

TANT VOUS AIMME (NJE 28.33)

The chanson survives only in Florence 2442. The scoring is for four voices with the following ranges: c¹–d² (superius), c¹–a¹ (altus), f–d¹ (tenor), Bflat–c¹ (bassus). Length: 38 measures.

This chanson survives in its only source without the lowest voice, and is published in the *NJE* with a reconstructed bassus. The text consists of four lines, the last two being repeated at the end of the poem. The musical setting follows this scheme: m. 1–13 = m. 26–38. The boy loves his little shepherdess so much that he picked three roses in his father's garden for her.[7] The simplicity of the text is mirrored in the unpretentious musical setting.

---

6   Osthoff, vol. 2, 175.

7   The poem has "trois fleurs d'amour".

The Virgil motets

The two settings of texts from Virgil's *Aeneid* are best designated as secular motets. Whether these works were composed when Josquin worked in Italy or in the Southern Netherlands is not clear. Since Isabella d'Este, who in 1490 had married the Duke of Mantua (see p. 24), showed a lively interest in the great Latin poet, born in the vicinity of that city, an Italian origin cannot be excluded.

DULCES EXUVIE (NJE 28.11)

The motet survives in 2 sources: one printed book and one manuscript. The scoring is for four voices with the following ranges: b–d^2 (superius), c–g^1 (altus), c–e^1 (tenor), G–a (bassus). Length: 85 measures.

The text, from Book 4, lines 651–654, is Dido's lament after Aeneas' unforeseen departure. Some anonymous settings of this fragment are known, along with settings by Marbriano de Orto, Johannes Ghiselin, and Jean Mouton. The superius of Mouton's setting is identical to the same voice part in Josquin's motet, but views diverge as to who borrowed from whom. Josquin's *Dulces exuvie* shows the hallmarks of the imitative-homophonic motet style from around the turn of the century. When the three lower voices are performed instrumentally, as suggested by Jaap van Benthem, a song in the style of the North-Italian *frottola* results rather than a secular motet.[8] The mood of the music expresses the plaintive character of the text. The last two lines run as follows: "I have lived my life and accomplished the course assigned by Fate, and now my shadow will pass in all its greatness under the earth." The motet concludes in the 3rd mode, which at that time was associated with distress.

FAMA MALUM (NJE 28.15)

The motet survives, entirely or in part, in 2 manuscripts. The scoring is for four voices with the following ranges: c^1–d^2 (superius), f–g^1 (altus), c–e^1 (tenor), A–c^1 (bassus). Length: 93 measures.

The text of lines 174–177 from Book 4 in the *Aeneid* describes how Rumour, of all evils the swiftest, becomes more persuasive as it circulates. At the opening of the motet, the *NJE* places the syllables of the word "malum" according to their position in the manuscript London 8 G.VII, thereby suggesting by the accentuation the influence of the hexameter (Fig. 42). It is nevertheless clear from other passages – particularly in m. 32f. and 60f. – that it has been Josquin's intention to remain independent of the Latin prosody rather than to aim at a metrically 'correct', humanistic approach. Such an approach would moreover have interfered with the imitative design of the counterpoint. In the passage "of all evils the swiftest", Josquin returns melodically to the beginning, setting the word "velocius" in a stretto-like motion (Ex. 77).

---

8   See Jaap van Benthem, 'Ist Josquins *Dulces exuvie* eine Motette?', in *TVNM* 56 (2006), 77–95; see also Michael Zywietz, '*Dulces exuviae* – Die Vergil-Vertonungen des Josquin des Prez', in *Archiv für Musikwissenschaft* 61 (2004), 245–254.

FIGURE 42: The opening of *Fama malum*. London, British Library, Ms. 8.G.VII, f. 15'-16.

EXAMPLE 77

The *frottole*

Two of the three following settings belong to the genre of the *frottola*, the most popular Italian secular song form of the late fifteenth and early sixteenth centuries. The third setting is a *canto carnascialesco*, a part song very similar to the *frottola* in style and form. The structural scheme of these songs is dependent on the poetic form of the text.

EL GRILLO (NJE *2812)

The song survives only in Petrucci's *Frottole libro tertio* (1504) and in the 1507 reprint. The scoring is for four voices with the following ranges: c'–a' (superius), g–g' (altus), d–e' (tenor), G–g (bassus). Length: 38 measures.

Nowadays, few of Josquin's works equal the popularity of his *El grillo*, which is often used as an encore after performances of Renaissance music. The text says that the cricket is a good singer, but behaves unlike birds because he always stays on one note, holding his song for a long time. The moral that can be drawn from the song is that, "in matters of love, sweet fanciful talk is worth less than endurance and fidelity."[9] After opening his song with the refrain ("El grillo, el grillo è bon cantore"), which also concludes the piece, Josquin creates an antithesis between the words "che tiene longo verso" (he holds his song a long time) and "dale breve grillo canta" (the cricket sings, starting from the *brevis*). The unbroken 'song' of the cricket is reflected in m. 7–11, and his chirp in the ever shorter notes in m. 12–17 (Ex. 78). The formal outline is A B C A D E D' E' F A. Unlike what is proposed in the *NJE*, the final refrain is best limited to m. 18–22. The gematric plan of the song is described on p. 94.

EXAMPLE 78

9   Marianne Hund, 'Fresh Light on Josquin Dascanio's Enigmatic *El grillo*', in *TVNM* 56 (2006), 5–16. Hund (see fn. 1 above) rejects the interpretation of the *frottola* given by Grantley McDonald in his article 'Josquin's Musical Cricket: *El grillo* as Humanist Parody', *AcM* 81 (2009), 39-53.

EXAMPLE 78 (continued)

IN TE, DOMINE, SPERAVI (NJE *28.18)

The song survives, entirely or in part, in 22 sources: two printed books and twenty manuscripts. Furthermore, five sources contain arrangements for lute. The scoring is for three or four voice parts with the following ranges: d^1-c^2 (superius), $f-f^1$ (altus and tenor), $F-c^1$ (bassus). Length: 34 measures.

No other *frottola* from the sixteenth century circulated more than *In te, domine, speravi*. This may be due to the text, which is of a sacred nature and contains, in each of the three strophes of the Italian poem, a reference in Latin to the Bible: in strophe 1 to verse 1 from Ps. 30 (31) or 70 (71) and Job 9:29; in strophe 2 to verse 6 from Ps. 141 (142); in strophe 3 to verse 1 from Ps. 122 (123). Having lived and laboured in vain (Job 9:29), the poet takes refuge in God. The plaintive tone of the text is expressed in the descending melodic lines of the superius. Considering what was said about this *frottola* in Chapter 4, p. 62, it could be assumed that the piece was originally in three, rather than four parts, with the tenor and bassus performed on instruments.

SCARAMELLA (NJE 28.30)

The song survives, entirely or in part, in 3 manuscripts. The scoring is for four voices with the following ranges: $a-a^1$ (superius), $d-e^1$ (altus and tenor), $G-a$ (bassus). Length: 38 measures.

With quick chord changes and lively syncopated rhythms, this song is a humoristic parody of soldierly customs. It may have been sung at the carnival processions in Florence under the reign of Lorenzo de' Medici (1469-1492). The pre-existing tune is quoted in the tenor, first beginning on the pitch of c^1, and then in the second strophe at the lower fifth. Compère's *Scaramella fa la galla* as well as Obrecht's *Missa Scaramella* also pay tribute to the tune.

Secular works with reconstructed texts

The texts of the following eight settings have been completed on the basis of a secondary source. If, in the poem "Comment peult avoir joye", the bird losing its prey is a metaphor, love is the subject of all these songs.

ACH HÜLFF MICH LEID (NJE *28.2)

The song survives, entirely or in part, in 6 sources: one printed book and five manuscripts. Furthermore, three sources contain arrangements for keyboard or viol. The scoring is for four voice parts with the following ranges: g–c² (superius), d–g¹ (altus), c–e¹ (tenor), F–bflat (bassus). Length: 73 measures.

This German song, a young woman's love complaint, consists of three lengthy strophes taken from the song book of Arnt von Aich, published in 1519 in Cologne. NJE *28.2 is ascribed in its sources to both Pierre de la Rue and Noel Bauldeweyn, as well as to 'Master hansen' (= Hans Buchner) in Fridolin Sicher's keyboard tablature book. Perhaps the intabulation was from Buchner's hand. In this last source, a later hand, however, wrote "Non. Josquin composuit". The song has therefore been adopted in the *NJE* as a dubious composition. If it is indeed by Josquin, it would be his only song in German. The tenor voice of Adam von Fulda's eponymous song, which according to Glarean was sung all over Germany, is quoted in the bassus, to which three new voice parts are added.

BERGERETTE SAVOYSIENNE (NJE 28.6)

The chanson survives, entirely or in part, in 4 sources: two printed books and two manuscripts. Furthermore, one source contains an arrangement for keyboard. The scoring is for four voice parts with the following ranges: g¹–g² (superius), g–a¹ (altus and tenor), B–c¹ (bassus). Length: 56 measures.

The text is taken from the fifteenth-century song book Paris 12744. The subject is a man's declaration of love to a shepherdess (Ex. 79):

EXAMPLE 79

Josquin quotes the melody of the above-mentioned pre-existing song in the superius, anticipating it up to m. 34 in the tenor an octave lower, then, from m. 39 onwards, in imitation in this same voice.

COMMENT PEULT AVOIR JOYE (NJE 28.7)

The chanson survives, entirely or in part, in 8 sources: five printed books and three manuscripts. Furthermore, two sources contain arrangements for lute. The scoring is for four voice parts with the following ranges: g¹–g² (superius), f–g¹ (altus), g–g¹ (tenor), Bflat–g¹ (bassus). Length: 60 measures.

Used as *cantus prius factus*, this song was known to the west of the Rhine as "Comment peult avoir joye" and to the east as "Wohlauf, gut G'sell, von hinnen" (Ex. 80).[10] The text adopted in the *NJE* is that from the eponymous chanson by Johannes de Vyzeto, preserved in London 35087. Both versions are about a bird: in the French text the bird bemoans the loss of its prey; in the German text it sings throughout the summer. Josquin quotes the beautiful melody in the superius, answering it canonically after two measures an octave lower in the tenor. Glarean included the

---

10   See the Critical Commentary to *NJE* vol. 24, 2.

chanson as a *contrafactum* in his *Dodecachordon* with the text "O Jesu, fili David", which consists of fragments from the story of the woman of Canaan (Matthew 15:22, 27-28). The theorist compares the superius and tenor with "a bridegroom leading his bride ...", while the altus and bassus "sing delightfully before them and with them, and play together so much that they might be considered as players who have been called to a wedding."[11]

EXAMPLE 80

Co -	ment	peult	a -	voir	jo -		ye	Qui	for -		tu- ne	con -	trent?	L oi-seau
Wohl -	auf,	gut	G sell,	von	hin -		nen!	Meins	blei - bens	ist	nim- mer		hie;	Der Mai

LA PLUS DES PLUS (NJE 27.22)

The chanson survives, entirely or in part, in 4 sources: three printed books and one manuscript. Furthermore, one source contains an arrangement for lute. The scoring is for three voice parts with the following ranges: a–d^2 (superius), c–f^1 (tenor), A–c^1 (bassus). Length: 57 measures.

The musical structure of this chanson suggests that the original text may have been a *rondeau cinquain*. There are several poems known to open with the words "La plus des plus". The one found in the Song Book of the Cardinal de Rohan (Berlin, Kupferstichkabinett) fits the music best. In the text, a man affirms that his love for a woman is without equal. The lowest voice serves as an instrumental basis for the predominantly imitative part-writing in the upper voices.

O VENUS BANT (NJE *27.29)

The song survives, entirely or in part, in 4 sources: one printed book and three manuscripts. Furthermore, one source contains an arrangement for lute. The scoring is for three voice parts with the following ranges: c^1–d^2 (superius), g–e^1 (tenor), F–d^1 (bassus). Length: 39 measures.

Eleven polyphonic settings of this popular Flemish song are known, among others by Alexander Agricola and Heinrich Isaac. A fifteenth-century manuscript in the library of the University of Amsterdam contains a text of six strophes that perfectly suits the tenor voice of the present setting. The *Antwerp Liedboek* of 1544 contains a version with no less than eighteen strophes. Whereas Petrucci attributes the song to Josquin, in Seville 5-I-43 it is given to Gaspar (van Weerbeke). Stylistically, the piece does not have much in common with Josquin's other secular works. But since Petrucci's attributions are in general reliable, it has been adopted in the *NJE*. Against the tenor, which states the text mostly in semibreves, the superius and bassus produce a lively counterpoint.

QUI BELLES AMOURS (NJE 28.29)

The chanson survives, entirely or in part, in 3 manuscripts. Furthermore, four

---

11   After Miller, vol. 2, 263.

sources contain arrangements for lute. The scoring is for four voice parts with the following ranges: d¹–c² (superius), g–g¹ (altus), d–c¹ (tenor), G–bflat (bassus). Length: 56 measures.

A text beginning with these words and consisting of three strophes is found in the fifteenth-century song book Paris 12744. It describes how a man on a black horse succeeds in attracting the attention of a chatelaine. The chanson melody, divided into short phrases, is mostly performed alternately, sometimes in imitation, by the superius and tenor; the two other parts provide a brisk counterpoint.

SE CONGIÉ PRENS (NJE *28.31)

The chanson survives in 2 manuscripts. The scoring is for four voices with the following ranges: f¹–d² (superius), c¹–a¹ (altus), f–e¹ (tenor), c–b (bassus). Length: 36 measures.

The manuscript Cappella Giulia XIII.27 only gives the incipit "Recordans de my segnora". Florence Magl. 178 is entirely wordless. The chanson's melodic material, however, is clearly related to Josquin's six-voice chanson *Se congié prens* (see p. 214), based on a folk song of unknown origin. The four-voice version is a canon 4 *ex* 2: both the bassus and altus are, after a half measure, answered at the upper fourth by the tenor and superius. Technically a *tour de force*, the setting produces some harmonic 'clashes' that prompted its editor to doubt Josquin's authorship.

UNE MUSQUE DE BISCAYE (NJE 28.35)

The chanson survives, entirely or in part, in 9 sources: one printed book and eight manuscripts. The scoring is for four voice parts with the following ranges: e¹–d² (superius), b–a¹ (altus), f–f¹ (tenor), Bflat–bflat (bassus). Length: 34 measures.

A text beginning with these words and consisting of four strophes is found in the fifteenth-century song book Paris 12744. It is in the form of a *ballade*. The spelling "une mousse" used in this chansonnier differs in other sources (e.g. *musque*, *moza*). There are contradictory explanations for the cryptic refrain "Soaz, soaz, ordonareqin". According to some scholars, the man is being encouraged by the girl, while others suppose, more probably, that she turns him down.[12] In Josquin's setting, the folk song opens in the altus, and after a half measure is answered canonically at the upper fourth in the superius. Contrary to the original tune, illustrated on p. 106, the composer begins most phrases with a dotted semibreve, thus intensifying the verve of the melody.

Chansons with no known text

HELAS MADAME (NJE *27.13)

The chanson survives, entirely or in part, in 4 manuscripts. The scoring is for three voice parts with the following ranges: a–c² (superius), c–f¹ (tenor), F–c¹ (bassus). Length: 143 measures.

---

12   See the Critical Commentary to *NJE* vol. 28, 427.

An originally strophic poem may have served as a text for this chanson. If so, the caesuras after m. 44 and 118 could mark the end of a strophe. Two of the sources preserve versions to which a fourth *si placet* voice is added. Notwithstanding the attribution to Josquin in a manuscript dating from the 1490s, the treatment of the musical material throws some doubt on his authorship.

JE ME (NJE *27.17)

The chanson survives only in Florence Magl. 178. The scoring is for three voice parts with the following ranges: d¹–d² (superius), d–g¹ (tenor), G–bflat (bassus). Length: 58 measures.

The opening of this chanson is clearly related to that of Ghiselin's *Je suis si trestourte* (I am so confused), which in London 35087 is found with the Dutch translation "Ic ben zo nau bedwonghen". The structure indicates that the original text may have been a *virelai* or a *bergerette*. However, none of the known poems with the incipit "Je me" can be combined with the music of NJE *27.17. Although there are no conflicting attributions, stylistically the piece has little in common with Josquin's genuine secular works.

JE N'OSE PLUS (NJE 27.19)

The chanson survives only in Florence Magl. 178. The scoring is for three voice parts with the following ranges: g¹–a² (superius), g–a¹ (tenor), c–f¹ (bassus). Length: 46 measures.

The original text may have been a *rondeau*, the setting of which has an *ouvert* (first-time ending) after m. 22. As with the previous chanson, no fifteenth-century poem is known to begin with this title. Although the plain counterpoint with 'empty' intervals of over two octaves between the outer voices in m. 34-36, together with the various unreliable attributions in its only source, might cast some doubt about Josquin's authorship, the piece has been published in the *NJE* as authentic.

JE SEY BIEN DIRE (NJE 28.20)

The chanson survives only in Petrucci's *Canti C* from 1504. The scoring is for four voice parts with the following ranges: f–c² (superius), c–f¹ (altus), e–e¹ (tenor), F–c¹ (bassus). Length: 57 measures.

This chanson may have been based on a monophonic strophic song in triple time, the melody of which appears as *cantus prius factus* in the tenor. The text must have numbered six phrases, schematically ordered as A A' B B A A'. The first five notes of the a-phrase are imitated an octave higher in the superius in m. 1, 7, 39 and 45. As such, the chanson shows some affinity with Josquin's *Bergerette savoysienne* (see p. 203). The seemingly homophonic, simple layout of the polyphony suggests that the music was meant to support an original text of narrative character.

LEAL SCHRAY TANTE (NJE *28.21)

The chanson survives in 3 manuscripts. Furthermore, one source contains an arrangement for keyboard. The scoring is for four voice parts with the following ranges: a–d² (superius), d–g¹ (altus), a–e¹ (tenor), F–a (bassus). Length: 35 measures.

The sources provide conflicting attributions to Josquin and La Rue, both of which are contested in the musicological literature. Although the formation of melodies and the use of stretto-like imitations in m. 19–23 and the final section seem to favour Josquin's authorship, the formless structure of the overall piece is an uncommon feature in his compositions. However, the musical features in La Rue's oeuvre likewise show few similarities with those of NJE *28.21.

MADAME HELAS (NJE *27.24)

The chanson survives in 5 sources: one printed book and four manuscripts. The scoring is for three voice parts with the following ranges: a–e²flat (superius), f–g¹ (tenor), Aflat–bflat (bassus). Length: 74 measures.

The original text may have been a *rondeau*, the setting of which has an *ouvert* (first-time ending) after m. 41. One of the manuscript sources gives the heading "Dux Carlus". According to the editors of the chanson, this could mean that the scribe wanted to identify the author of the text either as Charles, Duke of Orléans, or Charles I, Duke of Savoye. No source, however, is known to preserve a poem beginning with "Madame helas". Since the only attribution to Josquin – found in Petrucci's *Odhecaton* (1501) – was removed in the two reprints of this collection, and since, stylistically, the music has little in common with the composer's other chansons, there is reason to doubt its authenticity.

SCHANSON DE JOSQUIN (NJE 28.38, 'Textless piece')

The chanson survives only in Herdringen 9820. The scoring is for four voice parts with the following ranges: g–d² (superius), d–a¹ (altus), c–f¹ (tenor), G–b (bassus). Length: 49 measures.

In Herdringen 9820, NJE 28.38 carries the heading "Schanson de Josquin", a title that is reminiscent of NJE 27.15, which in its only source is called "Ile fantazies de Joskin". The musical structure of the chanson follows the pattern A B A', the A' section (m. 29-42) being a varied repeat of the opening, followed by a coda. The polyphony is predominantly imitative, and the brief motivic repeats in m. 13–18, 19–21 and 24–26 are characteristic of Josquin's musical language.

TEXTLESS PIECE (NJE *28.39)

The chanson survives only in Zwickau 78/2. The scoring is for four voice parts with the following ranges: c¹–d² (superius), d–g¹ (altus), c–d¹ (tenor), F–g (bassus). Length: 37 measures.

The song consists of eight short passages. The setting is predominantly homophonic, with the third, fifth and last passages running out in stepwise descending or ascending scales. Structurally, NJE *28.39 has no counterpart in Josquin's oeuvre – the layout is more reminiscent of some German songs, such as Isaac's well-known *Insprugk, ich muss dich lassen*. The attribution in Zwickau 78/2, a manuscript dating from 1531, must be regarded with great suspicion.

Secular works for five and six voices

As stated on p. 187, Josquin's chansons for five and six voices constitute a more homogeneous group than his works for three or four voices. This is due, among other things, to the fact that they all are settings of French texts and that, contrary to many of the three- and four-voice secular works, all voices are texted. As with the three- and four-voice works, we can draw a distinction between the chansons with a text following the courtly song tradition, and those with a text from the folk song tradition. Even more than the texts of the chansons for three and four voices, the courtly poems evoke a melancholic mood which Josquin always outstandingly expresses in his settings.

The most important sources for these chansons are prints published in Antwerp and Paris from 1544 onwards, i.e. long after the composer's death. It is generally accepted that nearly all of these chansons date from ca. 1500 onwards, and that Josquin was one of the first composers to explore this kind of polyphonic five- and six-voice writing. Only one of the chansons can be dated precisely: *Nymphes des bois*, composed in memory of Johannes Ockeghem, must have been written in 1497 or soon after.

The present group consists of 23 chansons, twelve of which are for five voices, the remaining eleven for six. (Since the five- and six-voice chansons have not yet been published in the *NJE*, it is possible that the selection of chansons discussed below may not entirely match the contents of the forthcoming volumes 29 and 30.) Except for the five-voice *Nymphes des bois*, *Je ne me puis tenir d'aimer*, *Tenez moy en voz bras*, and possibly *Fors seulement* (NJE 30.4) of which only one voice survives, all these chansons contain a two-part canon. These canons are always embedded in the polyphonic texture, the non-canonic voices of which sometimes derive their musical material from the canon melody. In contrast to the chansons for three and four parts, only seven chansons in this group are based on folk songs. For the chansons *Nymphes des bois* and *Nimphes, nappés*, Josquin took a Gregorian chant as a starting point.

Chansons from the courtly song tradition

CUEUR LANGOREULX (NJE 29.2; WW 1)

The chanson survives, entirely or in part, in 4 printed books. Furthermore, one source contains an arrangement for lute. The scoring is for five voices with the following ranges: d'–e² (superius), d–a' (altus), g–a' (quintus), c–e' (tenor), G–c' (bassus). Length: 60 measures.

The poet in the text addresses the sad lover with words of comfort: out of pity, his beautiful mistress will fulfil his desire. After four measures, the superius is answered canonically by the quinta vox, a fifth lower. Josquin creates an antithesis between the words "Cueur langoreulx ... plaindre, gémir" (Languishing heart ... weeping, sighing) and "Résiouys toy" (Be joyful) (Ex. 81). Since the *comes* of the canon only enters after the *dux* has sung "Résiouys toy", the cheerful motif is clearly audible four times in succession. Three voices end with the characteristic falling third, *f–d–d*.

EXAMPLE 81

DOULEUR ME BAT (NJE 29.4; WW 18)

The chanson survives in 3 sources: two printed books and one manuscript. The scoring is for five voices with the following ranges: c¹–d² (superius), a-f¹ (quintus), d–f¹ (altus), d–bflat (tenor), G–a (bassus). Length: 61 measures.

The narrator is overcome by grief, and sorrow makes him feel desperate. From the second measure, Josquin sets the mood of the chanson with a sharp suspended dissonance, and the 3rd mode of the piece as a whole stresses its sad character. The tenor begins the canon melody with the notes e–f–f–e, and, after two measures, these are answered by the quinta vox at the upper fifth. The text in the canon voices is entirely syllabic. The formal outline of the chanson can be indicated with the letters A A' B B C C + coda. C is exclusively reserved for the words "De vivre'ainsi, pour dieu, qu'on me décolle" (By God, I'd rather be beheaded than live in this way). By their continuous repeats, these are strongly emphasized. Willaert based a six-voice setting of the same text on Josquin's canon melody, changing the time interval between the *dux* and *comes* to three measures.[13]

DU MIEN AMANT (NJE 29.5; WW 23)

The chanson survives in 3 sources: two printed books and one manuscript. The scoring is for five voices with the following ranges: c¹–c² (superius), a-a¹ (quintus), d–g¹ (altus), d–d¹ (tenor), G–g (bassus). Length: 92 measures.

The text of the poem takes us back to *Mille regretz* (see p. 189), even though the narrator is now a woman. The departure of her friend is so painful that she will die, bequeathing her heart to him. The distressing mood of the text is masterfully expressed in the music. *Du mien amant* and *Mille regretz* have the head-motif of the superius in common, and end similarly (*Mille regretz* m. 38–40 = *Du mien amant* m. 53–55). The tenor enters with the canon melody, and begins with the notes of the head-motif. After two measures, it is answered canonically by the quinta vox, a fifth higher. The chanson is in the form of a *virelai*, unique among Josquin's five- and six-voice chansons (A B B' A' A). The text has the rhyme scheme *a a b b a* in part A, and *c d d c* in part B (see also *Que vous madame*, p. 191). Performed this way, the chanson is about twelve minutes long.

FORS SEULEMENT (NJE *30.4)

Only one voice survives in the tenor partbook Bologna R142. Length: 70 measures.

The superius of Ockeghem's famous three-voice eponymous *rondeau* serves as the tenor voice part of a chanson that, according to the first index of the manuscript, originally must have been for six voices. A four-voice instrumental setting of the same chanson is published in the *NJE* as a doubtful work (see NJE *28.16).

INCESSAMENT LIVRÉ SUIS (NJE 29.8; WW 6)

The chanson survives in 3 sources: two printed books and one manuscript. The scoring is for five voices with the following ranges: a-c² (superius), g-f¹ (tenor), d–f¹ (altus), c-bflat (quintus), G–a (bassus). Length: 68 measures.

---

13   See Eric Jas, 'Josquin, Willaert and *Douleur me bat*', in *'Recevez ce mien petit labeur'...*, 119–130.

The lover says that he will shortly be subjected to torture, because the one who could prevent this does not come to his help. In the first two lines of the poem, each of the voices enters with a descending triad, the same motif that opens Josquin's *Stabat mater*. It cannot be excluded that the similar subject matter of the two texts inspired Josquin to use the earlier Marian motet as a model. The melody of the tenor is answered canonically by the quinta vox after three measures, at the lower fifth. Lines 1–2 and 3–4 of the five-line poem are set in pairs to the same melodies, which results in the following formal outline: A A' B B' C + coda. The contratenor, which is occasionally musically related to the canonic voices, concludes at the words "mon malheur est de tous aultres le pire" (of all other sorrows, mine is the most awful) with the falling third, *f–d–d*.

JE NE ME PUIS TENIR D'AIMER (NJE 29.11; WW 31)

The chanson survives in 12 sources: three printed books and nine manuscripts. Furthermore, six sources contain arrangements for lute and one for organ. The scoring is for five voices with the following ranges: a–d² (superius), e–g¹ (altus), d–e¹ (tenor), c–e¹ (quintus), G–a (bassus). Length: 78 measures.

Though no less than eight sources transmit the chanson with a Latin text, there is no doubt that the original version was French. The song is about a man who is addressing his sovereign lady, but feels melancholic because his declarations of love are in vain. The mood of resignation is subtly expressed in downwards melodic lines, and the last phrase, "or he shall be half dead", is emphasized in a fourteen-measure conclusion. The five voices move mainly in free imitation, without the usual canonic frame.

NYMPHES DES BOIS (NJE 29.18; WW 22)

The chanson survives, entirely or in part, in 4 sources: two printed books and two manuscripts. The scoring is for five voices with the following ranges: d¹–d² (superius), Bflat–f¹ (altus and quintus), e–e¹ (tenor), E–a (bassus). (The notation in the sources is clefless; the pitch is to be deduced from the staff signatures.) Length: 155 measures.

Josquin's high esteem for Johannes Ockeghem is mirrored in what is considered his most impressive chanson, *Nymphes des bois*. In the elegiac poem, Jean Molinet exhorts the nymphs of the woods, goddesses of the springs, and singers of all nations to mourn Ockeghem, for Atropos – one of the Fates of Zeus – has taken him (see p. 33). The chanson consists of two parts, the first of which is based on the introit of the Gregorian Mass for the Dead (see p. 71). The first four measures of the superius quote the head-motif of Ockeghem's *Missa Cuiusvis toni* (Fig. 43), and the polyphonic progress of the following measures is reminiscent of the older composer's musical style. The second part is more chordal. The distinctly defined phrases contribute to the audibility of the text, which says that Josquin and three of his colleagues should weep over the loss of their "good father" (Ex. 82). In the setting of the final prayer, the sum of the notes equals the numerical value of Ockeghem's name (see p. 84–85]), while in the last measures, the falling third, Josquin's 'signature', is prominent in three of the five voices.

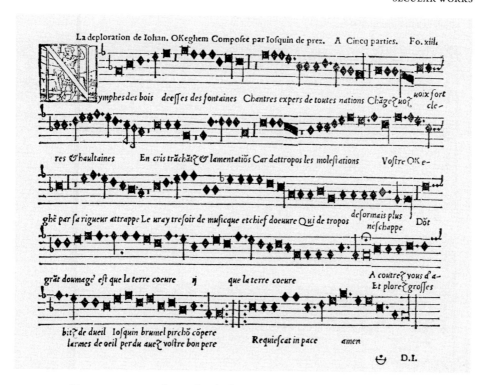

FIGURE 43: The superius voice of *Nymphes des bois*. Susato, *Septiesme livre* (Antwerp 1545), f. 13.

EXAMPLE 82

EXAMPLE 82 (continued)

NIMPHES, NAPPÉS (NJE 30.6; WW 21)

The chanson survives, entirely or in part, in 15 sources: four printed books and eleven manuscripts. Furthermore, three sources contain arrangements for lute. The scoring is for six voices with the following ranges: a–c² (superius), g–f¹ (sextus), Bflat–g¹ (altus), c–bflat (quintus), c–f¹ (tenor), F–f (bassus). Length: 66 measures.

In this chanson, the French text is combined with a Latin text. The narrator asks the nymphs of the waters and the woods to lament his sad state of mind, his spirits being dead rather than sick. In long note values and embedded in the six-voice texture, the quinta and sexta vox perform the Gregorian *cantus firmus* "Circumdederunt me gemitus mortis; dolores inferni circumdederunt me" (The sighs of Death surround me; the sorrows of hell surround me). This chant, derived from the liturgy for the Dead and based on verses 5 and 6 from psalm 17 (18), is treated canonically at the upper fifth (see also p. 21). The presence of this text may have been the key to the chanson's wide dissemination in Lutheran Germany, where it became known in no less than ten sources as a *contrafactum*.[14] Luther himself refers to it in his *Tischreden* (Table conversations). The contrafact text, "Haec dicit dominus", seems to have been written by Conrad Rupsch, Luther's musical adviser. Notwithstanding its polyphonic construction, the chanson has a strong harmonic foundation. False relations in m. 49 and 57 are intended to emphasize the textual content.[15] The last line, in seemingly endless repeats, brings the chanson to a climax. The word "malades" in the superius concludes with the falling third, a^1–f^1–f^1.

PARFONS REGRETZ (NJE 29.19; WW 3)

The chanson survives in 4 sources: three printed books and one manuscript. The scoring is for five voices with the following ranges: f^1–d^2 (superius), g–g^1 (altus), g–b^1flat (quintus), c–g^1 (tenor), G–bflat (bassus). Length: 66 measures.

The text could be by Claude Bouton, esquire in the service of Philip the Fair.[16] Profound sorrow and sad joy cause the narrator to ask for his heart to be put quickly to death. The bassus enters with the canon melody, which after three measures is answered by the superius, an octave higher. In the canon, the first and second text lines are identical, and the other voices are musically related to the melody. The setting has the same formal outline as *Douleur me bat* (see p. 209). The flat/natural oppositions might have been intended to 'paint' the plaintive mood of the text. In the last line, which takes up a third of the chanson, the words "deuil" and "larmes" are emphasized by threefold repetition. In the final chord, the superius introduces the falling third, b^1flat–g^1–g^1.

PLAINE DE DUEIL (NJE 29.20; WW 4)

The chanson survives in 4 sources: two printed books and two manuscripts. The scoring is for five voices with the following ranges: d^1–d^2 (superius), g–g^1 (quintus), d–g^1 (altus), d–e^1 (tenor), G–a (bassus). Length: 52 measures.

The narrator sees his/her pangs of love only increase, and therefore wants to devote the rest of his/her life to the beloved. The chanson opens imitatively in all voices with a four-note motif at the words "Plaine de dueil" which returns at the opening of the second line at "Voyant mon mal". The quinta vox and superius continue this motif canonically at the interval of the fifth. Apart from a few

---

14 See Martin Just, 'Josquins Chanson *Nymphes, napées* als Bearbeitung des Invitatoriums *Circumdederunt me* und als Grundlage für Kontrafaktur, Zitat und Nachahmung', in *Mf* 43 (1990), 305–335.

15 See Patrick Macey, 'An Expressive Detail in Josquin's *Nimphes, nappés*, in *EM* 31 (2003), 401–411.

16 See Osthoff, vol. 1, 68.

short melismas, the setting of the text is syllabic. The division of the chanson into two parts after m. 31 suggests the form of a *rondeau cinquain*. However, the only source to provide additional strophes, Brussels 228, appears incomplete. The doleful mood of the text is subtly expressed in the harmonic progress of the music.[17]

PLUSIEURS REGRETZ (NJE 29.21; WW 7)

The chanson survives, entirely or in part, in 8 sources: four printed books and four manuscripts. The scoring is for five voices with the following ranges: b–c² (superius), a–f¹ (quintus), d–g¹ (altus), d–bflat (tenor), G–a (bassus). Length: 59 measures.

The narrator declares that the many complaints and pains of other men and women on earth are pleasurable compared to what he/she must endure. The mournfulness of the text finds expression in the musical setting. Lines 1–2 and 3–4 of the five-line poem are set in pairs to the same melodies, resulting in the following formal outline: A A' B B' C + coda. (This outline is similar to that of *Incessament livré suis* (see p. 209). After two measures, the head-motif of the superius is taken up by the tenor, and the tenor, in turn, is answered canonically by the quinta vox, a fifth higher, after two measures. As in several of Josquin's other chansons, the altus covers a wide range and is the most virtuoso voice part.

REGRETZ SANS FIN (NJE 30.9; WW 5)

The chanson survives in the editions by Susato and Attaingnant. The scoring is for six voices with the following ranges: c¹–d² (superius), g–f¹ (sextus), d–f¹ (altus), A–d¹ (quintus), d–c¹ (tenor), F–a (bassus). Length: 130 measures.

The poem probably stems from the circle of the *grand rhétoriqueurs*. The narrator prefers a quick death above enduring the endless sadness of life any longer. The five-line refrain at the beginning of the text follows the rhyming scheme a a b b a. The next three lines rhyme with lines 1–3, after which the refrain returns. Except for the second line, which is a varied repeat of the first one, all the following lines are set to new music, resulting in the formal outline A A' B C D E F G [A A' B C D]. After three measures, the tenor is answered canonically by the sexta vox, a fourth higher. It is the top voice, in particular, that illustrates the poetical contents, notably in the subtle melismas at the word "endurer", m. 8–13.

SE CONGIÉ PRENS (NJE 30.10; WW 12)

The chanson survives, entirely or in part, in 10 sources: three printed books and seven manuscripts. The scoring is for six voices with the following ranges: d¹–d² (superius), c¹–a¹ (quintus), c–a¹ (altus), f–d¹ (sextus), c–d¹ (tenor), G–e¹ (bassus). Length: 99 measures.

The lover takes leave of his fair sweethearts, since because of them he has been suffering greater sorrows than those who swim in the sea [after a shipwreck]. The tuneful folk song on which the chanson is based is quoted by the sexta vox, and after two measures is answered canonically by the quinta vox, a fifth higher. The melody of the eight-line poem follows the formal outline A B A B' C D A B. Although

---

17 For a detailed analysis of the chanson, see Lawrence F. Bernstein, 'Chansons for Five and Six Voices', in *JosqComp*, 393–422, at 400–405.

this means that there are only four different melodic phrases, variety is achieved by the freely-composed voices. Fully embedded in the transparent polyphony, with a virtuoso altus part, the canon acts as the structural foundation. Three of the ten sources transmit the chanson with a sacred Latin text. Judging by the dates of the sources, NJE 30.10 is probably one of Josquin's earliest six-voice chansons.

VOUS L'AREZ (NJE 30.13; WW 16)

The chanson survives, entirely or in part, in 3 three printed books. The scoring is for six voices with the following ranges: g–c² (superius), d–g¹ (altus), c–g¹ (quintus), g–f¹ (tenor), d–c¹ (sextus), G–a (bassus). Length: 49 measures.

"My lady, if it pleases you, accept my heart, my body, my goods, my soul ..., and give me in exchange that which is sweeter than balm." All voices, including the two-part canon, open with the motif d^1–d^1–g (a–a–d). After four measures, the tenor is answered canonically by the sexta vox, at the lower fourth. While each line of the poem is repeated in a changing setting, Josquin dwells on the last line, where he emphasizes the sweetness of the balm by a harmonic change to c-minor (Ex. 83).

EXAMPLE 83

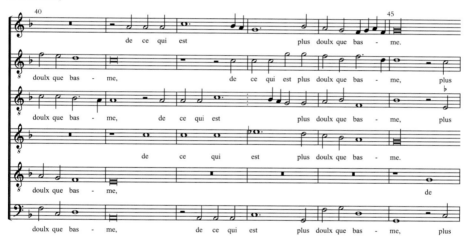

Chansons from the folk song tradition

ADIEU MES AMOURS (NJE *30.1)

The chanson survives incompletely in 2 manuscripts. Length: 69 measures.

The two sources originally belonged to two different sets of partbooks of which only three voice parts survive, the superius in Bologna R142, the second tenor and first bassus in Piacenza (3). The heading in Bologna is 'Josquin a7', in Piacenza 'Ave Maria a6'. Only the superius in Bologna contains a text, "Ave Maria, gratia plena ...". However, not only are the first five notes of this voice identical to the head-motif of Josquin's four-voice *Adieu mes amours*, but the canonic tenor and bassus in the Piacenza partbooks are also clearly moulded on the quasi-canonic lower voices in this same chanson (see p. 191–192). Hence, though both sources transmit the piece as a Marian motet, this is likely a *contrafactum* of an original six-voice setting of the famous folk song.[18] Since this incomplete setting cannot be evaluated stylistically, it is included in the *NJE* as doubtful.

ALLÉGEZ MOY (NJE 30.2; WW 14)

The chanson survives in 6 sources: four printed books and two manuscripts. Furthermore, one source contains an arrangement for two lutes. The scoring is for six voices with the following ranges: d^1–c^2 (superius), d–f^1 (quintus), d–f^1 (tenor), d–c^1 (altus), G–bflat (sextus and bassus). Length: 45 measures.

Although this chanson is also attributed to three other composers – Antoine Barbe, Jean Le Brung, and Adrian Willaert – the features of the musical style and compositional technique clearly point to Josquin as the composer. The five-line poem can be translated as follows: "Relieve me, dear sweet brunette, under the navel. Relieve me of all my grief. Your beauty holds me love-bound, under the navel." All voices open imitatively with the same six-note motif, thus emphasizing the narrator's need for 'relief'. The superius acts as the *dux* of the canon and after two measures is answered by the altus, at the lower octave. The structure is marked by a continuously alternating grouping of voices, and the 'sweet' harmony of sixth chords underlines the textual content. Notwithstanding the multivoiced scoring, the chanson keeps a cheerful character until the end. In the final chord, the superius introduces the falling third, *b'flat–g'–g'*.

FAULTE D'ARGENT (NJE 29.7; WW 15)

The chanson survives, entirely or in part, in 9 sources: four printed books and five manuscripts. Furthermore, three sources contain arrangements for lute or keyboard. The scoring is for five voices with the following ranges: a–d^2 (superius), a–g^1 (altus), c–g^1 (quintus), d–c^1 (tenor), G–bflat (bassus). Length: 72 measures.

Being impecunious was a popular theme in the poetry and music of the fifteenth century. François Villon alludes to it in his *Requeste à Monseigneur de Bourbon* – the last line of this poem reads "Que faulte d'argent si m'assault" (That I am so much assaulted by lack of money) – and the folk song "Faulte d'argent" forms the basis of chansons by N. Beauvois, Antoine de Févin and Josquin, as well as of a Mass setting by Mouton. Among the arrangements of Josquin's setting are Girolamo Cavazzoni's well-known canzona for organ and Willaert's six-voice chanson *Faulte d'argent*. Richafort quoted in his *Requiem* the phrase "C'est douleur non pareille" (It is a misfortune unequalled) from m. 12–24 of the superius and bassus (see p. 21) (Ex. 84). The last line, "A sleeping woman awakes at the clink of coins", musically corresponds with the first, giving the chanson the formal outline A B C A. The folk song is quoted in the altus, and after three measures is answered canonically by the quinta vox, a fifth lower.

EXAMPLE 84

C'est   dou - leur non pa - reil - le

---

18   See Martin Picker, 'Josquiniana in Some Manuscripts at Piacenza', in *ProcNY*, 247–260, at 247–255.

JE ME COMPLAINS (NJE 29.10; WW 11)

The chanson survives in 5 sources: three printed books and two manuscripts. The scoring is for five voices with the following ranges: d¹–b¹flat (superius), a-f¹ (quintus), Bflat–g¹ (tenor), c-a¹ (altus), G–bflat (bassus). Length: 56 measures.

The subject of the poem is a girl whose lover usually visits her at Prime, about six o'clock in the morning. Now Vespers, at six in the evening, are near, and he still has not appeared. The folkish melody is given to the superius, and after three measures is answered canonically by the quinta vox, at the lower fourth. While the canon melodies in lines 4 and 5 are nearly identical to those in the first two lines, their polyphonic elaboration differs. Line 6 forms the transition to the witty end. In these measures, Josquin refers to the popular song *La tricotée* (The little knitter).[19] It sounds as if he wanted to imitate the clicking of the knitting needles (Ex. 85).

EXAMPLE 85

---

19   See Alan Curtis, 'Josquin and *La belle tricotée*', in *Essays in Musicology in Honor of Dragan Plamenac...*, 1–8.

N'ESSE PAS UNG GRANT DESPLAISIR (NJE 29.17; WW 8)

The chanson survives in 10 sources: seven printed books and three manuscripts. The scoring is for five voices with the following ranges: c¹–c² (superius), d–f¹ (tenor and quintus), A–f¹ (altus), F–a (bassus). Length: 43 measures.

The narrator wants nothing but to indulge in the pleasures of life. The tenor enters the folkish melody, which only consists of two musical phrases, and is answered canonically after two measures by the quinta vox at the same pitch. The phrases are elaborated at different pitches according to a simple plan: line 1 A B; line 2 A; line 3 B; line 4 B; line 5 B, followed by a varied repeat of A. The airy tone of Josquin's setting seems to mirror the narrator's desire.

PETITE CAMUSETTE (NJE 30.7; WW 17)

The chanson survives, entirely or in part, in 8 sources: three printed books and five manuscripts. The scoring is for six voices with the following ranges: c¹–e² (superius and quintus), a–f¹ (altus and tenor), A–c¹ (sextus and bassus). Length: 41 measures.

"Little snub-nose, you have put me to death": with this phrase, the poem introduces Robin and Marion. They walk arm in arm into the woods, where they fall asleep. The graceful folk song enters in m. 5 in the tenor, and after one measure is answered canonically at the same pitch by the altus (Ex. 86). Josquin also borrows motifs from the song in the other voices, particularly in the opening, lending in this way the six-voice polyphonic texture a very lively character.

EXAMPLE 86

POUR SOUHAITTER (NJE 30.8; WW 10)

The chanson survives in 3 sources: two printed books and one manuscript. The scoring is for six voices with the following ranges: a–c² (superius), a–g¹ (sextus), d–f¹ (altus), d–e¹ (quintus), A–c¹ (tenor), D–g (bassus). Length: 45 measures.

The text of the four-line poem is as follows: "My only desire is to keep fit and have a long life, to be always happy and wealthy, and at the end to enter the kingdom of heaven." Except for the altus, all voices open with the motif *d–f–e–d* (*a–c–b–a*; the *b*flat accidental in the Smijers edition must be disregarded.) After four measures, the tenor enters with the canon melody, which in m. 7 is answered by the sexta vox, a fifth higher. In contrast to the other voices, the canon is entirely syllabic. The superius sets the key words "pour souhaitter", "demander", "longuement", "largement", and "royaulme" to lenghty, lively melismas. The chanson follows the formal outline A B C B D B. The last three sections (B D B) are reserved for the last line of the text.

TENEZ MOY EN VOZ BRAS (NJE *30.12; WW 13)

The chanson survives in 9 sources: four printed books and five manuscripts. The scoring is for six voices with the following ranges: d^1–d^2 (superius), e–a^1 (altus), c–f^1 (quintus), f–f^1 (tenor), F–g (bassus), F–a (sextus). Length: 76 measures.

All manuscripts transmit the chanson with a Latin text. In the certainly original French version, the subject of the poem is a woman who aks her lover to take her in his arms, for she feels sick. The chanson is based on an earlier anonymous three-voice setting of the same, pre-existing folk song, and has the formal outline A B C D E F A B C D. There is no canonic frame. Instead, the parts are written in free counterpoint around the tenor that quotes the folk tune and stands out from the other voices through the use of long note values. The tenor is anticipated in m. 1–17 of the superius.

VOUS NE L'AUREZ PAS (NJE 30.14; WW 2)

The chanson survives only in the editions by Susato and Attaingnant. The scoring is for six voices with the following ranges: c^1–c^2 (superius), a–g^1 (sextus), c–f^1 (altus), d–c^1 (tenor), A–f^1 (quintus), F–a (bassus). Length: 47 measures.

"For my part, you should not have what you desire, even if you had enough to fill an entire well." The canon melody used as a basis for the chanson consists of four different phrases, each setting one of the four text lines. Since the phrases are sung alternately by the tenor and sexta vox, at the pitches of *a* and *e^1*, the canon never overlaps.

Instrumental works

The twelve instrumental pieces form a category of their own. Although they are not identified as such in the sources, it can be deduced, from the character of the music and the absence of text, that they were meant to be performed by an instrumental ensemble. Seven of them are related to a pre-existing song, a dance tune or a polyphonic composition. The remaining five are autonomous.

DE TOUS BIENS PLAINE (NJE 27.6)

The piece survives only in Petrucci's *Odhecaton A* from 1502. The scoring is for three instruments with the following ranges: g–c^2 (superius), d–a^1 (tenor), G–d^1 (bassus). Length: 60 measures.

The top voice of Hayne van Ghizeghem's eponymous *rondeau*, a poetic ode to a woman, serves as superius. With its beautifully balanced melody, Hayne's song was one of the most widely disseminated songs of the fifteenth century. Josquin devised a new bass voice which, after a half measure, is answered canonically by the tenor, a fifth higher. Although the superius keeps its full original vocal character, the continuous motion in the canon voices in m. 28 does not allow for a stop, which would be obligatory for the performance of the text as a *rondeau*.

DE TOUS BIENS PLAINE (NJE 28.9)

The piece survives in 5 sources: four printed books and one manuscript. The scoring is for four instruments with the following ranges: g–c^2 (superius), d–e^1 (tenor), G–f^1 (bassus primus and secundus). Length: 61 measures.

This setting is based on the same chanson as NJE 27.6. This time, Josquin borrows both the superius and tenor from Hayne's chanson, and rewrites the bassus as a two-part canon at the unison, where the second part enters one minim later than the first part, posing herewith the performers for a *tour de force*. The canon is explained by the motto "Petrus & Joannes currunt In puncto" (Peter and John run after each other at the minim) (Ex. 87).

EXAMPLE 87

FORS SEULEMENT (NJE *28.16)

The piece survives in 3 sources: one printed book and two manuscripts. The scoring is for four instruments with the following ranges: a–f² (superius), f–d² (altus), d–f¹ (tenor), G–b (bassus). Length: 71 measures.

In the fifteenth century, Ockeghem's three-voice chanson *Fors seulement l'actente* rivalled Hayne's *De tous biens plaine* in popularity (see above). NJE *28.16 is anonymous in Petrucci's *Canti C* of 1504, attributed to Johannes Ghiselin in Florence 2439, and to Josquin in the song book of Fridolin Sicher (Saint Gall 461). The lowest voice part of the *rondeau* appears an octave higher in the top voice of the present setting. Moreover, as a fine example of counterpoint, the whole first phrase of the superius is quoted in m. 3–10 of the altus, and anticipated in m. 1 and 2 of the bassus and tenor. Characteristic of Josquin are the identical passages in the bassus, m. 11–16, 17–22 and 23–25. Nevertheless, his authorship is doubtful. It is defended by the older generation of musicologists but rejected in more recent studies. Furthermore, there is general agreement that the stylistic features of Ghiselin's music bear only a few similarities with those of NJE *28.16.

FORTUNA DESPERATA (NJE *27.11)

The piece survives only in Segovia s.s. The scoring is for three instruments with the following ranges: c¹–d² (superius), f–g¹ (tenor), A–d¹ (bassus). Length: 57 measures.

The piece is based on the three-voice, very popular song *Fortuna desperata*, in the same manuscript ascribed to Antoine Busnois. Against the two higher voices of the original setting, a new, unusually virtuoso bass part has been written. The two borrowed voices in the present setting deviate somewhat from the model used by Josquin in his *Missa Fortuna desperata* (see pp. 112–114). Since the attributions of several other compositions in the Segovia manuscript have been proven incorrect, the authenticity of NJE *27.11 is equally doubtful.

FORTUNA D'UN GRAN TEMPO (NJE 27.12)

The piece survives, entirely or in part, in 3 sources: two printed books and one manuscript. Furthermore, four sources contain arrangements for lute or keyboard. The scoring is for three instruments with the following ranges: c¹–c² (superius), Bflat–f¹ (tenor), Bflat–e¹flat (bassus). Length: 47 measures.

This *Fortuna* setting is based on an Italian song taken as a starting point by several other composers as well for a polyphonic piece. In Josquin's setting, the theme enters successively beginning on the pitches of *g*', *c*', and *f*. The piece has the following unusual staff signatures: none in the superius, *b*flat in the tenor, *b*flat and *e*flat in the bassus (see above, Fig. 14). Edward Lowinsky has argued that Josquin may have been inspired by the wheel of fortune, turning in a descending circle of fifths with a flat added at every turn, and that the piece could therefore represent a tonal experiment (Ex. 88).[20] If this was the case, then the piece recalls the motet *Absalon fili mi* (see p. 128-129). However, accepting several false relations, the editors of the piece in the *NJE* present a version without tonal adjustments.[21]

EXAMPLE 88

---

20   'The Goddess Fortuna in Music', in *The Musical Quarterly* 29 (1943), 45–77.

21   See Jaap van Benthem, 'Fortuna in Focus: Concerning 'Conflicting' Progressions in Josquin's *Fortuna dun gran tempo*', in *TVNM* 30 (1980), 1–50.

LE VILLAIN (NJE 28.22)

The piece survives only in Augsburg 142a. The scoring is for four instruments with the following ranges: a–f² (superius), d–a¹ (altus), c–a¹ (tenor), A–d¹ (bassus). Length: 67 measures.

Although some musical motifs in Mouton's chanson *Le villain jaloux* may be found in the present instrumental setting, it seems more likely that Josquin took a monophonic melody as a starting point. The piece, which has the character of a fantasia, is highly praised by some. For example, Ludwig Finscher refers to it as "ein wahres Feuerwerk motivischer Variationen und Kombinationen" (a real firework of motivic variations and combinations). On the other hand, Jaap van Benthem rejects its authenticity.[22] Comparing *Le villain* with Josquin's genuine fantasias *La Bernardina* and *Ile fantazies de Joskin* (see below), one cannot but admit that it lacks the driving force characteristic of these latter pieces. NJE 28.22 shows a lack of inspiration in the frequent repeats of the prominent motif, that is heard for the first time in m. 10–12.

L'HOMME ARMÉ (NJE *28.23)

The piece survives in 7 sources: five printed books and two manuscripts. The scoring is for four instruments with the following ranges: d¹–d² (superius), d–g¹ (altus), g–a¹ (tenor), G–c¹ (bassus). Length: 19 measures.

Each of the four parts opens with the notes *re–sol–fa–mi–re*, derived from the famous *L'homme armé* melody (see p. 108), a shortened version of which is used as *cantus prius factus* in the tenor. It may be tempting, when performing the piece, to restore the original A B A pattern of the song. In this case, the *e*flat in the bassus in m. 9 should be changed to *g* in the close. The remarkable thing about this setting is the instruction in the earliest source, Petrucci's *Canti B* from 1502, which opens with this piece. It runs: "Canon. Et sic de singulis", meaning that, like the first note in each of the four voices, every following note is to be dotted, augmenting its value by half. It would have been simpler to have used the *tempus imperfectum* sign and omit both the motto and the dot. In other words, the composer seems to have wanted, in a playful way, to test the performers' ability to solve a notation riddle. Because of the hidden parallel octaves and a rigid construction, the authenticity of NJE *28.23 has been doubted.[23] However, considering that Petrucci, in 1502, also published five Masses by Josquin and may have been in touch with the composer some time before, it would be strange for him to have given this piece a false attribution.

The following five pieces are freely composed

A L'HEURE (NJE 28.1)

The piece survives only in Petrucci's *Canti C* from 1503 (1504). The scoring is for four instruments with the following ranges: c¹–e²flat (superius), Bflat–a¹ (altus), c–g¹ (tenor), Bflat–d¹ (bassus). Length: 35 measures.

---

22   See the Critical Commentary to *NJE* vol. 28, 286.

23   See the Critical Commentary to *NJE* vol. 28, 298–299.

Although the opening phrase of the superius suggests a vocal composition, the stylistic features point clearly to an autonomous instrumental piece. After one measure, the superius is answered canonically by the bassus, a ninth lower. The melody is written in such a way that, to a large extent, the two parts move in parallel tenths. From m. 17 onwards, the outer voices form a stepwise ascending sequence for over six measures. The title in the only source may well be a corruption of what originally could have read "A l'heure que je vous prie" (At the time that I ask you). If so, this was perhaps intended as an invitation from the *dux* to the *comes* to enter.

CELA SANS PLUS (NJE 27.3)

The piece survives in 5 sources: two printed books and three manuscripts. The scoring is for three instruments with the following ranges: c¹–d² (superius), e–f¹ (tenor), Bflat–f¹ (bassus). Length: 55 measures.

The title seems to refer to a pre-existing chanson. Yet, musically there is no relation with eponymous chansons of the time. In *Cela sans plus*, the polyphony is determined by imitation, particularly in m. 1–27, where, after two measures, the superius is answered canonically by the tenor, a fifth lower. And as in *A l'heure*, there is an ascending sequence from m. 34 onwards in the outer voices, here for a duration of ten measures (Ex. 89).

EXAMPLE 89

ILE FANTAZIES DE JOSKIN (NJE 27.15)

The piece survives only in Rome 2856. The scoring is for three instruments with the following ranges: g–d² (superius), e–a¹ (tenor), c–g¹ (bassus). Length: 50 measures.

The title, more likely stemming from the scribe of the only source than from the composer himself, simply means 'a product of Josquin's imagination' (Fig. 44). NJE 27.15 is one of the first pieces to use 'fantasia' in its title. It starts with three parts in imitation (m. 1–5), after which superius and tenor continue with a descending sequence of a short motif in parallel thirds. Imitation and sequence techniques are also applied later in the piece. Josquin particularly shows his inventiveness in the variation of the musical motifs. Even though these are hardly related to one another, he combines them masterfully into coherent music.

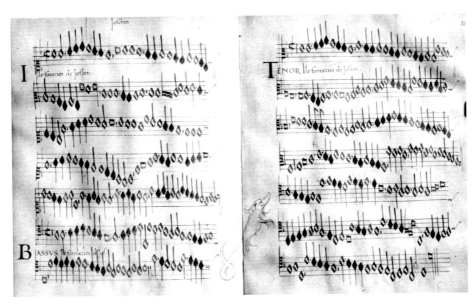

FIGURE 44: *Ile fantazies de Josquin*. Rome, Biblioteca Casanatense, Ms. 2856, f. 113ʹ-114.

LA BERNARDINA (NJE 27.21)

The piece survives in 4 sources: two printed books and two manuscripts. Furthermore, two sources contain arrangements for lute. The scoring is for three instruments with the following ranges: c¹–f² (superius), c–a¹ (tenor), A–g¹ (bassus). Length: 46 measures.

Shortly before 1500, some three-part instrumental pieces were composed in Italy with titles which seem to refer to particular (noble?) persons who have yet to be identified: *La Alfonsina* (Ghiselin), *La Martinella* (Johannes Martini and Isaac), *La Stangetta* (Van Weerbeke). Josquin's *La Bernardina* also belongs to this group. His trio is predominantly imitative, with stepwise ascending and descending melodies, often treated in sequence. With the breves in m. 15–23 and 29–35, the bassus and tenor form a backbone that is in marked contrast to the other parts.

VIVE LE ROY (NJE 28.36)

The piece survives only in Petrucci's *Canti C* from 1503 (1504). The scoring is for four instruments with the following ranges: g–d² (superius), d–a¹ (altus), g–g¹ (tenor), G–d¹ (bassus). Length: 41 measures.

This brilliant fanfare, possibly written for the accession of Louis XII in 1498, is a compositional *tour de force*. Petrucci offers a *resolutio* of what originally may have been a cryptic notation, i.e. an alto part with signs to indicate the canonically derived bassus and superius, which enter one after another after a half measure at the lower fifth and the upper fourth. The three canonic parts surround the tenor. The latter forms a *soggetto cavato* (see p. 118), where the vowels of the title are converted into the solmisation syllables of the Guidonian hexachord (the letter 'v' counting as 'u'): *ut–mi–ut–re–re–sol–mi*. This series of breves is played three times, starting on the pitches *c'*, *g*, and *c'*, always preceded by six breve rests (Ex. 90).

EXAMPLE 90

Epilogue

Five centuries separate us from the composer that is the subject of this book. To answer the question "Who was he?" we are dependent on sixteenth-century witnesses who, since they did not know Josquin personally, were certainly not always reliable. Moreover, they are so few in number that the following conclusion seems inescapable: Josquin's fame rests solely on the unparalleled quality of his music, a quality that had been recognized by the end of the fifteenth century and became legendary shortly after his death.

Josquin spoke the same musical language and used the same compositional techniques as his fellow composers, yet he fires the imagination so much more than they do. The secret lies within his music, but is not always easy to explain. An important factor is a greater attention to the meaning of the text in works written after approximately 1490, particularly in the motets about Jesus Christ and the Virgin Mary, and in the psalm settings. His stay in Italy, where humanism had left its mark on the music of Ciconia and Dufay in the early fifteenth century, undoubtedly contributed to the great expressivity of much of his oeuvre.[1] Another factor is the general transparency of his music. In all the works for more than four voices, one or more voices are structurally distinct from the others, either through the use of a *cantus prius factus* in long notes, an ostinato motif, a canon, or alternation between groups of voices.

Compared with his contemporaries, Josquin shows extraordinary musical inventiveness. To understand this, we should first compare works that are based on the same musical material. Josquin returned several times to a *cantus prius factus* – either a Gregorian chant or a secular song – that he had used earlier, as if he wanted to take up the challenge afresh. He devised different treatments for two *L'homme armé* Masses, the motets *Ave Maria*, *Ave maris stella*, *Inviolata* and *Salve regina*,

---

1   Willem Elders, 'Humanism and Early-Renaissance Music: A Study of the Ceremonial Music by Ciconia and Dufay', in *TVNM* 27 (1977), 65–101.

the chansons *A (En) l'ombre d'ung buissonnet* and *Entré(e je) suis*, and the instrumental settings of the song *De tous biens plaine*. His inventiveness is also apparent in ever-surprising twists of harmony and melody, and in the highly imaginative use of ostinato and sequence techniques.

Furthermore, Josquin's oeuvre displays a greater wealth of contrast than that of his contemporaries. In the sixteenth century, some of his works were unequalled in their spiritual and aesthetic quality, their variety of emotional expression and their technical brilliance. Many compositions also show a playful imagination, revealing Josquin to be a true 'homo ludens'.[2] Examples include the *Missa N'auray je jamais*, where the number of dice pips determines the factor by which note values must be augmented, the *Missa Faysant regretz* and the *Missa La sol fa re mi*, where a short motif is repeated endlessly at different pitches and with varying rhythms, the motet *Ut phebi radiis*, where the six notes of the hexachord form rising and falling scales with symbolic meaning, and the arrangement of *Fortuna dun gran tempo*, which poses many a harmonic riddle for the three instrumentalists. In the choice of such frivolous chanson texts as *Allégez moy* and *Baisiez moy*, or such trivial melodies as *L'ami Baudichon* and *Une mousse de Biscaye* as the basis for Mass settings, Josquin's sense of humour is undeniable.

The substantial problems of authenticity described in Chapter 4 and elsewhere in this book show that fully objective conclusions are rarely possible. Even musicologists specialising in this area often adopt a personal and emotional approach to Josquin's music. When the newly reconstructed motet *Obsecro te, domina* was performed in 2008, the reactions of two editors involved in the *NJE* were quite opposite. One said, "A beautiful piece, but not Josquin." The other said, "If this isn't Josquin, then I give up." Compositions by Josquin that depart too much from the prevailing consensus about his general style run the risk of being considered spurious. Examples include the Masses *Une mousse de Biscaye* and *Mater patris*, the motets *Ave maris stella* (NJE 23.8) and *Ave nobilissima creatura*, and the secular works *El grillo* and *Mille regretz*. However, we should remember that later composers also produced works that nobody would have recognized as being theirs from the music alone.[3]

When Josquin's work is taken as a whole, it is easy to find pieces that must have surprised his contemporaries by their technical mastery, or by their unusual scoring. The latter include, for example, the chanson *La belle se siet* for three basses, and the motet *Recordare, virgo mater* for three sopranos and alto.

Even though the extent of Josquin's oeuvre is impressive, we must realise that we certainly do not know it all. More than thirty compositions in the *NJE* survive in only one source, proving that the chance of survival was in some cases minimal. Mention can also be made of works transmitted anonymously that can be attributed to Josquin on stylistic grounds. Such is the case for the seven-voice motet *Proh dolor* surviving in Brussels 228, a four-voice chanson *Fors seulement* (NJE 28.40) and four chansons in Vienna 18746. Some non-musical sources refer to works by

---

2   *Homo ludens* is the title of a study by Johan Huizinga, the author of *The Waning of the Middle Ages*.

3   See for example Mozart's *Gigue* KV 574 or some of Beethoven's variations for piano.

Josquin, now unfortunately lost. For instance, in his *Le istitutioni harmoniche* (p. 265) from 1558, Zarlino mentions a six-voice motet by Josquin based on four different Marian texts: the antiphons *Alma redemptoris mater, Ave regina celorum, Regina celi* and the sequence *Inviolata*.[4] In his catalogue of all compositions attributed to Josquin, Ludwig Finscher names a *Missa pro defunctis*, a *Missa L'homme armé 8. toni*, several motets and a chanson as "lost but potentially authentic".[5]

In attempting to evaluate the significance of Josquin in Western European musical culture, it is worth pointing out that sources of his music are not only more numerous than those of Dufay, Ockeghem and Obrecht put together, but also more widespread. In this respect, he can be regarded as the first 'European' musician. None of his predecessors or contemporaries had such a broad or lasting influence on sixteenth-century music, no other Renaissance composer used such a variety of esoteric–symbolic tools at their disposal, and none of his colleagues created so many moments that can, in the true sense of the word, be called 'sublime'.[6]

---

4   Perhaps identical with the six-voice *Alma redemptoris mater* that is listed in the so-called "Heidelberger Kapellinventar"; see the Critical Commentary to *NJE* vol. 3, 51. In NJE 23.2, Josquin combined two Marian antiphons (see p. [174-175]). Nicolas Gombert went as far as to cram no less than seven different Marian chants into one motet; see Willem Elders, 'Music and Number in Token of the Holy Virgin', in Idem, *Symbolic Scores ...*, 169-171.

5   See the rubric 'Verschollene und möglicherweise echte Werke', *MGG2*, vol. 9, col. 1216–1246, at 1243–1244.

6   See *ProcM*.

Bibliography

The bibliography consists of two parts:
A. – a selective bibliography up to the publication in 2009 of David Fallows' Josquin monograph, which offers on pages 469–495 a comprehensive bibliography;
B. – a list of Josquin studies from 2008 onwards.

A.
Jaap van Benthem, 'Zur Struktur und Authenzität der Chansons à 5 & 6 von Josquin des Prez', in *TVNM* 21 (1968–70), 170–188 plus unpaginated musical examples
Jaap van Benthem, 'Einige wiedererkannte Josquin–Chansons im Codex 18746 der Österreichische Nationalbibliothek', in *TVNM* 22 (1972), 18–42
Jaap van Benthem, 'The Scoring of Josquin's Secular Music', in *TVNM* 35 (1985), 67–96
Bonnie Blackburn, 'Josquin's Chansons: Ignored and Lost Sources', in *JAMS* 29 (1976), 30–76
Willem Elders, 'Das Symbol in der Musik von Josquin des Prez', in *AcM* 41 (1969), 164–185
Willem Elders, 'Report of the First Josquin Meeting, Utrecht 1973', in *TVNM* 24 (1974), 20–82
Willem Elders, 'The Performance of *cantus firmi* in Josquin's Masses Based on Secular Monophonic Song', in *EM* 17 (1989), 330–341
Willem Elders, 'New Light on the Dating of Josquin's *Hercules* Mass', in *TVNM* 48 (1998), 112–149
Willem Elders, 'Symbolism in the Sacred Music of Josquin', in *JosqComp*, 531–568
David Fallows, 'The Performing Ensembles in Josquin's Sacred Music', in *TVNM* 35 (1985), 32–66
David Fallows, *Josquin* (Turnhout 2009)
Ludwig Finscher, 'Josquin des Prez', in *MGG2*, vol. 9 (2003), col. 1210–1282
Carlo Fiore, *Josquin des Prez* (Palermo 2003)
Irving Godt, 'The Restoration of Josquin's *Ave mundi spes, Maria*, and Some Observations on Restoration', in *TVNM* 26 (1976), 55–83

Paula Higgins, 'The Apotheosis of Josquin des Prez and Other Mythologies of Musical Genius', in *JAMS* 57 (2004), 443–510

Marianne Hund, 'Fresh Light on Josquin Dascanio's Enigmatic *El grillo*', in *TVNM* 56 (2006), 5–16

Martin Just, 'Josquins Chanson *Nymphes, Napées* als Bearbeitung des Invitatoriums *Circumdederunt me* und als Grundlage für Kontrafaktur, Zitat und Nachahmung', in *Mf* 43 (1990), 305–335

Kwee Him Yong, 'Sixteenth-century Printed Instrumental Arrangements of Works by Josquin des Prez', in *TVNM* 22 (1971–72), 43–66

Michael Long, 'Symbol and Ritual in Josquin's *Missa Di dadi*', in *JAMS* 42 (1989), 1–22

Patrick Macey, '*Celi enarrant*: An Inauthentic Psalm Motet Attributed to Josquin', in *ProcU*, 25–44

Patrick Macey, 'Josquin as Classic: *Qui habitat, Memor esto*, and Two Imitations Unmasked', in *Journal of the Royal Musical Association* 118 (1993), 1–43

Patrick Macey, 'Josquin and Musical Rhetoric: *Miserere mei, deus* and Other Motets', in *JosqComp*, 485–530

Patrick Macey, Jeremy Noble and Jeffrey Dean, 'Josquin (Lebloitte dit) des Prez', in *NGD2* (2001), vol. 13, 220–266

Jacqueline Mattfeld, 'Some Relationships between Texts and *cantus firmi* in the Liturgical Motets of Josquin des Pres', in *JAMS* 14 (1961), 159–183

Lora Matthews and Paul Merkley, 'Iudochus de Picardia and Jossequin Lebloitte dit Desprez: The Names of the Singer(s)', in *JM* 16 (1998), 200–226

Honey Meconi, 'Josquin and Musical Reputation', in *Essays on Music and Culture in Honor of Herbert Kellman*, ed. Barbara Haggh (Paris 2001), 280–297

John Milsom, 'Analysing Josquin', in *JosqComp*, 431–484

Jeremy Noble, 'The Function of Josquin's Motets', in *TVNM* 35 (1985), 9–31

Helmuth Osthoff, *Josquin Desprez*, 2 vols. (Tutzing 1962/65)

Jean–Pierre Ouvrard, *Josquin des Prez et ses contemporains: De l'écrit au sonore. Guide pratique d'interprétation* (Arles 1986)

Jessie Ann Owens, 'How Josquin Became Josquin: Reflections on Historiography and Reception', in *Music in Renaissance Cities and Courts: Studies in Honor of Lewis Lockwood*, edd. Eadem and Anthony M. Cummings (Warren, MI, 1997), 271–280

Leeman L. Perkins, 'Mode and Structure in the Masses of Josquin', in *JAMS* 26 (1973), 189–239

Stephanie Schlagel, 'The *Liber selectarum cantionum* and the "German Josquin Renaissance"', in *JM* 19 (2002), 564–615

Richard Sherr, '*Illibata dei virgo nutrix* and Josquin's Roman Style', in *JAMS* 41 (1988), 434–464

Edgar H. Sparks, 'Problems of Authenticity in Josquin's Motets', in *ProcNY* 345–359

Edward Stam, 'Die vierundzwanzigstimmige kanonische Psalmmotette *Qui habitat in adiutorio altissimi* von Josquin des Prez', in *TVNM* 22 (1971–72), 1–17

Rebecca Stewart, 'Voice Types in Josquin's Music', in *TVNM* 35 (1985), 97–193

Richard Taruskin, 'Josquin and the Humanists. Josquin des Prez in Fact and Legend; Parody Masses', in *The Oxford History of Western Music*, 6 vols., vol. 1 (Oxford 2005), 547–584

Rob Wegman, 'Who Was Josquin', in *JosqComp*, 21–50

B.

2008

Willem Elders, 'Josquin in the Sources of Spain. An Evaluation of Two Unique Attributions', in 'Recevez ce mien petit labeur': *Studies in Renaissance Music in Honour of Ignace Bossuyt*, edd. Mark Delaere and Pieter Bergé (Leuven 2008), 61–70

Eric Jas, 'Josquin, Willaert and *Douleur me bat*', in 'Recevez ce mien petit labeur', 119–130

Rob Wegman, 'The Other Josquin', in *TVNM* 58 (2008), 33–68 and 99

2009

Jeffrey J. Dean, 'Josquin's Teaching: Ignored and Lost Sources', in *Blackburn*, 741–750

Willem Elders, 'A New Case of Number Symbolism in Josquin?', in *EM* 37 (2009), 21–26

Willem Elders, 'Perfect Fifths and the Blessed Virgin's Immaculate Conception: On *Ficta* in Josquin's five-part *Inviolata*', in *Blackburn*, 403–411

Willem Elders, 'Which is Josquin's First Mass Based on a Gregorian Chant?', in *Littera NIGRO scripta manet. In honorem Jaromír Černý*, edd. Jan Bata, Jiří K. Kroupa, and Lenka Mráčková (Prague 2009), 59–70

David Fallows, 'Josquin and *Il n'est plaisir*', in *EM* 37 (2009), 3–8

Eric Jas, 'Multivoiced Canons Attributed to Josquin', in *Blackburn*, 593–603

Eric Jas, 'What's in a Quote? Josquin's (?) *Jubilate Deo, omnis terra* reconsidered', in *EM* 37 (2009), 9–19

Herbert Kellman, 'Dad and Granddad Were Cops: Josquin's Ancestry', in *Blackburn*, 183–200

Lewis Lockwood, '"It's true that Josquin composes better ...": The Short Unhappy Life of Gian de Artiganova', in *Blackburn*, 201–216

Patrick Macey, 'Josquin and Champion: Conflicting Attributions for the Psalm Motet *De profundis clamavi*', in *Blackburn*, 453–468

Grantley McDonald, 'Josquin's Musical Cricket: *El grillo* as Humanist Parody', in *AcM* 81 (2009), 39–53

John Milsom, 'Josquin and the Act of Self-Quotation: The Case of *Plusieurs regretz*, in *Blackburn*, 521–532

Jesse Rodin, 'When Josquin Became Josquin', in: *AcM* 81 (2009), 23–38

Jesse Rodin, 'A Most Laudible Competition? Hearing and Composing the *Beata Virgine* Masses of Josquin and Brumel', in *TVNM* 59 (2009), 3–24

Alice Tacaille, 'Notes sur la copie des messes de Josquin des Prés dans un manuscrit italien de la fin du XVIe siècle', in *Blackburn*, 335–350

Jennifer Thomas, '*Absalon fili mi*, Josquin, and the French Royal Court: Attribution, Authenticity, Context, and Conjecture', in *Blackburn*, 477–489

2010

Jacques Barbier, *Josquin Desprez* (no pl., Bleu Nuit Editeur, 2010)

Leeman L. Perkins, 'Josquin's *Qui habitat* and the Psalm Motets', in *JM* 26 (2010), 512–564

Christiane Wiesenfeldt, '*Cantus versus planus*. Überlegungen zu Josquins *Missa Hercules Dux Ferrariae*', in *Mf* 63 (2010), 379–389

2011

Jaap van Benthem, '*Domine, quis habitabit in tabernaculo tuo?* A Neglected Psalm Setting in Antico's *Motetti novi e chanzoni franciose*', in *ProcM*, 73–105

Willem Elders, 'On the Sublime in Josquin's Marian Motets', in *ProcM*, 7–26

Carlo Fiore, 'Josquin before 1919. Sources for a Reception History', in *ProcM*, 215–240

Fabrice Fitch, 'Josquin À l'ombre des buissonets. Arborescent Design and Popular Song in his Four-Voice Secular Music', in *ProcM*, 155–168

Richard Freedman, 'Josquin, the Multi-Voice Chanson, and the Sublime', in *ProcM*, 169–188

Martin Just, 'Two Singularly Transmitted Magnificat Settings', in *ProcM*, 121–139

Andrea Lindmayr-Brandl, 'Strange Polyphonic Borrowings. Josquin's *Missa Faysant regretz*', in *ProcM*, 107–119

John Milsom, 'Playing with Plainchant. Seven Motet Openings by Josquin and What We Can Learn From Them', in *ProcM*, 23–47

Stephanie P. Schlagel, 'Fortune's Fate. Josquin and the Nürnberg Mass Prints of 1539', in *ProcM*, 191–209

Nicole Schwindt, 'Josquin's Three-Part Chansons. A Case of the Sublime?', in *ProcM*, 141–153

Walter Testolin, 'Did Leonardo Paint Josquin? New Light on the 'Musician' in the Ambrosiana', in *ProcM*, 211–213

2012

Willem Elders, 'Josquin des Prez: ein "unbeschreibliches Genie" ', in *Logos et Musica. In honorem summi romani pontificis Benedicti XVI*, edd. E. Szczurko et alii (Frankfurt am Main 2012), 591–606

Willem Elders, 'Did Josquin Use a Musical 'Signature'?', in *TVNM* 62 (2012), 29–63

David Fiala, 'La collégiale royale de Saint-Quentin et la musique', in *La musique en Picardie du XIVe au XVIIe siècle*, edd. Camilla Cavicchi, Marie-Alexis Colin and Philippe Vendrix (Turnhout 2012), 189–227

Jesse Rodin, *Josquin's Rome: Hearing and Composing in the Sistine Chapel* (New York 2012)

Peter Urquhart, '*Ad fugam*, De Orto, and a Defense of the "Early Josquin" ', in *TVNM* 62 (2012), 3–27

2013

Marianne Hund and Willem Elders, 'Unravelling Josquin's *Quant je vous voy*. With a Postscript on *El grillo*', in *EM* 41 (2013; forthcoming)

Eric Jas, 'What Other Josquin?' (forthcoming)

Appendix A

New Josquin Edition: Summary of volumes and editors

Vol. 1 – The Sources: Compositions Attributed to Josquin in Manuscripts and Prints (Willem Elders and Eric Jas)
Vol. 2 – Facsimiles from the Sources of Compositions Attributed to Josquin (Willem Elders with Marnix van Berchum)
Vol. 3 – Masses Based on Gregorian Chants 1 (Willem Elders)
Vol. 4 – Masses Based on Gregorian Chants 2 (Willem Elders)
Vol. 5 – Masses Based on Secular Monophonic Songs 1 (Martin Just)
Vol. 6 – Masses Based on Secular Monophonic Songs 2 (Jesse Rodin)
Vol. 7 – Masses Based on Secular Polyphonic Songs 1 (Thomas Noblitt)
Vol. 8 – Masses Based on Secular Polyphonic Songs 2 (Barton Hudson)
Vol. 9 – Masses Based on Secular Polyphonic Songs 3 (Barton Hudson)
Vol. 10 – Masses Based on Sacred Polyphonic Songs (Willem Elders)
Vol. 11 – Masses Based on Solmisation Themes (James Haar and Lewis Lockwood)
Vol. 12 – Canonic Masses (Peter Urquhart and Theodor Dumitrescu)
Vol. 13 – Mass Movements (Barton Hudson)
Vol. 14 – Motets on Texts from the Old Testament 1 (Richard Sherr)
Vol. 15 – Motets on Texts from the Old Testament 2 (Patrick Macey)
Vol. 16 – Motets on Texts from the Old Testament 3 (Martin Picker)
Vol. 17 – Motets on Texts from the Old Testament 4 (Eric Jas)
Vol. 18 – Motets on Texts from the Old Testament 5 (Leeman L. Perkins)
Vol. 19 – Motets on Texts from the New Testament 1 (Martin Just)
Vol. 20 – Motets on Texts from the New Testament 2 (Martin Just)
Vol. 21 – Motets on Non-Biblical Texts 1 (Bonnie J. Blackburn)
Vol. 22 – Motets on Non-Biblical Texts 2 (Bonnie J. Blackburn)
Vol. 23 – Motets on Non-Biblical Texts 3 (Willem Elders)
Vol. 24 – Motets on Non-Biblical Texts 4 (Willem Elders)
Vol. 25 – Motets on Non-Biblical Texts 5 (Willem Elders)

Vol. 26 – Motets on Miscellaneous Texts (Ton Braas)
Vol. 27 – Secular Works for Three Voices (Jaap van Benthem and Howard Mayer Brown)
Vol. 28 – Secular Works for Four Voices (David Fallows)
Vol. 29 – Secular Works for Five Voices (Patrick Macey)
Vol. 30 – Secular Works for Six Voices (Patrick Macey)

Appendix B

List of authentic and doubtful works of Josquin

This list contains in alphabetic order all works by Josquin that are included in the *New Josquin Edition* as authentic or doubtful. Each title is followed by its number in the *NJE*. The number before the dot indicates the volume, the one after the dot the number of the composition in the volume. The number before the dot allows quick recognition of the category of works to which the composition belongs, as listed in Appendix A. Doubtful works are marked with an asterisk. The *NJE* number is followed by a reference to the Werken van Josquin des Prés, edited by A. Smijers (1922-1969) (Mi = Missen; Fm = Fragmenta missarum; Mo = Motetten; Ww = Wereldlijke werken; Su = Supplement).

A la mort (NJE 27.1) 66–67, 188
A l'heure (NJE 28.1; Ww 41) 222–223
A l'ombre d'ung buissonnet (NJE 27.2; Ww 61) 192, 228
Absalon fili mi (NJE *14.1; Su 5) 43, 60–61, 62, 128–129, 221
Absolve, quesumus, domine (NJE 26.1; Mo 82) 72, 74, 76, 85–86, 185–186
Ach hülff mich leid (NJE *28.2) 202–203
Adieu mes amours (NJE 28.3; Ww 35) 43, 191–192, 215
Adieu mes amours (= Ave Maria) (NJE *30.1) 215–216
Allégez moy (NJE 30.2; Ww 14) 216, 228
Alleluia. Laudate dominum (NJE *15.1) 133
Alma redemptoris mater (NJE 23.1; Mo 38) 79, 163–165
Alma redemptoris mater / Ave regina (NJE 23.2; Mo 21) 163–165
Ave Maria 4v (NJE 23.4; Mo 2) 68, 163, 165, 228\7
Ave Maria 4v (NJE 23.6; Mo 1) 43, 44, 78, 163, 176–177
Ave maris stella 4v (NJE 23.8; Mo 94) 66–68, 163, 174–175, 227, 228
Ave maris stella (Strophe 4) 4v (NJE 23.9; Su 1) 66–67, 163, 174–175, 227
Ave mundi spes Maria (NJE 23.10; Su 15) 49, 163, 165
Ave nobilissima creatura (NJE 23.11; Mo 34) 76, 161, 163, 178–179, 228

Index of names